The
"New Imperialism"

PROBLEMS IN
EUROPEAN CIVILIZATION

Under the editorial direction of
John Ratté
Amherst College

The "New Imperialism"

Analysis of Late-Nineteenth-Century Expansion

Second Edition

Edited and with an introduction by

Harrison M. Wright
Swarthmore College

D. C. HEATH AND COMPANY
Lexington, Massachusetts Toronto London

Published simultaneously in Canada.

Printed in the United States of America.

International Standard Book Number: 0-669-96008-X

Library of Congress Catalog Card Number: 75-18393

CONTENTS

INTRODUCTION

In the last decades of the nineteenth century, European states extended their formal political control over large areas of the world. Britain, which had the most extensive and widely dispersed empire to start with, in the end acquired the most new territory. France—also with worldwide commitments and ambitions—was, as usual, her major rival. Portugal and the Netherlands expanded already existing areas of imperial interest in Africa and Southeast Asia. Germany, Italy, and Belgium were new, but active, participants in the acquisition of overseas territory. Russia, not quite in the same category as the Western European states, continued her movement, primarily overland, to the east. Altogether it has been estimated that the Europeans extended their formal colonial empires by over 10 million square miles and 150 million people—about a fifth of the world's land area and perhaps a tenth of its population at the time—in about thirty years.

At first appearance this movement was also characterized by a kind of aggressive competition for territory that was quite unlike what had gone on before. Whether a state was simply gaining formal control over areas in which it had had previous interests, as in the Gold Coast or Madagascar; whether several states were competing for influence, as in China, the Sudan, or Morocco; or whether states were disputing over areas previously colonized, as in the Transvaal, they behaved in a fashion that kept them perpetually involved in diplomatic crises with each other and in exciting but usually one-sided conflicts ("sporting wars," Bismarck once called them) with peoples overseas. While small groups of competing Europeans worked their way across Africa and mainland Southeast Asia or sailed among innumerable Pacific islands inducing the inhabitants to sign treaties of protection or cession, the heads of state in Europe bickered ceaselessly among themselves and at the same time tried to establish effective control over the great areas so tenuously acquired. A climax developed, or at least appeared to develop, at the end of the century with the massacre of twenty thousand dervishes by Kitchener and his British troops at Obdurman, near Khartoum, in 1898; the tense meeting of French and British expeditions at Fashoda on the upper Nile, later that year, which resulted in a serious diplomatic crisis; the war between Spain and America; the outbreak in 1899 of the three-year conflict between the British and the Boers in South Africa; and the Boxer Rebellion in China in 1900.

Historians have generally agreed that modern European economic and political expansion overseas, taken as a whole, has constituted one of the great movements of world history. Its impact on both European and non-European peoples has been immense. But while historians have accepted its importance, they have been unable at the same time to agree about its causes, the motivations of its various participants, the nature of its different phases, and its particular relation to modern European and world history. Until a generation ago most historians at least accepted without question that the late nineteenth century, the period of the "new imperialism" as it is often called, was the most important phase of the expansion, that its propelling forces originated exclusively in Europe, and that it constituted a significant, unprecedented, and aggressive break with a previous half century of relative indifference and apathy toward expansion overseas. Even this is no longer agreed upon today. In the past twenty years some historians have begun to emphasize continuity rather than discontinuity in nineteenth-century expansion and events that took place overseas rather than in Europe itself. But such questions of periodization and perspective have merely added further complications to an already controversial subject.

To a certain extent the persistent and apparently irreconcilable debates about the period have been due to the difficulty of the problem involved. Satisfactory explanations and evaluations of any historical development are difficult to achieve because generalization always tends to do violence to details. The European overseas activities constituted, collectively, a development of extraordinary magnitude and complexity. Explanations of the period must account for an almost limitless number of complicating circumstances. Consider two of the most important: The late nineteenth century was a period not just of European, but of worldwide, expansion. In those years the United States, Japan, Australia, and other non-European states either took, or advocated taking, territories overseas. Are the European and non-European expansions connected? To what extent should a generalization about the European phenomenon be able to account for expansion elsewhere? The late nineteenth century was also a period of extensive tariff legislation. The era of free trade seemed to be over, and in the 1870s and 1880s Russia, Spain, Italy, Germany, and France drastically raised their duties on imports. Protectionists often argued for expansion and expansionists for protection. The two seemed linked. Yet the state that acquired the most new territory, Britain (along with Belgium and the Netherlands), remained free-trading. What connection was there, if any, between protection and expansion?

To such inherent difficulties must be added further complicating factors. From its beginning the late nineteenth-century expansion aroused an intense emotional and intellectual response. While many Europeans felt exhilarated by it, others, including leading liberal, socialist, and communist thinkers, attacked it bitterly. The "new imperialism" was highly controversial from the start, not only being analyzed historically but being used as an example in the development of general political and economic theories. The period is important to the neo-Marxist explanation of the basic weaknesses of capitalism. Other theorists have considered it as one indication that political action is motivated by the urge for power. Such general theorizing is not entirely appropriate to the historian's purposes: it is not historical in aim and it is sometimes not historically based. Nevertheless the various theories involving "imperialism" have been important ones by any criteria, and in attempting to understand the period the historian must be prepared to examine, if not all of their more abstract and general implications, at least their possible applications to the late nineteenth century.

One result of the various theoretical and interpretative disputes that have arisen is that apparently unimportant statements of detail often reflect basic differences of opinion. Even the date cited for the beginning of the period of European expansion may imply an interpretation of the period as a whole. Writers following nationalistic interpretations tend to favor 1870, that great watershed in the history of modern European nations. Those who emphasize diplomacy often consider 1878, the year of the Congress of Berlin, or 1884–85, the time of the Berlin Conference on Africa, to be more appropriate. Lenin, in his economic interpretation, used the year 1876, when, he argued, "the pre-monopolist stage of development of West European capitalism can be said to have been completed, in the main. . . ."

The use of that much-abused word "imperialism" also reflects basic differences. The word has been applied to the period for almost a century, usually more as a term of polemic than of analysis. When one finds Joseph Schumpeter, the economist, saying that "imperialism" is "the objectless disposition on the part of a state to unlimited forcible expansion," while Lenin says that it is "the monopoly stage of capitalism," and Langer, the historian, that it is "in a sense, synonymous with the appropriation by the western nations of the largest part of the rest of the world," it is apparent that a consideration of an author's definition is a prerequisite to the study of his interpretation. In many cases the mere acceptance of a particular definition of "imperialism" is tantamount to accepting a position about the nature of the period, and this even though the events themselves presumably may be studied and interpreted without the use of the word at all.

It is the purpose of this book to consider the historical debate over the origins and nature of late nineteenth-century European expansion taken as a whole. The issues involved are obviously closely related to those concerning the policies of specific European countries (such as Britain or Germany), the partitions of particular overseas areas (such as Africa or Southeast Asia), and the activities of certain individuals both in Europe and overseas at the time. They are also obviously closely related in a broader sense to those concerning mid-twentieth-century expansion and, for that matter, expansionism in general. But while the issues are indeed related, they are not the same. The problem of European expansion as a whole in the late nineteenth century implies, like any historical problem, its own distinct questions, perspectives, and levels of generalization. This book presents in roughly chronological order the positions—analytically contrasting and historically linked—of some of the most important participants in this particular debate.

The first author represented, J. Holland Rose, was not directly

involved in the theoretical or historiographical controversies outlined above. Few professional historians at the turn of the century
spent much time trying to analyze the period of expansion in a
broad and sweeping way. They were too concerned with recording
the specific events that had taken place and, in any case, they had
not at that time traveled far from the traditional historical emphasis
on politics and individuals. Rose's discussion of 1905 did, however,
list three "prerequisites" to expansion that some later authors have
not mentioned: that Europe was at peace, that exploration had
provided necessary information, that technological changes facili-
tated the acquisition and maintenance of large empires. These
somewhat prosaic reasons were largely disregarded in the heated
ideological controversies of later years. The problem still remains,
however, as to whether such "prerequisites" are a necessary or
important part of an explanation of the period.

The next three authors, Hobson, Lenin, and Woolf, were not professional historians. All were concerned to a great extent with
matters of economic theory. All attacked European expansion as a
function, in one way or another, of capitalistic greed. Their differences stemmed from the fact that there are a number of economic
schools of thought and many shades of doctrine within each of
them. Communists and most socialists, for example, claim direct
intellectual descent from the works of Marx; but Marx, who died in
1883, left writings on European overseas expansion that can be interpreted in different ways. And so disagreements even about the
nature of Marx's own position on capitalist "imperialism" have
almost inevitably come about.

Economic explanations of the immediate needs that drove European capitalist states into political activities overseas in the late
nineteenth century have usually followed one, or more, of three lines
of argument: that the capitalists wanted to be sure of having the
raw materials they needed to supply their rapidly growing industrial
complexes; that they needed markets because their industries were
producing far more goods than could be profitably sold at home;
and that they had to find undeveloped areas for investment in order
to absorb the great amounts of capital which had accumulated in
the form of profits from their industrial and financial concerns. Although some economic interpretations have emphasized one or

another of these arguments to the virtual exclusion of the others, most have mentioned more than one, since the three are not necessarily incompatible.

Economic interpreters have differed most bitterly over other aspects of the problem. While all the communists and socialists and some of the liberals apparently agree that "imperialism"—past or present—represents something seriously wrong with capitalism, they have disagreed over just what this dislocation is: whether or not it is inevitable; whether (and, if so, how) it might be corrected; and what the ultimate economic goal should be. They have also argued over just how economic interests requiring or desiring overseas expansion force or persuade a government to undertake it and how these interests are related to the social structure as a whole.

The logical place to start in any economic analysis of late nineteenth-century overseas expansion is J. A. Hobson's *Imperialism*, published in 1902. Of the many books and articles being written on the subject at the time, this book became by far the most famous and influential. To put it very briefly, Hobson considered "imperialism" to be engineered primarily by that "central ganglion" of international capitalism—finance. The interlocking network of great financiers promoted overseas expansion in order to generate profitable financial activity, in particular to have places to invest the surplus capital that resulted from maldistribution in the domestic economy. The financiers profited; the body politic (and the peoples overseas) paid the price. But while Hobson has probably been the person most consistently associated with theories of "economic imperialism," he was no economic determinist. He believed in laissez faire and in free trade. Like most economic liberals, he felt that the political and economic system of his time was basically sound and that with proper adjustment it could produce peace and plenty for all. Furthermore, he pointed out a number of noneconomic pressures tending toward empire-building, and subtly combined these with the financial ones. Historians have found in *Imperialism* the inspiration for many different views, and every historian who has come after Hobson has had to reckon with his interpretation of the period. In the last three-quarters of a century his thesis has been subjected to much praise and much criticism, perhaps not all of it based on a reasonable summary of what he actually said.

One of the most rigorous economic interpretations of European expansion, Lenin's *Imperialism, The Highest Stage of Capitalism* (1916), contains warm praise for Hobson's argument about investments and borrows some of his analysis—even as it chides him for advocating "bourgeois social reformism and pacifism." To Lenin, "imperialism" was an inevitable and predictable catastrophe, one of the culminating crises resulting from the internal contradictions of the capitalist system and leading to its final breakdown. Lenin's argument is important not only because of its author but because of its influence on neo-Marxist theory. Whatever one's final judgment about it, it deserves closer consideration than it often receives: not infrequently it is simply dismissed out-of-hand or with criticism that is hastily contrived and inappropriate.

The economic interpretation of Leonard Woolf, the English Fabian socialist who wrote *Empire and Commerce in Africa* (1919), was less doctrinaire than Lenin's and, in some ways, Hobson's. Some non-theorists have felt that by and large this makes it more effective. Economic self-interest in general was Woolf's concern. Along with its general arguments, his book contained some of the variety of evidence that must be dealt with by anyone critical of economic interpretations as a whole. It also discussed, with assured self-confidence, the problem of motivation. Motivation is, in fact, an almost insoluble problem. Historians considering the subject have had to ask whether a statesman says what he thinks is true or what he thinks will be effective, whether he himself really knows what his ultimate motivations are, and whether in any case it is possible for historians, with considerably less information (although perhaps with more objectivity), to come to any firm conclusions about it.

The critics of the economic interpretation of the "new imperialism" have been, like their opponents, vehement and vigorous. One of the most famous of them was, himself, a noted economist. Joseph A. Schumpeter included late-nineteenth-century expansion in a study of "the sociology of imperialisms" that he published in 1919. To Schumpeter, "imperialism" as a general phenomenon was an "atavism," the result of culturally inherited political and social forces that hung on from a previous age, when they had a purposeful existence, to a later period, in which their impact was dysfunctional. Schumpeter saw Egypt, for example, as having been a peaceful society until it needed to organize militarily, during the period of the New Kingdom, to expel the ruling Hyksos. At the end of this period of purposeful struggle the war-making machine had to continue fighting in order to exist, even though there was no longer any particular occasion for it to do so. "Created by wars that required it," as Schumpeter put it, "the machine now created the wars it required." So Egypt, in "objectless" fashion, aggressively built an empire. Likewise, primitive instincts toward war based on religion led the later Assyrians, even though they had settled in circumstances different from those of their ancestors, to cruel, unwarranted, and continuous conquering and expansion. One could, Schumpeter argued, find structurally similar explanations for the various empires that have followed.

The particular "atavism" that Schumpeter thought responsible for late-nineteenth-century expansion was the continuation in certain European states of the precapitalist "war-oriented" nobility, as shaped by the "absolute" autocracy of earlier centuries. The theory was abstractly stated and, except for a section on England, it made little factual reference to the events of the period. It also may have reflected to a certain degree a pro-British, anti-German attitude which Schumpeter held during World War I, when it was written. The argument has nevertheless become probably the most influential of all criticisms of the economic interpretation. While it patently accepts the importance of economic forces in history, it not only criticizes the economic interpretations of nineteenth-century European expansion but defends pure capitalism as anti-imperialistic and provides a challenging alternative explanation as well.

Critics have argued that Schumpeter had so particular and irrelevant a definition of imperialism as to exclude from it the greatest imperial power, Britain; that he limited his causal explanation to one narrow and uninclusive phenomenon; and that his defense of capitalism as anti-imperialistic was simply theoretical rhapsodizing. Still, one who compares Schumpeter with Hobson may find the basic positions of the two men not so very far apart as they may at first seem, and one must follow carefully the connections that each one makes between economic theory and specific historical interpretation. Whether Schumpeter's explanation is or is not more satisfactory than its economic predecessors is still a matter of considerable debate.

William L. Langer, the diplomatic historian, took up the debate in a well-known article first published in *Foreign Affairs* in 1935. The questions, assumptions, evidence, and arguments Langer used in his comparison of Hobson and Schumpeter were those of a professional historian and were characteristic of that method of approach. Evidence on both sides was carefully presented and judiciously weighed. Other historians have since argued over the issues to be found in Langer's article. Is Lenin's contention that the European overseas rivalry was to satisfy prospective future, as well as immediate, needs a satisfactory answer to Langer's point that many states did not extensively invest in or trade with their newly acquired territories? Does the existence of a nonindustrialized expansionist state, such as Russia, really destroy the economic argument? Despite its apparent judiciousness, is Langer's historical analysis in fact so closely related to his own contemporary political concerns as to affect the validity of his remarks?

To the historian Carlton J. H. Hayes, writing just before America entered World War II, the European expansion was essentially nationalistic and based on wide popular support. Hayes explained the undeniably economic pronouncements and activities of the period (such as one finds in Woolf) by maintaining that economic arguments were usually *ex post facto* and by implying that there can be economic self-interest in a venture without its being the primary motive. If one accepts Hayes's many facts (some of which, such as France's relatively sluggish industrial development, Lenin also used for *his* argument), it is still necessary to consider why the nationalistic publicists decided to use economic arguments and whether any other influences lay behind the apparently nationalistic fervor. Proponents of the economic interpretation, for example, have argued that nationalism was simply a cover by which the economic forces obscured their real motives. Schumpeter, on the other hand, believed that the fervor of a nationalistic appeal lay in the fact that it called into play "instincts that carry over from the life habits of the dim past."

Nicholas Mansergh, a British historian writing in the mid-1940s, had a more precise explanation than Hayes—and one tied not to popular opinion but to the decisions of a few political leaders. Germany had become, by its victory over France in the Franco-Prussian War, the pivot around which European diplomacy revolved. In *The Coming of the First World War* Mansergh maintained that the international position of Germany dominated the thinking not only of the German but of all the other European governments, and that therefore any overseas expansion was primarily an adjunct to the crucial diplomatic maneuvering in Europe. In considering this thesis critics have asked whether the explanation of expansion as a vehicle of European diplomacy applies as well to Britain and to France as to Germany—and how far beyond these countries it might have had significance. (Indeed, one might ask: How far does or should any explanation of the expansion rely primarily on one particular country for its example?) Critics have also had to weigh the importance of the diplomatic decisions of a few political leaders against the evidence both of great popular support for expansion, as suggested by Hayes, and of economic pressure, as mentioned by Woolf.

Unlike Mansergh, Hannah Arendt, the political philosopher, found virtual unanimity in favor of expansion among the various social and economic elements within each European country (including capitalists and the "mob"), but she argued that these different elements reached that common attitude from widely different directions. Her argument was published in her controversial book, *The Origins of Totalitarianism* (1951), which not only recognized both economic and nationalistic pressures for expansion in the late nineteenth century, but incorporated them into a larger assessment of the period as a whole. It was an all-encompassing approach, both assertive and stimulating. And it exemplified the general problem of assessing the specific relations among the different elements of late-nineteenth-century society that were involved in determining a country's course of action.

About the time that Arendt wrote, the major assumptions of the interpretation of European expansion were beginning to be questioned and to shift: from discontinuity to continuity, from the center to the periphery, from popular movements to reasons of state, from motives of aggression to motives of defense. This movement, while anticipated in some earlier thinking, was ultimately the result of postwar changes in perspective. The main precipitating influence was the work of the British historians Ronald Robinson and John Gallagher. In their article, "The Imperialism of Free Trade," published in the *Economic History Review* in 1953, Robinson and Gallagher argued that there was no significant break in British expansion from the early Victorian period through the end of the century. They maintained, rather, that if expansion is considered to be not just the acquisition of territory but the aggressive extension of trade and of informal control, there may actually have been a decline in the vigor of late Victorian expansion. The territorial acquisition at the end of the century reflected more a change of tactics—a defensive posture to meet rising European competition—than a change of attitude. In *Africa and the Victorians* (1961), a book written with Alice Denny, Robinson and Gallagher took their arguments further. They minimized the importance of nationalistic and economic pressure groups and of popular demand in order to emphasize the significance of the "official mind," the thinking of those statesmen and senior civil servants who maintained a continuity of attitude in British policy from early in the century until its end. And they argued that it was not so much events in Europe that precipitated the partition of Africa as it was events in Africa itself: notably, the crises in the Transvaal (1877–81) and, particularly, in Egypt (1882). In both cases British statesmen, compelled by a vital strategic interest in those areas that guarded the lines of empire to India, undertook action which led to countermoves by the other European countries and to the ultimate division of the African continent.

No doubt the ideas of previous authors influenced Robinson and Gallagher to some extent. They referred to Schumpeter explicitly, for example, in their analysis of the nature of official thinking, while the picture of a Britain basically reluctant to occupy territory was not inconsistent with Schumpeter's interpretation of British nineteenth-century anti-imperialism. There were overtones of Mansergh's school of thinking in their emphasis on diplomacy and on the important role of a few statesmen. But fundamentally the theory was a bold and fresh reinterpretation of European expansion. And it had immediate appeal to the new generation of historians, both those who saw Eurocentric bias in previous explanations and those who felt that the discontinuity or "break" between the early and late nineteenth century had been grossly exaggerated.

Africa and the Victorians was quickly subjected to intense and detailed analysis. It contained an enormous amount of information, and specialists in African history found occasional inaccuracies of fact. These were not, in the view of most historians, by themselves enough to damage its overall factual or interpretative reliability. But the book was so large and had so many ramifications and insights that it was also possible to find within it serious inconsistencies of interpretation and doubtful uses of method. Were the assumptions of rational action on the part of British statesmen true to the fact, or were they simply retroactive rationalization on the authors' part? Since the authors gave evidence both ways, did they or did they not finally consider as significant the change from "informal" to "formal" empire? Despite the authors' intentions, was there in fact significant evidence in the book supporting more orthodox interpretations of the expansion? Can one separate a strategically-motivated action (the occupation of Egypt) from the presumably economic interest (India), which it was designed to protect? If nationalism was not a vital factor in late-nineteenth-century Europe, why did the British actions in Egypt and the Transvaal spark such a vigorous continental response?

Perhaps most important to a consideration of Robinson and Gallagher with respect to the late-nineteenth-century expansion of Europe as a whole, however, was the particular emphasis they placed on Britain as a metropolitan power, and on Africa as an object of overseas expansion. Britain certainly acquired more territory than any other European power—but was it typical in its motivation? Africa was certainly more thoroughly and completely divided by European powers than any other continent—but was its division typical of what happened elsewhere? How well can an interpretation of Britain and Africa be transferred to Europe and to the overseas world in general? Robinson and Gallagher themselves suggested in *Africa and the Victorians* that the nature of Britain's motives might not be those of the rest of Europe; and at the end of their 1953 essay they criticized Hobson for his distorting emphasis on Africa. In short, one must be cautious in applying broadly the Robinson and Gallagher thesis, even assuming one thinks it appropriate for Britain and for Africa, as one tries to explain why the general European expansion of the late nineteenth century took place when and how it did.

One response to Robinson and Gallagher has been to reassert or rearrange older interpretations, but with explicit reference to the new theses, in order to defend positions that formerly were accepted without examination. The distinguished British historian Geoffrey Barraclough has done this in passing in his *An Introduction to Contemporary History* (1964). Barraclough not only believes that there was a break between the first three-quarters and the last quarter of the nineteenth century with respect to expansion, but that there was a break in most other aspects of European (and by extension world) development as well. Barraclough deliberately looks for discontinuity rather than continuity in order to support his contention that the "modern" age of European history ended and the "contemporary" age began in a transition period extending from the late nineteenth century to about 1960. In an argument that in some ways recalls Rose, Barraclough points to the technological innovations, the growth of industry and of industrial needs, and the other forces of the late nineteenth century that altered many aspects of European life. Though by no means a Marxist historian, Barraclough uses arguments which support a number of the contentions of the economic interpreters of European expansion. And through his emphasis on economic change across Europe he also emphasizes and brings together the continent-wide nature of the movement.

A more specific form of attack on Robinson and Gallagher is represented in the work of D. C. M. Platt. In his article "The 'Imperialism of Free Trade': Some Reservations" (1968), Platt uses Latin America and China as examples to show how scrupulously the British government limited overseas political action in the mid-nineteenth century. He thereby attempts to demonstrate that the later period of British expansion constituted a real break in governmental attitudes. Robinson and Gallagher might contend that Platt's definition of "imperialism" is too narrow, but Platt would respond that the change in attitudes was nonetheless real and that the causes for it must be found elsewhere than in Robinson and Gallagher's explanations.

D. K. Fieldhouse, the author of *Economics and Empire 1830–1914* (1973), from which the last selection in this volume is drawn, was born in India and has lived in New Zealand. Perhaps for that reason, as he observes in his book, he has been led to look at the problem of expansion from the imperial periphery. In the last decade or two, as many recent histories of Asia and Africa demonstrate, emphasis away from the metropolitan centers of Europe to the actual sites of imperial action has been growing rapidly. But Fieldhouse is one of the few historians to have considered the issue in general terms—to have considered the periphery not just in relation to one European country or one overseas area, but as a whole. Still, as Fieldhouse recognizes, peripheral events cannot by themselves be used to provide a general explanation of European expansion. One must account for the reasons impelling Europeans to respond to them. For this reason Fieldhouse is driven back to a reconsideration of economic and other theories. Here the validity of his distinction between "political" and "economic" causes is liable to be questioned. So also is his balance between peripheral and metropolitan forces. Indeed his book must be taken not as the final word but simply as one stage in a still progressing and developing debate.

If the most recent analyses of the European expansion of the late nineteenth century have not resolved the debate, they have made it, although more complex, at the same time less theoretical and more substantial. Some of the real analytical difficulties of the problem —such as those of distinguishing the precipitating from the underlying causes of an event, of determining motives through the statements and actions of participants, of deciding whether one should emphasize continuities or discontinuities over a period of years, of using a limited set of examples as the basis for a general conclusion—are now being more squarely faced than they ever were before. And yet the more realistically the problem is faced, the more difficult it appears to be, to some historians, to accept any single, broad explanation.

Nevertheless historians will always have to reckon with the period as a whole because of its particular historical importance—to modern European history, to the histories of large parts of Africa, Asia, and other sections of the world, and to the similar, worldwide problems of today. Intensity of feeling about the period does and will remain strong. Broad, conflicting, and often polemical generalizations will continue to be made about it. Indeed, even with careful historical analysis changing interpretations are inevitable.* But then the study of historical problems has always had this challenging and rewarding quality. As circumstances and perspectives change, historians must continually confront all historical problems anew as they turn to the past to try to understand the world and the relation of their own generation to it.

*Indeed, several of the writers represented in this book have in other writings made clearly different interpretations of the period than are included here. See, for example, for Hobson and Schumpeter, in E. M. Winslow, *The Pattern of Imperialism* (New York, 1948), pp. 100–103, 235–36; for Hayes, his *Contemporary Europe since 1870* (rev. ed.; New York, 1958), pp. 267–70; for Langer, his *European Alliances and Alignments, 1871–1890* (New York, 1931), pp. 283–90; for Fieldhouse, his *Economics and Empire, 1830–1914* (Ithaca, N.Y., 1973), Preface.

Note: In order to save space all but a few of the authors' footnotes have been eliminated from the texts of the following readings.

Conflict of Opinion

Analysis of the actual course of modern Imperialism has laid bare the combination of economic and political forces which fashions it. These forces are traced to their sources in the selfish interests of certain industrial, financial, and professional classes, seeking private advantages out of a policy of imperial expansion, and using this same policy to protect them in their economic, political, and social privileges against the pressure of democracy.

J. A. HOBSON

We have seen that the economic quintessence of imperialism is monopoly capitalism. This very fact determines its place in history, for monopoly that grew up on the basis of free competition, and precisely out of free competition, is the transition from the capitalist system to a higher social-economic order.

V. I. LENIN

. . . It follows that capitalism is by nature anti-imperialist. Hence we can not readily derive from it such imperialist tendencies as actually exist, but must evidently see them only as alien elements, carried into the world of capitalism from the outside, supported by noncapitalist factors in modern life.

J. A. SCHUMPETER

. . . The postulates of the socialist theory undoubtedly existed. There is no mentionable reason why the development of the capitalist system should not have had the results attributed to it. But, as it happens, the actual course of history refutes the thesis."

W. L. LANGER

Basically the new imperialism was a nationalistic phenomenon. . . . Some capitalists undoubtedly promoted imperialism, and more profited by it. But in the last analysis it was the nationalistic masses who made it possible and who most vociferously applauded it and most constantly backed it.

C. J. H. HAYES

The rulers of Europe thought primarily in terms of political not economic advantage and . . . the colonial policies of the Continental states were formulated in the light of the European balance of power and designed to serve European ends. When they no longer served those ends the colonial scene slips unobtrusively into the background.

N. MANSERGH

There are good reasons for regarding the mid-Victorian period as the golden age of British expansion, and the late-Victorian as an age which saw the beginnings of contraction and decline.

R. ROBINSON AND J. GALLAGHER

It was . . . a stupendous movement, without parallel in history, which completely changed the shape of things to come, and to argue, as historians have recently done, that there was "no break in continuity after 1870" or, still more, that it was an age not of expansion but of "contraction and decline," does less than justice to its importance.

G. BARRACLOUGH

There would seem . . . to be a strong case for approaching the problem of modern imperialism from the standpoint of problems developing outside Europe and on the assumption that colonization may have constituted a response by the metropolitan powers to external stimuli rather than the expression of economic or other problems within Europe.

D. K. FIELDHOUSE

MAPS

MAP 1
Africa in 1870

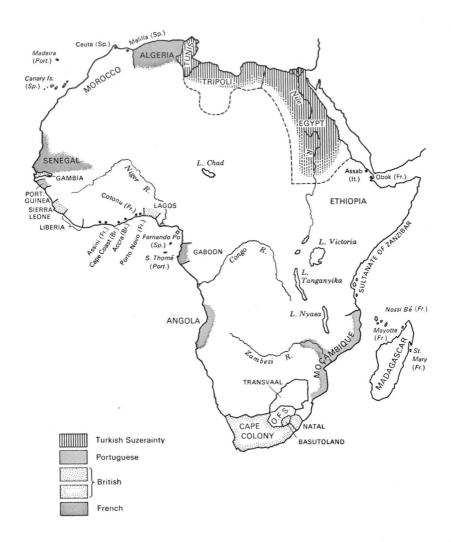

Madeira (Port.)

Canary Is. (Sp.)

Ceuta (Sp.)   Melilla (Sp.)

MOROCCO

ALGERIA

TUNIS

TRIPOLI

Nile

EGYPT

R.

L. Chad

Assab (It.)   Obok (Fr.)

SENEGAL

GAMBIA

PORT. GUINEA

SIERRA LEONE

LIBERIA

Niger R.

Cotonu (Fr.)

LAGOS

Assini (Fr.)
Cape Coast (Br.)
Accra (Br.)
Porto Novo (Fr.)

Fernando Po (Sp.)

S. Thomé (Port.)

GABOON

Congo R.

ETHIOPIA

SULTANATE OF ZANZIBAR

L. Victoria

L. Tanganyika

ANGOLA

L. Nyasa

Nossi Bé (Fr.)

Mayotte (Fr.)

MADAGASCAR

St. Mary (Fr.)

Zambezi R.

MOÇAMBIQUE

TRANSVAAL

O. F. S.

CAPE COLONY

NATAL

BASUTOLAND

Turkish Suzerainty

Portuguese

British

French

MAP 2
Africa in 1914

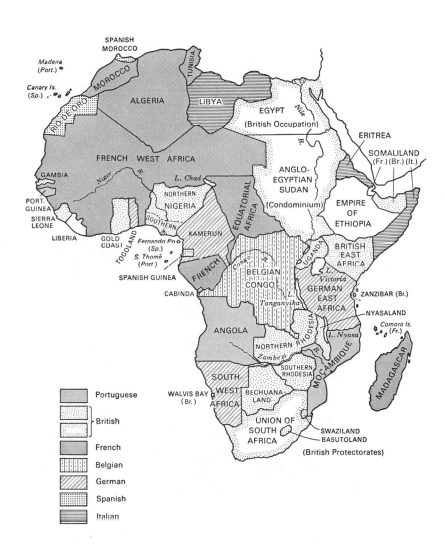

Madeira (Port.)

Canary Is. (Sp.)

RÍO DE ORO

SPANISH MOROCCO

MOROCCO

TUNISIA

ALGERIA

LIBYA

EGYPT (British Occupation)

Nile R.

ERITREA

SOMALILAND (Fr.) (Br.) (It.)

FRENCH WEST AFRICA

GAMBIA

Niger R.

L. Chad

ANGLO-EGYPTIAN SUDAN (Condominium)

EMPIRE OF ETHIOPIA

PORT. GUINEA

SIERRA LEONE

LIBERIA

NORTHERN NIGERIA

SOUTHERN

EQUATORIAL AFRICA

GOLD COAST

TOGOLAND

Fernando Po (Sp.)

S. Thomé (Port.)

KAMERUN

SPANISH GUINEA

FRENCH

CABINDA

Congo R.

BELGIAN CONGO

L. Tanganyika

L. Victoria

UGANDA

BRITISH EAST AFRICA

GERMAN EAST AFRICA

ZANZIBAR (Br.)

NYASALAND

Comoro Is. (Fr.)

ANGOLA

RHODESIA

L. Nyasa

NORTHERN RHODESIA

Zambezi R.

MOÇAMBIQUE

SOUTHERN RHODESIA

MADAGASCAR

WALVIS BAY (Br.)

SOUTH WEST AFRICA

BECHUANA-LAND

SWAZILAND

BASUTOLAND

UNION OF SOUTH AFRICA

(British Protectorates)

Portuguese

British

French

Belgian

German

Spanish

Italian

MAP 3
Asia in 1870

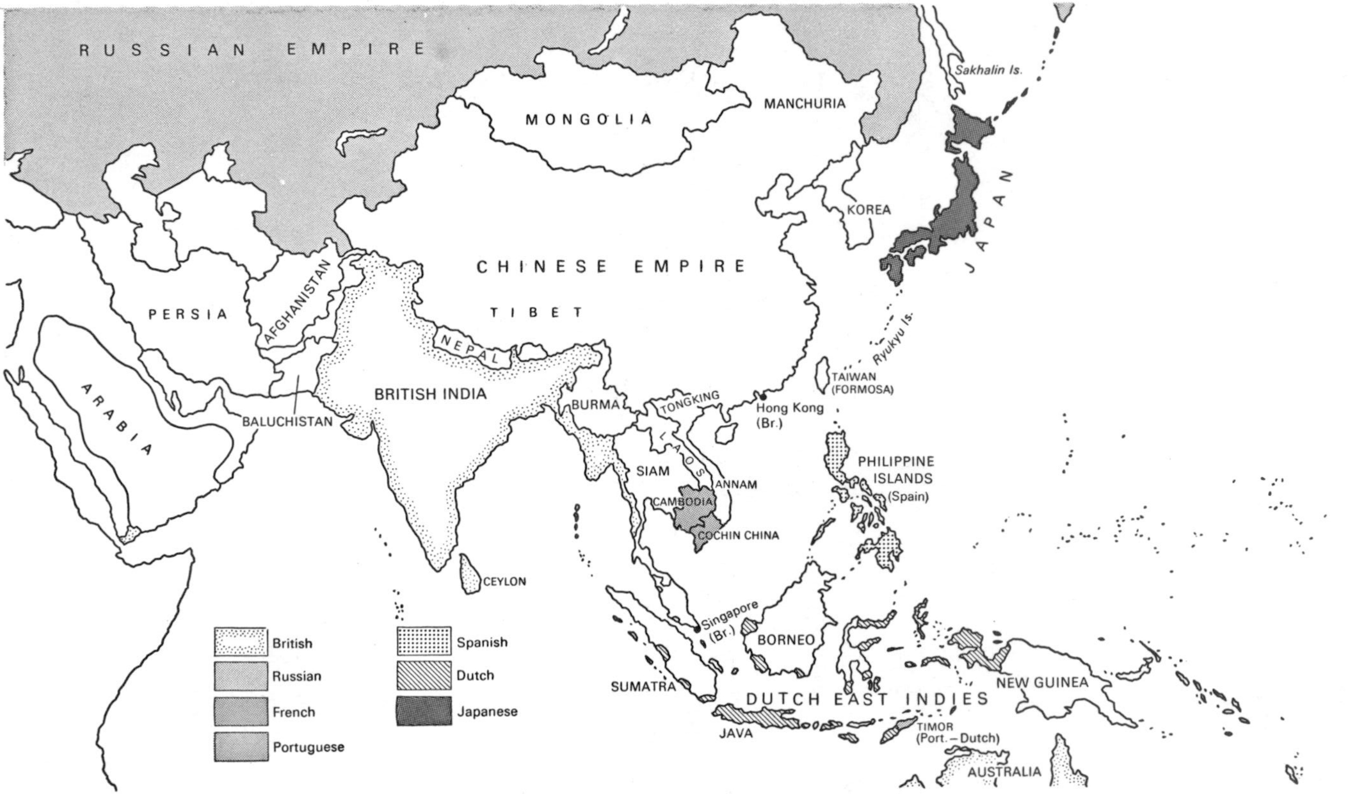

RUSSIAN EMPIRE

MONGOLIA

MANCHURIA

KOREA

JAPAN

Sakhalin Is.

Ryukyu Is.

TAIWAN (FORMOSA)

PHILIPPINE ISLANDS (Spain)

NEW GUINEA

AUSTRALIA

TIMOR (Port—Dutch)

DUTCH EAST INDIES

BORNEO

JAVA

SUMATRA

Singapore (Br.)

COCHIN CHINA

CAMBODIA

ANNAM

LAOS

SIAM

TONGKING

Hong Kong (Br.)

BURMA

TIBET

CHINESE EMPIRE

NEPAL

BRITISH INDIA

CEYLON

AFGHANISTAN

BALUCHISTAN

PERSIA

ARABIA

Spanish

Dutch

Japanese

British

Russian

French

Portuguese

MAP 4

Asia in 1914

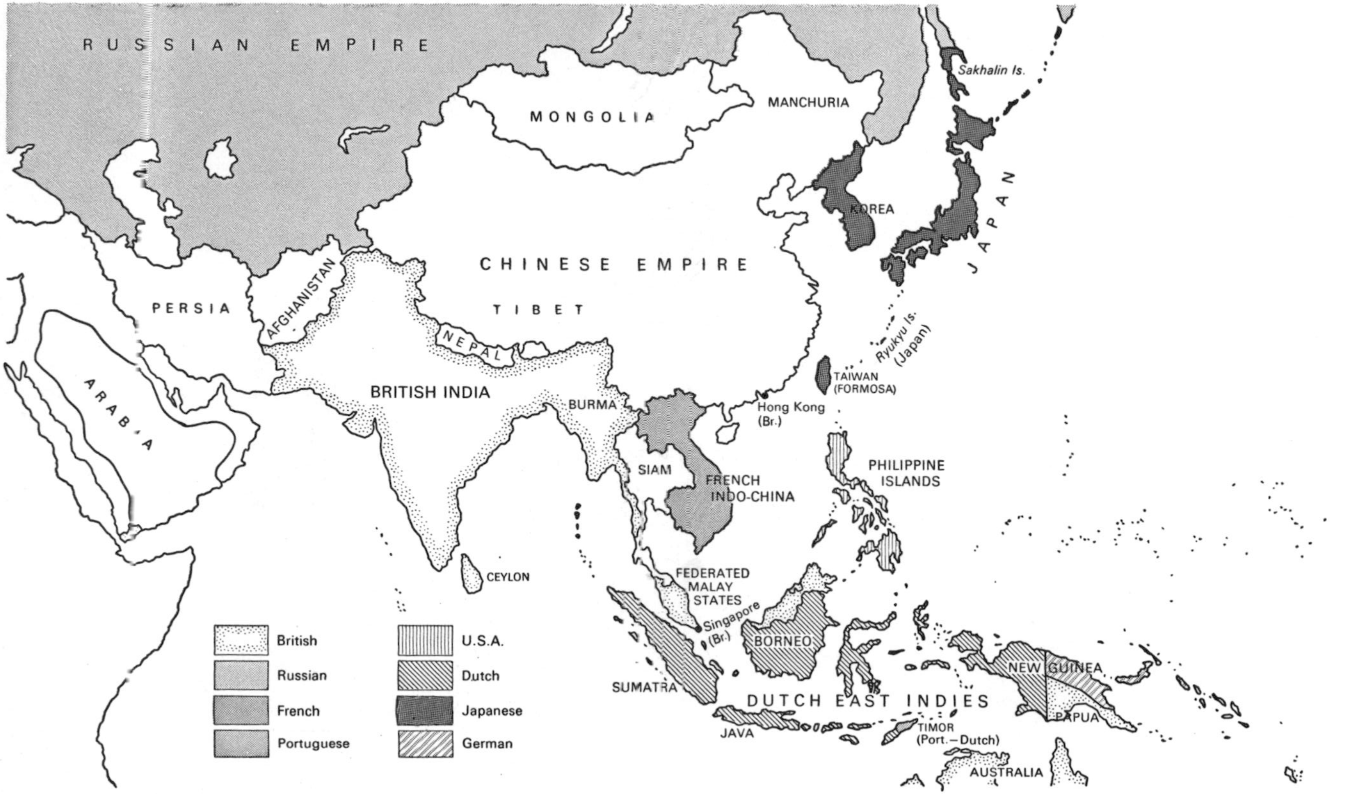

RUSSIAN EMPIRE

MONGOLIA

MANCHURIA

JAPAN

Sakhalin Is.

KOREA

Ryūkyū Is. (Japan)

TAIWAN (FORMOSA)

CHINESE EMPIRE

TIBET

Hong Kong (Br.)

FRENCH INDO-CHINA

SIAM

PHILIPPINE ISLANDS

DUTCH EAST INDIES

NEW GUINEA

PAPUA

AUSTRALIA

TIMOR (Port.–Dutch)

BORNEO

Singapore (Br.)

FEDERATED MALAY STATES

SUMATRA

JAVA

BURMA

NEPAL

BHUTAN

BRITISH INDIA

AFGHANISTAN

PERSIA

ARABIA

CEYLON

MONGOLIA

British

Russian

French

Portuguese

U.S.A.

Dutch

Japanese

German

J. Holland Rose

THREE CONDITIONS OF EXPANSION

John Holland Rose (1855–1942) was one of the most eminent British historians in the first third of the twentieth century. Best known, perhaps, for his series of works on the French Revolution and the Napoleonic Era (including distinguished biographies of Napoleon and Pitt), he wrote as well on nationalism and on diplomatic affairs. His works were based on careful scholarship and were written with style and distinction. The Development of the European Nations, 1870–1900, *from which the following selection is drawn, was first published in 1905. It is a detailed account of European international relations—both within Europe and in areas overseas.*

In the opening up of new lands by European peoples the order of events is generally somewhat as follows: first come explorers, pioneers, or missionaries. These having thrown some light on the character of a land or of its people, traders follow in their wake; and in due course factories are formed and settlements arise. The ideas of the newcomers as to the rights of property and landholding differ so widely from those of the natives, that quarrels and strifes frequently ensue. Warships and soldiers then appear on the scene; and the end of the old order of things is marked by the hoisting of the Union Jack, or the French or German tricolor. In the case of the expansion of Russia as we have seen, the procedure is far otherwise. But Africa has been for the most part explored, exploited, and annexed by agencies working from the sea and proceeding in the way just outlined.

The period since the year 1870 has for the most part witnessed the operation of the last and the least romantic of these so-called civilizing efforts. The great age of African exploration was then drawing to a close. In the year 1870 that devoted missionary explorer, David Livingstone, was lost to sight for many months owing to his earnest longing peacefully to solve the great problem of the waterways of Central Africa, and thus open up an easy path for the suppression of the slave-trade. But when, in 1871, Mr. H. M. Stanley, the enterprising correspondent of the *New York Herald,* at the head of a rescue expedition, met the grizzled, fever-stricken veteran near

From J. Holland Rose, *The Development of the European Nations, 1870–1900* (London, 1905), pp. 508–512. By permission of Constable & Company, Ltd.

Ujiji and greeted him with the words—"Mr. Livingstone, I presume," the age of mystery and picturesqueness vanished away.

A change in the spirit and methods of exploration naturally comes about when the efforts of single individuals give place to collective enterprise, and that change was now rapidly to come over the whole field of African exploration. The day of the Mungo Parks and Livingstones was passing away, and the day of associations and companies was at hand. In 1876, Leopold II, King of the Belgians, summoned to Brussels several of the leading explorers and geographers in order to confer on the best methods of opening up Africa. The specific results of this important Conference will be considered in the next chapter; but we may here note that, under the auspices of the "International Association for the Exploration and Civilization of Africa" then founded, much pioneer work was carried out in districts remote from the River Congo. The vast continent also yielded up its secrets to travelers working their way in from the south and the north, so that in the late seventies the white races opened up to view vast and populous districts which imaginative chartographers in other ages had diversified with the Mountains of the Moon or with signs of the Zodiac and monstrosities of the animal creation.

The last epoch-marking work carried through by an individual was accomplished by a Scottish explorer, whose achievements almost rivaled those of Livingstone. Joseph Thomson, a native of Dumfriesshire, succeeded in 1879 to the command of an exploring party which sought to open up the country around the lakes of Nyassa and Tanganyika. Four years later, on behalf of the Royal Geographical Society, he undertook to examine the country behind Mombasa which was little better known than when Vasco da Gama first touched there. In this journey Thomson discovered two snow-capped mountains, Kilimanjaro and Kenia, and made known the resources of the country as far inland as the Victoria Nyanza. Considering the small resources he had at hand, and the cruel and warlike character of the Masai people through whom he journeyed, this journey was by far the most remarkable and important in the annals of exploration during the eighties. Thomson afterwards undertook to open a way from the Benuë, the great eastern affluent of the Niger, to Lake Chad and the White Nile. Here again he succeeded beyond all expectation, while his tactful management of the natives led to political results of the highest importance, as will shortly appear.

These explorations and those of French, German, and Portuguese travelers served to bring nearly the whole of Africa within the ken of the civilized world, and revealed the fact that nearly all parts of tropical Africa had a distinct commercial value.

This discovery, we may point out, is the necessary preliminary to any great and sustained work of colonization and annexation. Three conditions may be looked on as essential to such an effort. First, that new lands should be known to be worth the labor of exploitation or settlement; second, that the older nations should possess enough vitality to pour settlers and treasure into them; and thirdly, that mechanical appliances should be available for the overcoming of natural obstacles.

Now, a brief glance at the great eras of exploring and colonizing activity will show that in all these three directions the last thirty years have presented advantages which are unique in the history of the world. A few words will suffice to make good this assertion. The wars which constantly devastated the ancient world, and the feeble resources in regard to navigation wielded by adventurous captains, such as Hanno the Carthaginian, grievously hampered all the efforts of explorers by sea, while mechanical appliances were so weak as to cripple man's efforts at penetrating the interior. The same is true of the medieval voyagers and travelers. Only the very princes among men, Columbus, Magellan, Vasco da Gama, Cabot, Cabral, Gilbert, and Raleigh, could have done what they did with ships that were mere playthings. Science had to do her work of long and patient research before man could hopefully face the mighty forces and malignant influences of the tropics. Nor was the advance of knowledge and invention sufficient by itself to equip man for successful war against the ocean, the desert, the forest, and the swamp. The political and social development of the older countries was equally necessary. In order that thousands of settlers should be able and ready to press in where the one great leader had shown the way, Europe had to gain something like peace and stability. Only thus, when the natural surplus of the white races could devote itself to the task of peacefully subduing the earth rather than to the hideous work of mutual slaughter, could the life-blood of Europe be poured forth in fertilizing streams into the waste places of the other continents.

The latter half of the eighteenth century promised for a brief space to inaugurate such a period of expansive life. The close of the Seven Years' War seemed to be the starting point for a peaceful campaign against the unknown; but the efforts of Cook, d'Entrecasteaux, and others then had little practical result, owing to the American War of Independence, and the great cycle of the Revolutionary and Napoleonic Wars. These in their turn left Europe too exhausted to accomplish much in the way of colonial expansion until the middle of the nineteenth century. Even then, when the steamship and the locomotive were at hand to multiply man's powers, there was, as yet, no general wish, except on the part of the more fortunate English-speaking peoples, to enter into man's new heritage. The problems of Europe had to be settled before the age of expansive activity could dawn in its full radiance. As has been previously shown, Europe was in an introspective mood up to the years 1870–1878.

Our foregoing studies have shown that the years following the Russo-Turkish War of 1877-8 brought about a state of political equilibrium which made for peace and stagnation in Europe; and the natural forces of the Continent, cramped by the opposition of equal and powerful forces, took the line of least resistance—away from Europe. For Russia, the line of least resistance was in Central Asia. For all other European States it was the sea, and the new lands beyond.

Furthermore, in that momentous decade the steamship and locomotive were constantly gaining in efficiency; electricity was entering the arena as a new and mighty force; by this time medical science had so far advanced as to screen man from many of the ills of which the tropics are profuse; and the repeating rifle multiplied the power of the white man in his conflicts with savage peoples. When all the advantages of the present generation are weighed in the balance against the meager equipment of the earlier discoverers, the nineteenth century has scant claim for boasting over the fifteenth. In truth, its great achievements in this sphere have been practical and political. It has only fulfilled the rich promise of the age of the great navigators. Where they could but wonderingly skirt the fringes of a new world, the moderns have won their way to the heart of things and found many an Eldorado potentially richer than that which tempted the cupidity of Cortes and Pizarro.

In one respect the European statesmen of the recent past tower above their predecessors of the centuries before. In the eighteenth century the "mercantilist" craze for seizing new markets and shutting out all possible rivals brought about most of the wars that desolated Europe. In the years 1880–1890 the great Powers put forth sustained and successful efforts to avert the like calamity, and to cloak with the mantle of diplomacy the eager scrambles for the unclaimed lands of the world.

J. A. Hobson
IMPERIALISM: A STUDY

John A. Hobson (1858–1940) was an economist and publicist of unusual powers and reputation. He wrote constantly—as a regular contributor to the British Nation *for many years and as author of some three dozen books on a wide variety of economic, political, and social topics. In the course of his career he developed a theory of underconsumption which maintained that the weaknesses of contemporary capitalism resulted primarily from the maldistribution of wealth—especially oversaving by the wealthy. Hobson's solution to this economic problem included the nationalization of certain industries and the retention of private enterprise in others—which left him somewhere between the socialists and the liberals of his time. His interest in "imperialism" (which reflected an important part of his general economic theory) stemmed most directly from a trip to South Africa as a correspondent for the* Manchester Guardian *just before the Boer War. Hobson was a severe critic of British policy in South Africa, and especially of the war itself. In the selections from* Imperialism *(probably his most famous book), the reader will encounter Hobson's remarkable talents of analysis and exposition.*

The Measure of Imperialism

Quibbles about the modern meaning of the term Imperialism are best resolved by reference to concrete facts in the history of the last thirty years. During that period a number of European nations, Great Britain being first and foremost, have annexed or otherwise asserted political sway over vast portions of Africa and Asia, and over numer-

From J. A. Hobson, *Imperialism: A Study* (London, 1902), pp. 15–26, 30–31, 42–44, 46, 47–48, 50–68, 76–79, 85–86, 207–211, 224–234. Reprinted by permission of George Allen & Unwin Ltd.

ous islands in the Pacific and elsewhere. The extent to which this policy of expansion has been carried on, and in particular the enormous size and the peculiar character of the British acquisitions, are not adequately realized even by those who pay some attention to Imperial politics.

The following lists [see Table 1], giving the area and, where possible, the population of the new acquisitions, are designed to give definiteness to the term Imperialism. Though derived from official sources, they do not, however, profess strict accuracy. The sliding scale of political terminology along which no-man's land, or hinterland, passes into some kind of definite protectorate is often applied so as to conceal the process; "rectification" of a fluid frontier is continually taking place; paper "partitions" of spheres of influence or protection in Africa and Asia are often obscure, and in some cases the area and the population are highly speculative.

In a few instances it is possible that portions of territory put down as acquired since 1870 may have been earmarked by a European Power at some earlier date. But care is taken to include only such territories as have come within this period under the definite political control of the Power to which they are assigned. The figures in the case of Great Britain are so startling as to call for a little further interpretation. I have thought it right to add to the recognized list of colonies and protectorates the "veiled Protectorate" of Egypt, with its vast Soudanese claim, the entire territories assigned to Chartered Companies, and the native or feudatory States in India which acknowledge our paramountcy by the admission of a British Agent or other official endowed with real political control.

All these lands are rightly accredited to the British Empire, and if our past policy is still pursued, the intensive as distinct from the extensive Imperialism will draw them under an ever-tightening grasp.

In a few other instances, as, for example, in West Africa, countries are included in this list where some small dominion had obtained before 1870, but where the vast majority of the present area of the colony is of recent acquisition. Any older colonial possession thus included in Lagos or Gambia is, however, far more than counterbalanced by the increased area of the Gold Coast Colony, which is not included in this list, and which grew from 29,000 square miles in 1873 to 39,000 square miles in 1893.

The list is by no means complete. It takes no account of several

TABLE 1

	Date of Acquisition	Area: Square Miles	Population
EUROPE—			
Cyprus	1878	3,584	227,900
AFRICA—			
Zanzibar and Pemba	1888 ⎱	1,000,000	⎰ 200,000
East Africa Protectorate	1895 ⎰		⎱ 2,500,000
Uganda Protectorate	1894–1896	140,000	3,800,000
Somali Coast Protectorate	1884–1885	68,000	(?)
British Central Africa Protectorate	1889	42,217	688,049
Lagos	to 1899	21,000	3,000,000
Gambia	to 1888	3,550	215,000
Ashantee	1896–1901	70,000	2,000,000
Niger Coast Protectorate	1885–1898	400,000 to 500,000	25,000,000 to 40,000,000
Egypt	1882	400,000	9,734,405
Egyptian Soudan	1882	950,000	10,000,000
Griqualand West	1871–1880	15,197	83,373
Zululand	1879–1897	10,521	240,000
British Bechuanaland	1885	51,424	72,736
Bechuanaland Protectorate	1891	213,000	200,000
Transkei	1879–1885	2,535	153,582
Tembuland	1885	4,155	180,130
Pondoland	1894	4,040	188,000
Griqualand East	1879–1885	7,511	152,609
British South Africa Charter	1889	750,000	321,000
Transvaal	1900	119,139	870,000
Orange River Colony	1900	48,826	207,503
ASIA—			
Hong Kong (littoral)	1898	376	100,000
Wei-hai-wei	. . .	270	118,000
Socotra	1886	1,382	10,000
Upper Burma	1887	83,473	2,046,933
Baluchistan	1876–1889	130,000	500,000
Sikkim	1890	2,818	30,000
Rajputana (States)	⎧	128,022	12,186,352
Burma (States)	⎨ since 1881	62,661	785,800
Jammu and Kashmir	⎩	80,000	2,543,952
Malay Protected States	1883–1895	24,849	620,000
North Borneo Company	1881	31,106	175,000
North Borneo Protectorate	1888	. . .	. . .
Sarawak	1888	50,000	500,000
British New Guinea	1888	90,540	350,000
Fiji Islands	1874	7,740	122,676

large regions which have passed under the control of our Indian Government as native or feudatory States, but of which no statistics of area or population, even approximate, are available. Such are the Shan States, the Burma Frontier, and the Upper Burma Frontier, the districts of Chitral, Bajam, Swat, Waziristan, which came under our "sphere of influence" in 1893, and have been since taken under a closer protectorate. The increase of British India itself between 1871 and 1891 amounted to an area of 104,993 square miles, with a population of 25,330,000, while no reliable measurement of the formation of new native States within that period and since is available. Many of the measurements here given are in round numbers, indicative of their uncertainty, but they are taken, wherever available, from official publications of the Colonial Office, corroborated or supplemented from the "Statesman's Year-book." They will by no means comprise the full tale of our expansion during the thirty years, for many enlargements made by the several colonies themselves are omitted. But taken as they stand they make a formidable addition to the growth of an Empire whose nucleus is only 120,000 square miles, with 40 million population.

For so small a nation to add to its domains in the course of a single generation an area of 4,754,000 square miles, with an estimated population of 88 million, is a historical fact of great significance.

Accepting Sir Robert Giffen's estimate[1] of the size of our Empire (including Egypt and the Soudan) at about 13 million square miles, with a population of some 400 to 420 million (of whom about 50 million are of British race and speech), we find that one-third of this Empire, containing quite one-fourth of the total population of the Empire, has been acquired within the last generation. This is in tolerably close agreement with other independent estimates.

The character of this Imperial expansion is clearly exhibited in the list of new territories.

Though, for convenience, the year 1870 has been taken as indicative of the beginning of a conscious policy of Imperialism, it will be evident that the movement did not attain its full impetus until the middle of the eighties. The vast increase of territory, and the method

---

[1] Sir Robert Griffen was chief of the statistical department of the Board of Trade in the late nineteenth century.—Ed.

of wholesale partition which assigned to us great tracts of African land, may be dated from about 1884. Within fifteen years some three and three-quarter millions of square miles have been added to the British Empire.

Nor does Great Britain stand alone in this enterprise. The leading characteristic of modern Imperialism, the competition of rival Empires, is the product of this same period. The close of the Franco-German war marks the beginning of a new colonial policy in France and Germany, destined to take effect in the next decade. It was not unnatural that the newly founded German Empire, surrounded by powerful enemies and doubtful allies, and perceiving its more adventurous youth drawn into the United States and other foreign lands, should form the idea of a colonial empire. During the seventies a vigorous literature sprang up in advocacy of the policy which took shape a little later in the powerful hands of Bismarck. The earliest instance of official aid for the promotion of German commerce abroad occurred in 1880 in the Government aid granted to the "German Commercial and Plantation Association of the Southern Seas." German connection with Samoa dates from the same year, but the definite advance of Germany upon its Imperialist career began in 1884, with a policy of African protectorates and annexations of Oceanic islands. During the next fifteen years she brought under her colonial sway about 1 million square miles, with an estimated population of 14 million. Almost the whole of this territory is tropical, and the white population forms a total of a few thousands.

Similarly in France a great revival of the old colonial spirit took place in the early eighties, the most influential of the revivalists being the eminent economist, M. Paul Leroy-Beaulieu. The extension of empire in Senegal and Sahara in 1880 was followed next year by the annexation of Tunis, and France was soon actively engaged in the scramble for Africa in 1884, while at the same time she was fastening her rule on Tonking and Laos in Asia. Her acquisitions since 1880 (exclusive of the extension of New Caledonia and its dependencies) amount to an area of over three and a half million square miles, with a native population of some 37 million, almost the whole tropical or subtropical, inhabited by lower races and incapable of genuine French colonization.

Italian aspirations took similar shape from 1880 onwards, though the disastrous experience of the Abyssinian expeditions has given a check to Italian Imperialism.[2] Her possessions in East Africa are confined to the northern colony of Eritrea and the protectorate of Somaliland.

Of the other European States, two only, Portugal and Belgium, enter directly into the competition of the new Imperialism. The African arrangements of 1884–6 assigned to Portugal the large district of Angola on the Congo Coast, while a large strip of East Africa passed definitely under her political control in 1891. The anomalous position of the great Congo Free State, ceded to the King of Belgium in 1883, and growing since then by vast accretions, must be regarded as involving Belgium in the competition for African empire.

Spain may be said to have definitely retired from imperial competition. The large and important possessions of Holland in the East and West Indies, though involving her in imperial politics to some degree, belong to older colonialism: she takes no part in the new imperial expansion.

Russia, the only active expansionist country of the North, stands alone in the character of her imperial growth, which differs from other Imperialism in that it has been principally Asiatic in its achievements and has proceeded by direct extension of imperial boundaries, partaking to a larger extent than in the other cases of a regular colonial policy of settlement for purposes of agriculture and industry. It is, however, evident that Russian expansion, though of a more normal and natural order than that which characterizes the new Imperialism, comes definitely into contact and into competition with the claims and aspirations of the latter in Asia, and has been advancing rapidly during the period which is the object of our study.

The recent entrance of the powerful and progressive nation of the United States of America upon Imperialism by the annexation of Hawaii and the taking over of the relics of ancient Spanish empire not only adds a new formidable competitor for trade and territory, but changes and complicates the issues. As the focus of political attention and activity shifts more to the Pacific States, and the commercial aspirations of America are more and more set upon

---

[2] In 1887–89 and 1895–96, the Italians undertook two major expeditions into Ethiopia, both militarily undistinguished. At Adowa (or Adua) in 1896, the advancing Italian forces were virtually destroyed in one of the most crushing European defeats by a non-European army in modern times.—Ed.

trade with the Pacific islands and the Asiatic coast, the same forces which are driving European States along the path of territorial expansion seem likely to act upon the United States, leading her to a virtual abandonment of the principle of American isolation which has hitherto dominated her policy.

The following comparative table of colonization, compiled from the "Statesman's Year-book" for 1900 by Mr. H. C. Morris, marks the present expansion of the political control of Western nations [see Table 2].

The political nature of the new British Imperialism may be authoritatively ascertained by considering the governmental relations which the newly annexed territories hold with the Crown.

Officially, British "colonial possessions" fall into three classes— (1) "Crown colonies, in which the Crown has the entire control of legislation, while the administration is carried on by public officers under the control of the Home Government; (2) colonies possessing representative institutions, but not responsible government, in which the Crown has no more than a veto on legislation, but the Home Government retains the control of public affairs; (3) colonies possessing representative institutions and responsible government, in

TABLE 2

	Number of Colonies	Area: Square Miles		Population	
		Mother Country	Colonies, etc.	Mother Country	Colonies, etc.
United Kingdom	50	120,979	11,605,238	40,559,954	345,222,239
France	33	204,092	3,740,756	38,517,975	56,401,860
Germany	13	208,830	1,027,120	52,279,901	14,687,000
Netherlands	3	12,648	782,862	5,074,632	35,115,711
Portugal	9	36,038	801,100	5,049,729	9,148,707
Spain	3	197,670	243,877	17,565,632	136,000
Italy	2	110,646	188,500	31,856,675	850,000
Austria-Hungary	2	241,032	23,570	41,244,811	1,568,092
Denmark	3	15,289	86,634	2,185,335	114,229
Russia	3	8,660,395	255,550	128,932,173	15,684,000
Turkey	1	1,111,741	403,000	23,834,500	14,956,236
China	5	1,336,841	2,881,560	386,000,000	16,680,000
U.S.A.	6	3,557,000	172,091	77,000,000	10,544,617
Total	136	15,813,201	22,273,858	850,103,317	521,108,791

which the Crown has only a veto on legislation, and the Home Government has no control over any officer except the Governor."

Now, of the thirty-nine separate areas which have been annexed by Great Britain since 1870 as colonies or protectorates, not a single one ranks in class 2 or 3. The new Imperialism has established no single British colony endowed with responsible government or representative institutions. Nor, with the exception of the three new States in South Africa, where white settlers live in some numbers, is it seriously pretended that any of these annexed territories is being prepared and educated for representative, responsible self-government; and even in these South African States there is no serious intention, either on the part of the Home Government or of the colonists, that the majority of the inhabitants shall have any real voice in the government.

It is true that some of these areas enjoy a measure of self-government, as protectorates or as feudatory States, under their own native princes. But all these in major matters of policy are subject to the absolute rule of the British Government, or of some British official, while the general tendency is towards drawing the reins of arbitrary control more tightly over protectorates, converting them into States which are in substance, though not always in name, Crown colonies. With the exception of a couple of experiments in India, the tendency everywhere has been towards a closer and more drastic imperial control over the territories that have been annexed, transforming protectorates, company rule, and spheres of influence into definite British States of the Crown colony order.

This is attributable, not to any greed of tyranny on the part of the Imperial Government, but to the conditions imposed upon our rule by considerations of climate and native population. Almost the whole of this new territory is tropical, or so near to the tropics as to preclude genuine colonization of British settlers, while in those few districts where Europeans can work and breed, as in parts of South Africa and Egypt, the preoccupation of the country by large native populations of "lower races" precludes any considerable settlement of British workers and the safe bestowal of the full self-government which prevails in Australasia and Canada.

The same is true to an even more complete extent of the Imperialism of other continental countries. The new Imperialism has nowhere extended the political and civil liberties of the mother country to any part of the vast territories which, since 1870, have fallen under the government of Western civilized Powers. Politically, the new Imperialism is an expansion of autocracy.

Taking the growth of Imperialism as illustrated in the recent expansion of Great Britain and of the chief continental Powers, we find the distinction between Imperialism and colonization, set forth in the opening chapter, closely borne out by facts and figures, and warranting the following general judgments:

First—Almost the whole of recent imperial expansion is occupied with the political absorption of tropical or subtropical lands in which white men will not settle with their families.

Second—Nearly all the lands are thickly peopled by "lower races."

Thus this recent imperial expansion stands entirely distinct from the colonization of sparsely peopled lands in temperate zones, where white colonists carry with them the modes of government, the industrial and other arts of the civilization of the mother country. The "occupation" of these new territories is comprised in the presence of a small minority of white men, officials, traders, and industrial organizers, exercising political and economic sway over great hordes of population regarded as inferior and as incapable of exercising any considerable rights of self-government, in politics or industry.

The Commercial Value of Imperialism

The absorption of so large a proportion of public interest, energy, blood and money in seeking to procure colonial possessions and foreign markets would seem to indicate that Great Britain obtains her chief livelihood by external trade. Now this is not the case. Large as is our foreign and colonial trade in volume and in value, essential as is much of it to our national well-being, nevertheless it furnishes a small proportion of the real income of the nation.

Although the volume and value of home industries are not directly calculable, the total income of the nation, comprising profits, wages, rents, and other gains from all sources, is approximately estimated at £1.7 billion per annum. This sum, of course, covers all payments, not only for productive services of land, capital and labor in the making and distributing of material wealth, but for professional and personal services as well. Real income in the shape of goods or services to this amount is consumed or saved within the year.

Now the total value of the import and export trade of Great Britain in 1898 (we take this year as the latest normal one for the purpose, later years being disturbed by the war factor) amounted to £765 million. If we were to take the very liberal allowance of 5 percent as profit upon this turnover of trade, the annual income directly derived from our external trade would amount to a little over £38 million, or about one forty-fifth part of our total income.

*　　*　　*

... Taking under survey our whole Empire, we reach the conclusion that, excluding our commerce with India, the smallest, least valuable, and most uncertain trade is that done with our tropical possessions, and in particular with those which have come under imperial control since 1870. The only considerable increase of our import trade since 1884 is from our genuine colonies in Australasia, North America, and Cape Colony; the trade with India has been stagnant, while that with our tropical colonies in Africa and the West Indies has been in most cases irregular and dwindling. Our export trade exhibits the same general character, save that Australia and Canada show a growing resolution to release themselves from dependence upon British manufactures; the trade with the tropical colonies, though exhibiting some increase, is very small and very fluctuating.

As for the territories acquired under the new Imperialism, except in one instance, no serious attempt to regard them as satisfactory business assets is possible. Egypt alone yields a trade of some magnitude; of the other possessions, three only—Lagos, Niger Coast Protectorate, and North Borneo—are proved to do a trade with Great Britain exceeding one million pounds in value. In fact, excluding Egypt, the whole volume of this trade, so far as it is officially recorded, does not amount to ten million pounds; and though the actual trade is doubtless in excess of this sum, it forms an infinitesimal addition to the commercial resources of our nation. Apart from its quantity, the quality of the new tropical export trade is of the lowest, consisting for the most part, as the analysis of the Colonial Office shows, of the cheapest metal goods of Birmingham and Sheffield, and large quantities of gunpowder, spirits, and tobacco.

Such evidence leads to the following conclusions bearing upon the economics of the new Imperialism. First, the external trade of Great Britain bears a small and diminishing proportion to its internal industry and trade. Secondly, of the external trade, that with British possessions bears a diminishing proportion to that with foreign countries. Thirdly, of the trade with British possessions, the tropical trade, and in particular the trade with the new tropical possessions, is the smallest, least progressive, and most fluctuating in quantity, while it is lowest in the character of the goods which it embraces.

Imperialism as an Outlet for Population

There is a widely prevalent belief that imperial expansion is desirable, or even necessary, in order to absorb and utilize the surplus of our ever-growing population. . . .

. . . What validity does it possess as an argument for recent imperial expansion? Let me first ask: Is England overpopulated now, and is the prospect of further increase such as to compel us to "peg out claims for posterity" in other parts of the world? The facts are these. Great Britain is not so thickly populated as certain prosperous industrial areas in Germany, the Netherlands, and China: along with every recent growth of population has come a far greater growth of wealth and of the power to purchase food and other subsistence. The modern specialization of industry has caused a congestion of population upon certain spots which may be injurious in some ways to the well-being of the nation, but it cannot be regarded as overpopulation in the sense of a people outgrowing the means of subsistence. Nor have we reason to fear such overpopulation in the future. It is true that our manufactures and commerce may not continue to grow as rapidly as in the past, though we have no clear warrant from industrial statistics for this judgment: but if this be so, neither is our population likely to increase so fast. Of this we have clear statistical evidence: the diminution of the rate of growth of our population, as disclosed by the two latest censuses, is such as to justify the conclusion that, if the same forces continue to operate, the population of Great Britain will be stationary by the middle of the century.

There exists, then, no general necessity for a policy of expansion in order to provide for overpopulation, present or prospective. But supposing it were necessary for an increasing surplus of our population to emigrate, is it necessary for us to spend so large a part of our national resources, and to incur such heavy risks, in seizing new territory for them to settle upon?. . .

No substantial settlement of Britons is taking place upon any of the areas of the Empire acquired since 1870, excepting the Transvaal and the Orange River Colony, nor is it likely that any such settlement will take place. The tropical character of most lands acquired under the new Imperialism renders genuine colonization impossible: there is no true British settlement in these places; a small number of men spend a short broken period in precarious occupations as traders, engineers, missionaries, overseers. The new Empire is even more barren for settlement than for profitable trade.

Economic Parasites of Imperialism

I

Seeing that the Imperialism of the last three decades is clearly condemned as a business policy, in that at enormous expense it has procured a small, bad, unsafe increase of markets, and has jeopardized the entire wealth of the nation in rousing the strong resentment of other nations, we may ask, "How is the British nation induced to embark upon such unsound business?" The only possible answer is that the business interests of the nation as a whole are subordinated to those of certain sectional interests that usurp control of the national resources and use them for their private gain. This is no strange or monstrous charge to bring; it is the commonest disease of all forms of government. The famous words of Sir Thomas More are as true now as when he wrote them: "Everywhere do I perceive a certain conspiracy of rich men seeking their own advantage under the name and pretext of the commonwealth."

Although the new Imperialism has been bad business for the nation, it has been good business for certain classes and certain trades within the nation. The vast expenditure on armaments, the costly wars, the grave risks and embarrassments of foreign policy, the stoppage of political and social reforms within Great Britain, though fraught with great injury to the nation, have served well the present business interests of certain industries and professions.

It is idle to meddle with politics unless we clearly recognize this central fact and understand what these sectional interests are which are the enemies of national safety and the commonwealth. We must put aside the merely sentimental diagnosis which explains wars or other national blunders by outbursts of patriotic animosity or errors of statecraft. Doubtless at every outbreak of war not only the man in the street but the man at the helm is often duped by the cunning with which aggressive motives and greedy purposes dress themselves in defensive clothing. There is, it may be safely asserted, no war within memory, however nakedly aggressive it may seem to the dispassionate historian, which has not been presented to the people who were called upon to fight as a necessary defensive policy, in which the honor, perhaps the very existence, of the State was involved.

The disastrous folly of these wars, the material and moral damage inflicted even on the victor, appear so plain to the disinterested spectator that he is apt to despair of any State attaining years of discretion, and inclines to regard these natural cataclysms as implying some ultimate irrationalism in politics. But careful analysis of the existing relations between business and politics shows that the aggressive Imperialism which we seek to understand is not in the main the product of blind passions of races or of the mixed folly and ambition of politicians. It is far more rational than at first sight appears. Irrational from the standpoint of the whole nation, it is rational enough from the standpoint of certain classes in the nation. A completely socialist State which kept good books and presented regular balance-sheets of expenditure and assets would soon discard Imperialism; an intelligent laissez-faire democracy which gave duly proportionate weight in its policy to all economic interests alike would do the same. But a State in which certain well-organized business interests are able to outweigh the weak, diffused interest of the community is bound to pursue a policy which accords with the pressure of the former interests.

In order to explain Imperialism on this hypothesis we have to answer two questions. Do we find in Great Britain today any well-organized group of special commercial and social interests which stand to gain by aggressive Imperialism and the militarism it involves? If such a combination of interests exists, has it the power to work its will in the arena of politics?

What is the direct economic outcome of Imperialism? A great

expenditure of public money upon ships, guns, military and naval equipment and stores, growing and productive of enormous profits when a war, or an alarm of war, occurs; new public loans and important fluctuations in the home and foreign Bourses; more posts for soldiers and sailors and in the diplomatic and consular services; improvement of foreign investments by the substitution of the British flag for a foreign flag; acquisition of markets for certain classes of exports, and some protection and assistance for trades representing British houses in these manufactures; employment for engineers, missionaries, speculative miners, ranchers and other emigrants.

Certain definite business and professional interests feeding upon imperialistic expenditure, or upon the results of that expenditure, are thus set up in opposition to the common good, and, instinctively feeling their way to one another, are found united in strong sympathy to support every new imperialist exploit.

If the £60 million which may now be taken as a minimum expenditure on armaments in time of peace were subjected to a close analysis, most of it would be traced directly to the tills of certain big firms engaged in building warships and transports, equipping and coaling them, manufacturing guns, rifles, and ammunition, supplying horses, wagons, saddlery, food, clothing for the services, contracting for barracks, and for other large irregular needs. Through these main channels the millions flow to feed many subsidiary trades, most of which are quite aware that they are engaged in executing contracts for the services. Here we have an important nucleus of commercial Imperialism. Some of these trades, especially the shipbuilding, boilermaking, and gun and ammunition making trades, are conducted by large firms with immense capital, whose heads are well aware of the uses of political influence for trade purposes.

These men are Imperialists by conviction; a pushful policy is good for them.

With them stand the great manufacturers for export trade, who gain a living by supplying the real or artificial wants of the new countries we annex or open up. Manchester, Sheffield, Birmingham, to name three representative cases, are full of firms which compete in pushing textiles and hardware, engines, tools, machinery, spirits, guns, upon new markets. The public debts which ripen in our colonies, and in foreign countries that come under our protectorate or influence, are largely loaned in the shape of rails, engines, guns, and other materials of civilization made and sent out by British firms. The making of railways, canals, and other public works, the establishment of factories, the development of mines, the improvement of agriculture in new countries, stimulate a definite interest in important manufacturing industries which feeds a very firm imperialist faith in their owners.

The proportion which such trade bears to the total industry of Great Britain is very small, but some of it is extremely influential and able to make a definite impression upon politics, through chambers of commerce, Parliamentary representatives, and semipolitical, semicommercial bodies like the Imperial South African Association or the China League.

The shipping trade has a very definite interest which makes for Imperialism. This is well illustrated by the policy of State subsidies now claimed by shipping firms as a retainer, and in order to encourage British shipping for purposes of imperial safety and defense.

The services are, of course, imperialist by conviction and by professional interest, and every increase of the army and navy enhances their numerical strength and the political power they exert. The abolition of purchase in the army, by opening the profession to the upper middle classes, greatly enlarged this most direct feeder of imperial sentiment. The potency of this factor is, of course, largely due to the itch for glory and adventure among military officers upon disturbed or uncertain frontiers of the Empire. This has been a most prolific source of expansion in India. The direct professional influence of the services carries with it a less organized but powerful sympathetic support on the part of the aristocracy and the wealthy classes, who seek in the services careers for their sons.

To the military services we may add the Indian Civil Service and the numerous official and semiofficial posts in our colonies and protectorates. Every expansion of the Empire is also regarded by these same classes as affording new openings for their sons as ranchers, planters, engineers, or missionaries. This point of view is aptly summarized by a high Indian official, Sir Charles Crossthwaite, in discussing British relations with Siam. "The real question was who was to get the trade with them, and how we could make the most of them, so as to find fresh markets for our goods and also employment for those superfluous articles of the present day, our boys."

From this standpoint our colonies still remain what James Mill cynically described them as being, "a vast system of outdoor relief for the upper classes."

In all the professions, military and civil, the army, diplomacy, the church, the bar, teaching and engineering, Greater Britain serves for an overflow, relieving the congestion of the home market and offering chances to more reckless or adventurous members, while it furnishes a convenient limbo for damaged characters and careers. The actual amount of profitable employment thus furnished by our recent acquisitions is inconsiderable, but it arouses that disproportionate interest which always attaches to the margin of employment. To extend this margin is a powerful motive in Imperialism.

These influences, primarily economic, though not unmixed with other sentimental motives, are particularly operative in military, clerical, academic, and Civil Service circles, and furnish an interested bias towards Imperialism throughout the educated classes.

II

By far the most important economic factor in Imperialism is the influence relating to investments. The growing cosmopolitanism of capital is the greatest economic change of this generation. Every advanced industrial nation is tending to place a larger share of its capital outside the limits of its own political area, in foreign countries, or in colonies, and to draw a growing income from this source.

No exact or even approximate estimate of the total amount of the income of the British nation derived from foreign investments is possible. We possess, however, in the income-tax assessments an indirect measurement of certain large sections of investments, from which we can form some judgment as to the total size of the income from foreign and colonial sources, and the rate of its growth [see Table 3].

From this table it appears that the period of energetic Imperialism has been coincident with a remarkable growth in the income from external investments. The income from these sources has nearly doubled in the period 1884–1900, while the portion derived from

TABLE 3

Income from Foreign Investments Assured to Income-Tax

	1884	1888	1892	1896	1900
	£	£	£	£	£
From Indian public revenue	2,607,942	3,130,959	3,203,573	3,475,751	3,587,919
Indian rails	4,544,466	4,841,647	4,580,797	4,543,969	4,693,795
Colonial and foreign public securities, etc.	13,233,271	16,757,736	14,949,017	16,419,933	18,394,380
Railways out of United Kingdom	3,777,592	4,178,456	8,013,838	13,032,556	14,043,107
Foreign and colonial investments	9,665,853	18,069,573	23,981,545	17,428,870	19,547,685
	33,829,124	46,978,371	54,728,770	54,901,079	60,266,886

foreign railways and foreign and colonial investments has increased at a still more rapid rate.

These figures only give the foreign income which can be identified as such. To them must be added a large amount of income which escapes these income-tax returns, including considerable sums which would appear as profits of businesses carried on in the United Kingdom, such as insurance companies, investment trusts, and land mortgage companies, many of which derive a large part of their income from foreign investments. How rapid is the growth of this order of investment is seen from the published returns of investments of life insurance companies, which show that their investments in mortgages outside the United Kingdom had grown from about £6 million in 1890 to £13 million in 1898.

Sir R. Giffen estimated the income derived from foreign sources as profit, interest and pensions in 1882 at £70 million, and in a paper read before the Statistical Society in March 1899 he estimated the income from these same sources for the current year at £90 million. It is probable that this last figure is an underestimate, for if the items of foreign income not included as such under the income-tax returns bear the same proportion to those included as in 1882, the present total of income from foreign and colonial investments should be £120 million rather than £90 million. Sir R. Giffen hazards the calculation that the new public investments abroad in the sixteen years 1882–1898 amounted to over £800 million, "and though part of the sum may have been nominal only, the real investment must have been enormous."

Mr. Mulhall[3] gives the following estimate of the size and growth of our foreign and colonial investments since 1862:

Year	Amount	Annual Increase
	£	Percent
1862	144,000,000	. . .
1872	600,000,000	45.6
1882	875,000,000	27.5
1893	1,698,000,000	74.8

This last amount is of especial interest, because it represents the most thorough investigation made by a most competent economist for the "Dictionary of Political Economy." The investments included under this figure may be classified under the following general heads:

Loans	Million £	Railways	Million £	Sundries	Million £
Foreign	525	U.S.A.	120	Banks	50
Colonial	225	Colonial	140	Lands	100
Municipal	20	Various	128	Mines, etc.	390
	770		388		540

In other words, in 1893 the British capital invested abroad represented about 15 percent of the total wealth of the United Kingdom: nearly one-half of this capital was in the form of loans to foreign and colonial Governments; of the rest a large proportion was invested in railways, banks, telegraphs, and other public services, owned, controlled, or vitally affected by Governments, while most of the remainder was placed in lands and mines, or in industries directly dependent on land values.

Income-tax returns and other statistics descriptive of the growth of these investments indicate that the total amount of British invest-

---

[3] Michael G. Mulhall was a British editor and statistician.—Ed.

ments abroad at the end of the nineteenth century cannot be set down at a lower figure than £2 billion. Considering that Sir R. Giffen regarded as "moderate" the estimate of £1.7 billion in 1892, the figure here named is probably below the truth.

Now, without placing any undue reliance upon these estimates, we cannot fail to recognize that in dealing with these foreign investments we are facing by far the most important factor in the economics of Imperialism. Whatever figures we take, two facts are evident. First, that the income derived as interest upon foreign investments enormously exceeds that derived as profits upon ordinary export and import trade. Secondly, that while our foreign and colonial trade, and presumably the income from it, are growing but slowly, the share of our import values representing income from foreign investments is growing very rapidly.

In a former chapter I pointed out how small a proportion of our national income appeared to be derived as profits from external trade. It seemed unintelligible that the enormous costs and risks of the new Imperialism should be undertaken for such small results in the shape of increase to external trade, especially when the size and character of the new markets acquired were taken into consideration. The statistics of foreign investments, however, shed clear light upon the economic forces which are dominating our policy. While the manufacturing and trading classes make little out of their new markets, paying, if they knew it, much more in taxation than they get out of them in trade, it is quite otherwise with the investor.

It is not too much to say that the modern foreign policy of Great Britain is primarily a struggle for profitable markets of investment. To a larger extent every year Great Britain is becoming a nation living upon tribute from abroad, and the classes who enjoy this tribute have an ever-increasing incentive to employ the public policy, the public purse, and the public force to extend the field of their private investments, and to safeguard and improve their existing investments. This is, perhaps, the most important fact in modern politics, and the obscurity in which it is wrapped constitutes the gravest danger to our State.

What is true of Great Britain is true likewise of France, Germany, the United States, and of all countries in which modern capitalism has placed large surplus savings in the hands of a plutocracy or of a thrifty middle class. A well-recognized distinction is drawn between creditor and debtor countries. Great Britain has been for some time by far the largest creditor country, and the policy by which the investing classes use the instrument of the State for private business purposes is most richly illustrated in the recent history of her wars and annexations. But France, Germany, and the United States are advancing fast along the same path. The nature of these imperialist operations is thus set forth by the Italian economist Loria:

> *When a country which has contracted a debt is unable, on account of the slenderness of its income, to offer sufficient guarantee for the punctual payment of interest, what happens? Sometimes an out-and-out conquest of the debtor country follows. Thus France's attempted conquest of Mexico during the second empire was undertaken solely with the view of guaranteeing the interest of French citizens holding Mexican securities. But more frequently the insufficient guarantee of an international loan gives rise to the appointment of a financial commission by the creditor countries in order to protect their rights and guard the fate of their invested capital. The appointment of such a commission literally amounts in the end, however, to a veritable conquest. We have examples of this in Egypt, which has to all practical purposes become a British province, and in Tunis, which has in like manner become a dependency of France, who supplied the greater part of the loan. The Egyptian revolt against the foreign domination issuing from the debt came to nothing, as it met with invariable opposition from capitalistic combinations, and Tel-el-Kebir's[4] success, bought with money, was the most brilliant victory wealth has ever obtained on the field of battle.*

But, though useful to explain certain economic facts, the terms "creditor" and "debtor," as applied to countries, obscure the most significant feature of this Imperialism. For though, as appears from the analysis given above, much, if not most, of the debts are "public," the credit is nearly always private, though sometimes, as in the case of Egypt, its owners succeed in getting their Government to enter a most unprofitable partnership, guaranteeing the payment of the interest, but not sharing in it.

Aggressive Imperialism, which costs the taxpayer so dear, which is of so little value to the manufacturer and trader, which is fraught with such grave incalculable peril to the citizen, is a source of great gain to the investor who cannot find at home the profitable use he

---

[4] Site of British victory over Egyptians, 1882.—Ed.

seeks for his capital, and insists that his Government should help him to profitable and secure investments abroad.

If, contemplating the enormous expenditure on armaments, the ruinous wars, the diplomatic audacity of knavery by which modern Governments seek to extend their territorial power, we put the plain, practical question, *Cui bono?* the first and most obvious answer is, The investor.

The annual income Great Britain derives from commissions on her whole foreign and colonial trade, import and export, is estimated by Sir R. Giffen at £18 million for 1899, taken at $2\frac{1}{2}$ percent, upon a turnover of £800 million. This is the whole that we are entitled to regard as profits on external trade. Considerable as this sum is, it cannot serve to yield an economic motive-power adequate to explain the dominance which business considerations exercise over our imperial policy. Only when we set beside it some £90 million or £100 million, representing pure profit upon investments, do we understand whence the economic impulse to Imperialism is derived.

Investors who have put their money in foreign lands, upon terms which take full account of risks connected with the political conditions of the country, desire to use the resources of their Government to minimize these risks, and so to enhance the capital value and the interest of their private investments. The investing and speculative classes in general also desire that Great Britain should take other foreign areas under her flag in order to secure new areas for profitable investment and speculation.

III

If the special interest of the investor is liable to clash with the public interest and to induce a wrecking policy, still more dangerous is the special interest of the financier, the general dealer in investments. In large measure the rank and file of the investors are, both for business and for politics, the cat's-paws of the great financial houses, who use stocks and shares not so much as investments to yield them interest, but as material for speculation in the money market. In handling large masses of stocks and shares, in floating companies, in manipulating fluctuations of values, the magnates of the Bourse find their gain. These great businesses—banking, broking, bill discounting, loan floating, company promoting—form the central ganglion of international capitalism. United by the strongest bonds of organization, always in closest and quickest touch with one another, situated in the very heart of the business capital of every State, controlled, so far as Europe is concerned, chiefly by men of a single and peculiar race, who have behind them many centuries of financial experience, they are in a unique position to control the policy of nations. No great quick direction of capital is possible save by their consent and through their agency. Does anyone seriously suppose that a great war could be undertaken by any European State, or a great State loan subscribed, if the house of Rothschild and its connections set their face against it?

Every great political act involving a new flow of capital, or a large fluctuation in the values of existing investments, must receive the sanction and the practical aid of this little group of financial kings. These men, holding their realized wealth and their business capital, as they must, chiefly in stocks and bonds, have a double stake, first as investors, but secondly and chiefly as financial dealers. As investors, their political influence does not differ essentially from that of the smaller investors, except that they usually possess a practical control of the businesses in which they invest. As speculators or financial dealers they constitute, however, the gravest single factor in the economics of Imperialism.

To create new public debts, to float new companies, and to cause constant considerable fluctuations of values are three conditions of their profitable business. Each condition carries them into politics, and throws them on the side of Imperialism.

The public financial arrangements for the Philippine war put several millions of dollars into the pockets of Mr. Pierpont Morgan and his friends; the China-Japan war, which saddled the Celestial Empire for the first time with a public debt, and the indemnity which she will pay to her European invaders in connection with the recent conflict, bring grist to the financial mills in Europe; every railway or mining concession wrung from some reluctant foreign potentate means profitable business in raising capital and floating companies. A policy which rouses fears of aggression in Asiatic states, and which fans the rivalry of commercial nations in Europe, evokes vast expenditure on armaments, and ever-accumulating public debts, while the doubts and risks accruing from this policy promote that constant oscillation of values of securities which is so profitable to the skilled financier. There is not a war, a revolution, an anarchist assassination, or any other public shock, which is not gainful to these men; they are harpies who suck their gains from every new forced expenditure and every sudden disturbance of public credit. To the financiers "in the know" the Jameson raid [5] was a most advantageous coup, as may be ascertained by a comparison of the "holdings" of these men before and after that event; the terrible sufferings of England and South Africa in the war, which is a sequel of the raid, is a source of immense profit to the big financiers who have best held out against the uncalculated waste, and have recouped themselves by profitable war contracts and by "freezing out" the smaller interests in the Transvaal. These men are the only certain gainers from the war, and most of their gains are made out of the public losses of their adopted country or the private losses of their fellow-countrymen.

The policy of these men, it is true, does not necessarily make for war; where war would bring about too great and too permanent a damage to the substantial fabric of industry, which is the ultimate and essential basis of speculation, their influence is cast for peace, as in the dangerous quarrel between Great Britain and the United States regarding Venezuela. But every increase of public expenditure, every oscillation of public credit short of this collapse, every risky enterprise in which public resources can be made the pledge of private speculations, is profitable to the big money-lender and speculator.

The wealth of these houses, the scale of their operations, and their cosmopolitan organization make them the prime determinants of imperial policy. They have the largest definite stake in the business of Imperialism, and the amplest means of forcing their will upon the policy of nations.

In view of the part which the noneconomic factors of patriotism, adventure, military enterprise, political ambition, and philanthropy play in imperial expansion, it may appear that to impute to financiers so much power is to take a too narrowly economic view of history. And it is true that the motor-power of Imperialism is not chiefly financial: finance is rather the governor of the imperial engine,

---

[5] This disastrous attempt by Cape Colony leaders (with some connivance in London) to help overthrow the government of the Transvaal in December 1895 seriously exacerbated British-Boer relations.—Ed.

directing the energy and determining its work: it does not constitute the fuel of the engine, nor does it directly generate the power. Finance manipulates the patriotic forces which politicians, soldiers, philanthropists, and traders generate; the enthusiasm for expansion which issues from these sources, though strong and genuine, is irregular and blind; the financial interest has those qualities of concentration and clear-sighted calculation which are needed to set Imperialism to work. An ambitious statesman, a frontier soldier, an overzealous missionary, a pushing trader, may suggest or even initiate a step of imperial expansion, may assist in educating patriotic public opinion to the urgent need of some fresh advance, but the final determination rests with the financial power. The direct influence exercised by great financial houses in "high politics" is supported by the control which they exercise over the body of public opinion through the Press, which, in every "civilized" country, is becoming more and more their obedient instrument. While the specifically financial newspaper imposes "facts" and "opinions" on the business classes, the general body of the Press comes more and more under the conscious or unconscious domination of financiers. The case of the South African Press, whose agents and correspondents fanned the martial flames in this country, was one of open ownership on the part of South African financiers, and this policy of owning newspapers for the sake of manufacturing public opinion is common in the great European cities. In Berlin, Vienna, and Paris many of the influential newspapers are held by financial houses, which use them, not primarily to make direct profits out of them, but in order to put into the public mind beliefs and sentiments which will influence public policy and thus affect the money market. In Great Britain this policy has not gone so far, but the alliance with finance grows closer every year, either by financiers purchasing a controlling share of newspapers, or by newspaper proprietors being tempted into finance. Apart from the financial Press, and financial ownership of the general Press, the City notoriously exercises a subtle and abiding influence upon leading London newspapers, and through them upon the body of the provincial Press, while the entire dependence of the Press for its business profits upon its advertising columns involves a peculiar reluctance to oppose the organized financial classes with whom rests the control of so much advertising business. Add to this the natural sympathy with a sensational policy which a cheap Press always manifests, and it becomes evident that the Press is strongly biased towards Imperialism, and lends itself with great facility to the suggestion of financial or political Imperialists who desire to work up patriotism for some new piece of expansion.

Such is the array of distinctively economic forces making for Imperialism, a large loose group of trades and professions seeking profitable business and lucrative employment from the expansion of military and civil services, from the expenditure on military operations, the opening up of new tracts of territory and trade with the same, and the provision of new capital which these operations require, all these finding their central guiding and directing force in the power of the general financier.

The play of these forces does not openly appear. They are essentially parasites upon patriotism, and they adapt themselves to its protecting colors. In the mouths of their representatives are noble phrases, expressive of their desire to extend the area of civilization, to establish good government, promote Christianity, extirpate slavery, and elevate the lower races. Some of the businessmen who hold such language may entertain a genuine, though usually a vague, desire to accomplish these ends, but they are primarily engaged in business, and they are not unaware of the utility of the more unselfish forces in furthering their ends. Their true attitude of mind is expressed by Mr. Rhodes in his famous description of "Her Majesty's Flag" as "the greatest commercial asset in the world." . . .

The Economic Taproot of Imperialism

No mere array of facts and figures adduced to illustrate the economic nature of the new Imperialism will suffice to dispel the popular delusion that the use of national force to secure new markets by annexing fresh tracts of territory is a sound and a necessary policy for an advanced industrial country like Great Britain. It has indeed been proved that recent annexations of tropical countries, procured at great expense, have furnished poor and precarious markets, that our aggregate trade with our colonial possessions is virtually stationary, and that our most profitable and progressive trade is with rival industrial nations, whose territories we have no desire to annex, whose markets we cannot force, and whose active antagonism we are provoking by our expansive policy.

But these arguments are not conclusive. It is open to Imperialists to argue thus: "We must have markets for our growing manufactures, we must have new outlets for the investment of our surplus capital and for the energies of the adventurous surplus of our population: such expansion is a necessity of life to a nation with our great and growing powers of production. An ever larger share of our population is devoted to the manufactures and commerce of towns, and is thus dependent for life and work upon food and raw materials from foreign lands. In order to buy and pay for these things we must sell our goods abroad. During the first three-quarters of the century we could do so without difficulty by a natural expansion of commerce with continental nations and our colonies, all of which were far behind us in the main arts of manufacture and the carrying trades. So long as England held a virtual monopoly of the world markets for certain important classes of manufactured goods, Imperialism was unnecessary. During the last thirty years this manufacturing and trading supremacy has been greatly impaired: other nations, especially Germany, the United States, and Belgium, have advanced with great rapidity, and while they have not crushed or even stayed the increase of our external trade, their competition is making it more and more difficult to dispose of the full surplus of our manufactures at a profit. The encroachments made by these nations upon our old markets, even in our own possessions, make it most urgent that we should take energetic means to secure new markets. These new markets must lie in hitherto undeveloped countries, chiefly in the tropics, where vast populations live capable of growing economic needs which our manufacturers and merchants can supply. Our rivals are seizing and annexing territories for similar purposes, and when they have annexed them close them to our trade. The diplomacy and the arms of Great Britain must be used in order to compel the owners of the new markets to deal with us: and experience shows that the safest means of securing and developing such markets is by establishing "protectorates" or by annexation. The present value of these markets must not be taken as a final test of the economy of such a policy; the process of educating civilized needs which we can supply is of necessity a gradual one, and the cost of such imperialism must be regarded as a capital outlay, the fruits of which posterity will reap. The new markets may not be large, but they form serviceable outlets for the overflow of our great textile and metal industries, and, when the vast Asiatic and African populations of the interior are reached, a rapid expansion of trade may be expected to result.

"Far larger and more important is the pressure of capital for external fields of investment. Moreover, while the manufacturer and trader are well content to trade with foreign nations, the tendency for investors to work towards the political annexation of countries which contain their more speculative investments is very powerful. Of the fact of this pressure of capital there can be no question. Large savings are made which cannot find any profitable investment in this country; they must find employment elsewhere, and it is to the advantage of the nation that they should be employed as largely as possible in lands where they can be utilized in opening up markets for British trade and employment for British enterprise.

"However costly, however perilous, this process of imperial expansion may be, it is necessary to the continued existence and progress of our nation; if we abandoned it we must be content to leave the development of the world to other nations, who will everywhere cut into our trade, and even impair our means of securing the food and raw materials we require to support our population. Imperialism is thus seen to be, not a choice, but a necessity."

The practical force of this economic argument in politics is strikingly illustrated by the recent history of the United States. Here is a country which suddenly breaks through a conservative policy, strongly held by both political parties, bound up with every popular instinct and tradition, and flings itself into a rapid imperial career for which it possesses neither the material nor the moral equipment, risking the principles and practices of liberty and equality by the establishment of militarism and the forcible subjugation of peoples which it cannot safely admit to the condition of American citizenship.

Is this a mere wild freak of spread-eaglism, a burst of political ambition on the part of a nation coming to a sudden realization of its destiny? Not at all. The spirit of adventure, the American "mission of civilization," are, as forces making for Imperialism, clearly subordinate to the driving force of the economic factor....

...American Imperialism is the natural product of the economic

pressure of a sudden advance of capitalism which cannot find occupation at home and needs foreign markets for goods and for
investments.

The same needs exist in European countries, and, as is admitted,
drive Governments along the same path. Overproduction in the
sense of an excessive manufacturing plant, and surplus capital
which cannot find sound investments within the country, force Great
Britain, Germany, Holland, France to place larger and larger portions of their economic resources outside the area of their present
political domain, and then stimulate a policy of political expansion
so as to take in the new areas. The economic sources of this movement are laid bare by periodic trade-depressions due to an inability
of producers to find adequate and profitable markets for what they
can produce. The Majority Report of the Commission upon the
Depression of Trade in 1885 put the matter in a nutshell. "That,
owing to the nature of the times, the demand for our commodities
does not increase at the same rate as formerly; that our capacity
for production is consequently in excess of our requirements, and
could be considerably increased at short notice; that this is due
partly to the competition of the capital which is being steadily
accumulated in the country." The Minority Report straightly imputes
the condition of affairs to "overproduction." Germany is at the
present time suffering severely from what is called a glut of capital
and of manufacturing power: she must have new markets; her
Consuls all over the world are "hustling" for trade; trading settlements are forced upon Asia Minor; in East and West Africa, in China
and elsewhere the German Empire is impelled to a policy of colonization and protectorates as outlets for German commercial energy.

Every improvement of methods of production, every concentration of ownership and control, seems to accentuate the tendency.
As one nation after another enters the machine economy and adopts
advanced industrial methods, it becomes more difficult for its manufacturers, merchants, and financiers to dispose profitably of their
economic resources, and they are tempted more and more to use
their Governments in order to secure for their particular use some
distant undeveloped country by annexation and protection.

The process we may be told is inevitable, and so it seems upon a
superficial inspection. Everywhere appear excessive powers of production, excessive capital in search of investment. It is admitted by

all businessmen that the growth of the powers of production in their country exceeds the growth in consumption, that more goods can be produced than can be sold at a profit, and that more capital exists than can find remunerative investment.

It is this economic condition of affairs that forms the taproot of Imperialism. If the consuming public in this country raised its standard of consumption to keep pace with every rise of productive powers, there could be no excess of goods or capital clamorous to use Imperialism in order to find markets: foreign trade would indeed exist, but there would be no difficulty in exchanging a small surplus of our manufactures for the food and raw material we annually absorbed, and all the savings that we made could find employment, if we chose, in home industries. . . .

Moral and Sentimental Factors

I

Analysis of the actual course of modern Imperialism has laid bare the combination of economic and political forces which fashions it. These forces are traced to their sources in the selfish interests of certain industrial, financial, and professional classes, seeking private advantages out of a policy of imperial expansion, and using this same policy to protect them in their economic, political, and social privileges against the pressure of democracy. It remains to answer the question, "Why does Imperialism escape general recognition for the narrow, sordid thing it is?" Each nation, as it watches from outside the Imperialism of its neighbors, is not deceived; the selfish interests of political and commerical classes are seen plainly paramount in the direction of the policy. So every other European nation recognizes the true outlines of British Imperialism and charges us with hypocrisy in feigning blindness. This charge is false; no nation sees its own shortcomings; the charge of hypocrisy is seldom justly brought against an individual, against a nation never. Frenchmen and Germans believe that our zeal in promoting foreign missions, putting down slavery, and in spreading the arts of civilization is a false disguise conveniently assumed to cover naked national self-assertion. The actual case is somewhat different.

There exists in a considerable though not a large proportion of the British nation a genuine desire to spread Christianity among the heathen, to diminish the cruelty and other sufferings which they believe exist in countries less fortunate than their own, and to do good work about the world in the cause of humanity. Most of the churches contain a small body of men and women deeply, even passionately, interested in such work, and a much larger number whose sympathy, though weaker, is quite genuine. Ill-trained for the most part in psychology and history, these people believe that religion and other arts of civilization are portable commodities which it is our duty to convey to the backward nations, and that a certain amount of compulsion is justified in pressing their benefits upon people too ignorant at once to recognize them.

Is it surprising that the selfish forces which direct Imperialism should utilize the protective colors of these disinterested movements? Imperialist politicians, soldiers, or company directors, who push a forward policy by portraying the cruelties of the African slave raids or the infamous tyranny of a Prempeh or a Thebaw,[6] or who open out a new field for missionary enterprise in China or the Soudan, do not deliberately and consciously work up these motives in order to incite the British public. They simply and instinctively attach to themselves any strong, genuine elevated feeling which is of service, fan it and feed it until it assumes fervor, and utilize it for their ends. The politician always, the businessman not seldom, believes that high motives qualify the political or financial benefits he gets: it is certain that Lord Salisbury[7] really believes that the South African war, for which his Government is responsible, has been undertaken for the benefit of the people of South Africa and will result in increased liberty and happiness; it is quite likely that Earl Grey[8] thinks that the Chartered Company which he directs is animated by a desire to improve the material and moral condition of the natives of Rhodesia and that it is attaining this object.

So Leopold, King of the Belgians, has claimed for his government

---

[6] Prempeh: Asantehene (leading chief) of the Ashanti in West Africa. Thebaw (or Thibaw): last king of Burma (deposed 1885). Both men were well-known opponents of the British in the late nineteenth century.—Ed.

[7] Salisbury: British prime minister in 1885–86, 1886–92, and 1895–1902.—Ed.

[8] Earl Grey: British Statesman (Governor-General of Canada, 1904–11) and, for a time, member of the board of directors of the British South Africa Company and administrator of Rhodesia. Not to be confused with his cousin, Sir Edward Grey: foreign secretary, 1905–16.—Ed.

of the Congo—"Our only program is that of the moral and material regeneration of the country." It is difficult to set any limit upon the capacity of men to deceive themselves as to the relative strength and worth of the motives which affect them: politicians, in particular, acquire so strong a habit of setting their projects in the most favorable light that they soon convince themselves that the finest result which they think may conceivably accrue from any policy is the actual motive of that policy. As for the public, it is only natural that it should be deceived. All the purer and more elevated adjuncts of Imperialism are kept to the fore by religious and philanthropic agencies: patriotism appeals to the general lust of power within a people by suggestions of nobler uses, adopting the forms of self-sacrifice to cover domination and the love of adventure. So Christianity becomes "imperialist" to the Archbishop of Canterbury, a "going out to all the world to preach the gospel"; trade becomes "imperialist" in the eyes of merchants seeking a world market.

It is precisely in this falsification of the real import of motives that the gravest vice and the most signal peril of Imperialism reside. When, out of a medley of mixed motives, the least potent is selected for public prominence because it is the most presentable, when issues of a policy which was not present at all to the minds of those who formed this policy are treated as chief causes, the moral currency of the nation is debased. The whole policy of Imperialism is riddled with this deception. Although no candid student of history will maintain for a moment that the entrance of British power into India, and the chief steps leading to the present British Empire there, were motived by considerations other than our own political and commercial aggrandizement, nothing is more common than to hear the gains which it is alleged the natives of the country have received from British rule assigned as the moral justification of our Indian Empire. The case of Egypt is a still more striking one. Though the reasons openly assigned for the British occupation of Egypt were military and financial ones affecting our own interests, it is now commonly maintained that we went there in order to bestow the benefits which Egyptians have received from our sway, and that it would be positively wicked of us to keep the pledge we gave to withdraw within a short term of years from the country. When the ordinary Englishman reads how "at no previous period of his history has the fellah lived under a Government so careful to promote his interests or to preserve his rights," he instinctively exclaims, "Yes, that is what we went to Egypt for," though, in point of fact, the play of "Imperialism" which carried us there was determined by quite other considerations. Even if one supposes that the visible misgovernment of Egypt, in its bearing on the life of the inhabitants, did impart some unselfish element to our conduct, no one would suggest that as an operative force in the direction of our imperial policy such motive has ever determined our actions. Not even the most flamboyant Imperialist contends that England is a knight-errant, everywhere in search of a quest to deliver oppressed peoples from oppressive governments, regardless of her own interests and perils. Though perhaps not so inefficient, the Russian tyranny is quite as oppressive and more injurious to the cause of civilization than the government of the Khedive,[9] but no one proposes that we should coerce Russia, or rescue Finland from her clutches. The case of Armenia, again, attests the utter feebleness of the higher motives. Both the Government and the people of Great Britain were thoroughly convinced of the atrocious cruelties of Turkey, public opinion was well informed and thoroughly incensed, Great Britain was expressly pledged by the Cyprus Convention to protect Armenia; but the "cause of humanity" and the "mission of civilization" were power-less either for interference or for effective protest. . . .

III

. . . The controlling and directing agent of the whole process, as we have seen, is the pressure of financial and industrial motives, op-erated for the direct, short-range, material interests of small, able, and well-organized groups in a nation. These groups secure the active cooperation of statesmen and of political cliques who wield the power of "parties" partly by associating them directly in their business schemes, partly by appealing to the conservative instincts of members of the possessing classes, whose vested interests and class dominance are best preserved by diverting the currents of political energy from domestic on to foreign politics. The acquies-cence, even the active and enthusiastic support, of the body of a nation in a course of policy fatal to its own true interests is secured

[9] Khedive: title of Turkish viceroys in Egypt, after 1867.—Ed.

partly by appeals to the mission of civilization, but chiefly by playing upon the primitive instincts of the race.

The psychology of these instincts is not easy to explore, but certain prime factors easily appear. The passion which a French writer describes as kilometritis, or milomania, the instinct for control of land, derives back to the earliest times when a wide range of land was necessary for a food supply for men or cattle, and is linked on to the "trek" habit, which survives more powerfully than is commonly supposed in civilized peoples. The "nomadic" habit bred of necessity survives as a chief ingredient in the love of travel, and merges into "the spirit of adventure" when it meets other equally primitive passions. This "spirit of adventure," especially in the Anglo-Saxon, has taken the shape of "sport," which in its stronger or "more adventurous" forms involves a direct appeal to the lust of slaughter and the crude struggle for life involved in pursuit. The animal lust of struggle, once a necessity, survives in the blood, and just in proportion as a nation or a class has a margin of energy and leisure from the activities of peaceful industry, it craves satisfaction through "sport," in which hunting and the physical satisfaction of striking a blow are vital ingredients. The leisured classes in Great Britain, having most of their energy liberated from the necessity of work, naturally specialize on "sport," the hygienic necessity of a substitute for work helping to support or coalescing with the survival of a savage instinct. As the milder expressions of this passion are alone permissible in the sham or artificial encounters of domestic sports, where wild game disappears and human conflicts more mortal than football are prohibited, there is an ever stronger pressure to the frontiers of civilization in order that the thwarted "spirit of adventure" may have strong, free play. These feelings are fed by a flood of the literature of travel and of imaginative writing, the security and monotony of the ordinary civilized routine imparting an ever-growing fascination to the wilder portions of the earth. The milder satisfactions afforded by sport to the upper classes in their ample leisure at home are imitated by the industrial masses, whose time and energy for recreation have been growing, and who, in their passage from rural to town conditions, have never abandoned the humbler sports of feudal country life to which from time immemorial they had been addicted. "Football is a good game, but better than it, better than any other game, is that of man-hunting."

The sporting and military aspects of Imperialism form, therefore, a very powerful basis of popular appeal. The desire to pursue and kill either big game or other men can only be satisfied by expansion and militarism. It may indeed be safely said that the reason why our army is so inefficient in its officers, as compared with its rank and file, is that at a time when serious scientific preparation and selection are required for an intellectual profession, most British officers choose the army and undertake its work in the spirit of "sport." While the average "Tommy" is perhaps actuated in the main by similar motives, "science" matters less in his case, and any lack of serious professional purpose is more largely compensated by the discipline imposed on him.

But still more important than these supports of militarism in the army is the part played by "war" as a support of Imperialism in the noncombatant body of the nation. Though the active appeal of "sport" is still strong, even among townsmen, clear signs are visible of a degradation of this active interest of the participant into the idle excitement of the spectator. How far sport has thus degenerated may be measured by the substitution everywhere of a specialized professionalism for a free amateur exercise, and by the growth of the attendant vice of gambling, which everywhere expresses the worst form of sporting excitement, drawing all disinterested sympathy away from the merits of the competition, and concentrating it upon the irrational element of chance in combination with covetousness and low cunning. The equivalent of this degradation of interest in sport is Jingoism in relation to the practice of war. Jingoism is merely the lust of the spectator, unpurged by any personal effort, risk, or sacrifice, gloating in the perils, pains, and slaughter of fellow-men whom he does not know, but whose destruction he desires in a blind and artificially stimulated passion of hatred and revenge. In the Jingo all is concentrated on the hazard and blind fury of the fray. The arduous and weary monotony of the march, the long periods of waiting, the hard privations, the terrible tedium of a prolonged campaign, play no part in his imagination; the redeeming factors of war, the fine sense of comradeship which common personal peril educates, the fruits of discipline and self-restraint, the respect for the personality of enemies whose courage he must admit and whom he comes to realize as fellow-beings—all these moderating elements in actual war are eliminated from the passion of the

Jingo. It is precisely for these reasons that some friends of peace maintain that the two most potent checks of militarism and of war are the obligation of the entire body of citizens to undergo military service and the experience of an invasion.

Whether such expensive remedies are really effectual or necessary we are not called on to decide, but it is quite evident that the spectatorial lust of Jingoism is a most serious factor in Imperialism. The dramatic falsification both of war and of the whole policy of imperial expansion required to feed this popular passion forms no small portion of the art of the real organizers of imperialist exploits, the small groups of businessmen and politicians who know what they want and how to get it.

Tricked out with the real or sham glories of military heroism and the magnificent claims of empire-making, Jingoism becomes a nucleus of a sort of patriotism which can be moved to any folly or to any crime.

IV

Where this spirit of naked dominance needs more dressing for the educated classes of a nation, the requisite moral and intellectual decorations are woven for its use; the church, the press, the schools and colleges, the political machine, the four chief instruments of popular education, are accommodated to its service. From the muscular Christianity of the last generation to the imperial Christianity of the present day it is but a single step; the temper of growing sacerdotalism and the doctrine of authority in the established churches well accord with militarism and political autocracy. Mr. Goldwin Smith has rightly observed how "force is the natural ally of superstition, and superstition knows it well." As for the most potent engine of the press, the newspaper, so far as it is not directly owned and operated by financiers for financial purposes (as is the case to a great extent in every great industrial and financial center), it is always influenced and mostly dominated by the interests of the classes which control the advertisements upon which its living depends; the independence of a paper with a circulation so large and firm as to "command" and to retain advertisements in the teeth of a policy disliked by the advertising classes is becoming rarer and more precarious every year, as the cluster of interests which form the business nucleus of Imperialism becomes more consolidated and more conscious in its politics. The political machine is an hireling, because it is a machine, and needs constant repair and lubrication from the wealthy members of the party; the machinist knows from whom he takes his pay, and cannot run against the will of those who are in fact the patrons of the party, the tightening of whose purse-strings will automatically stop the machine. The recent Imperialism both of Great Britain and America has been materially assisted by the lavish contributions of men like Rockefeller, Hanna, Rhodes, Beit to party funds for the election of "imperialist" representatives and for the political instruction of the people.

Most serious of all is the persistent attempt to seize the school system for Imperialism masquerading as patriotism. To capture the childhood of the country, to mechanize its free play into the routine of military drill, to cultivate the savage survivals of combativeness, to poison its early understanding of history by false ideals and pseudo-heroes and by a consequent disparagement and neglect of the really vital and elevating lessons of the past, to establish a "geocentric" view of the moral universe in which the interests of humanity are subordinated to that of the "country" (and so, by easy, early, natural inference, that of the "country" to that of the "self"), to feed the always overweening pride of race at an age when self-confidence most commonly prevails, and by necessary implication to disparage other nations, so starting children in the world with false measures of value and an unwillingness to learn from foreign sources—to fasten this base insularity of mind and morals upon the little children of a nation and to call it patriotism is as foul an abuse of education as it is possible to conceive. Yet the power of Church and State over primary education is being bent consistently to this purpose, while the blend of clericalism and autocratic academicism which dominates the secondary education of this country pours its enthusiasm into the same evil channel. Finally, our centers of highest culture, the universities, are in peril of a new perversion from the path of free inquiry and expression, which is the true path of intellectual life. A new sort of "pious founder" threatens intellectual liberty. Our colleges are, indeed, no longer to be the subservient defenders of religious orthodoxy, repressing science, distorting history, and molding philosophy to conserve the interests of Church and King. The academic studies and their teachers are to employ the same methods, but directed to a different end: philosophy, the natural sciences, history, economics, sociology, are to be employed in setting up new earthworks against the attack of the disinherited masses upon the vested interests of the plutocracy. I do not of course represent this perversion as destructive of the educational work of the colleges: the services rendered in defense of "conservatism" may even be regarded in most cases as incidental: only perhaps in philosophy and economics is the bias a powerful and pervasive one, and even there the individuality of strong independent natures may correct it. Moreover, it is needless to charge dishonesty against the teachers, who commonly think and teach according to the highest that is in them. But the actual teaching is nonetheless selected and controlled, wherever it is found useful to employ the arts of selection and control, by the business interests playing on the vested academic interests. No one can follow the history of political and economic theory during the last century without recognizing that the selection and rejection of ideas, hypotheses, and formulae, the molding of them into schools or tendencies of thought, and the propagation of them in the intellectual world, have been plainly directed by the pressure of class interests. In political economy, as we might well suspect, from its close bearing upon business and politics, we find the most incontestable example. The "classical" economics in England were the barely disguised formulation of the mercantile and manufacturing interests as distinguished from, and opposed to, the landowning interest on the one hand, the laboring interest on the other, evoking in later years other class economics of "protection" and of "socialism" similarly woven out of sectional interests.

The real determinants in education are given in these three questions: "Who shall teach? What shall they teach? How shall they teach?" Where universities are dependent for endowments and incomes upon the favor of the rich, upon the charity of millionaires, the following answers will of necessity be given: "Safe teachers. Safe studies. Sound (i.e., orthodox) methods." The coarse proverb which tells us that "he who pays the piper calls the tune" is quite as applicable here as elsewhere, and no bluff regarding academic dignity and intellectual honesty must blind us to the fact.

The interference with intellectual liberty is seldom direct, seldom personal, though of late both in the United States and Canada some instances of the crudest heresy-hunting have occurred. The real danger consists in the appointment rather than in the dismissal of teachers, in the determination of what subjects shall be taught, what relative attention shall be given to each subject, and what textbooks and other apparatus of instruction shall be used. The subservience to rank and money, even in our older English universities, has been of late evinced so nakedly, and the demands for monetary aid in developing new faculties necessarily looms so large in academic eyes, that the danger here indicated is an ever-growing one. It is not so much the weight of the "dead hand" that is to be feared as that of the living: a college so unfortunate as to harbor teachers who, in handling vital issues of politics or economics, teach truths deeply and obviously antagonistic to the interests of the classes from whom financial aid was sought, would be committing suicide. Higher education has never been economically self-supporting; it has hardly ever been fully organized from public funds; everywhere it has remained parasitic on the private munificence of wealthy persons. The peril is too obvious to need further enforcement: it is the hand of the prospective, the potential donor that fetters intellectual freedom in our colleges, and will do so more and more so long as the duty of organizing public higher education for a nation out of public funds fails of recognition.

The area of danger is, of course, far wider than Imperialism, covering the whole field of vested interests. But, if the analysis of previous chapters is correct, Imperialism stands as a first defense of these interests: for the financial and speculative classes it means a pushing of their private businesses at the public expense, for the export manufacturers and merchants a forcible enlargement of foreign markets and a related policy of Protection, for the official and professional classes large openings of honorable and lucrative employment, for the Church it represents the temper and practice of authority and the assertion of spiritual control over vast multitudes of lower people, for the political oligarchy it means the only effective diversion of the forces of democracy and the opening of great public careers in the showy work of empire-making.

This being so, it is inevitable that Imperialism should seek intellectual support in our seats of learning, and should use the sinews of education for the purpose. The millionaire who endows Oxford does not buy its men of learning outright, need not even stipulate what should be taught. But the practical pressure of Imperialism is such that when a professional appointment is made in history it is becoming more difficult for a scholar with the intellectual outlook of a John Morley, a Frederick Harrison, or a Goldwin Smith to secure election, or for a political economist with strong views on the necessity of controlling capital to be elected to a chair in economics. No formal tests are necessary; the instinct of financial self-preservation will suffice. The price which universities pay for preferring money and social position to intellectual distinction in the choice of chancellors and for touting among the millionaires for the equipment of new scientific schools is this subservience to the political and business interests of their patrons: their philosophy, their history, their economics, even their biology must reflect in doctrine and method the consideration that is due to patronage, and the fact that this deference is unconscious enhances the damage done to the cause of intellectual freedom.

Thus do the industrial and financial forces of Imperialism, operating through the party, the press, the church, the school, mold public opinion and public policy by the false idealization of those primitive lusts of struggle, domination, and acquisitiveness which have survived throughout the eras of peaceful industrial order and whose stimulation is needed once again for the work of imperial aggression, expansion, and the forceful exploitation of lower races. For these business politicians biology and sociology weave thin convenient theories of a race struggle for the subjugation of the inferior peoples, in order that we, the Anglo-Saxon, may take their lands and live upon their labors; while economics buttresses the argument by representing our work in conquering and ruling them as our share in the division of labor among nations, and history devises reasons why the lessons of past empire do not apply to ours, while social ethics paints the motive of "Imperialism" as the desire to bear the "burden" of educating and elevating races of "children." Thus are the "cultured" or semicultured classes indoctrinated with the intellectual and moral grandeur of Imperialism. For the masses there is a cruder appeal to hero-worship and sensational glory, adventure and the sporting spirit: current history falsified in coarse flaring colors, for the direct stimulation of the combative instincts. But while various methods are employed, some delicate and indirect, others coarse and flamboyant, the operation everywhere resolves itself into an incitation and direction of the brute lusts of human domination which are everywhere latent in civilized humanity, for the pursuance of a policy fraught with material gain to a minority of cooperative vested interests which usurp the title of the commonwealth.

V. I. Lenin

THE HIGHEST STAGE OF CAPITALISM

The Communist leader of the Russian Revolution, V. I. Lenin (1870–1924), wrote Imperialism: The Highest Stage of Capitalism *while still in exile in Switzerland in 1916. It has been argued that he was probably motivated in this more by a desire to justify certain of his political programs and activities than to present a balanced analysis of contemporary European expansion— though certainly many writers have also argued that he achieved the latter as well. The work is extremely theoretical. Lenin later maintained that he had been unable to be as specific and explicit on political matters as he could have been had the essay been written after he achieved power. As it was, he relied to a great extent on the theoretical position of the Austrian-trained economist, Rudolph Hilferding, and on Hobson. Much of the text is made up of criticism of the writings of Karl Kautsky, a fellow Marxist who, as a late convert to a more moderate point of view than Lenin's, was one of the "opportunists" whose position Lenin was always trying to destroy.*

The Division of the World among the Great Powers

In his book, *The Territorial Development of the European Colonies,* A. Supan, the geographer, gives the following brief summary of this development at the end of the nineteenth century [see Table 1].

"The characteristic feature of this period," he concludes, "is, therefore, the division of Africa and Polynesia."

As there are no unoccupied territories—that is, territories that do not belong to any state—in Asia and America, Mr. Supan's conclusion must be carried further, and we must say that the characteristic

From V. I. Lenin, *Imperialism: The Highest Stage of Capitalism,* new, revised translation (New York, 1939), pp. 76–84, 88–92, 123–127. By permission of the International Publishers Co., Inc.

TABLE 1

Percentage of Territories Belonging to the European Colonial Powers (Including United States)

	1876	1900	Increase or Decrease
Africa	10.8	90.4	+79.6
Polynesia	56.8	98.9	+42.1
Asia	51.5	56.6	+ 5.1
Australia	100.0	100.0	. . .
America	27.5	27.2	− 0.3

feature of this period is the final partition of the globe—not in the sense that a *new* partition is impossible—on the contrary, new partitions are possible and inevitable—but in the sense that the colonial policy of the capitalist countries has *completed* the seizure of the unoccupied territories on our planet. For the first time the world is completely divided up, so that in the future *only* redivision is possible; territories can only pass from one "owner" to another, instead of passing as unowned territory to an "owner."

Hence, we are passing through a peculiar period of world colonial policy, which is closely associated with the "latest stage in the development of capitalism," with finance capital. For this reason, it is essential first of all to deal in detail with the facts, in order to ascertain exactly what distinguishes this period from those preceding it, and what the present situation is. In the first place, two questions of fact arise here. Is an intensification of colonial policy, an intensification of the struggle for colonies, observed precisely in this period of finance capital? And how, in this respect, is the world divided at the present time?

The American writer, Morris, in his book on the history of colonization, has made an attempt to compile data on the colonial possessions of Great Britain, France and Germany during different periods of the nineteenth century. The following [Table 2] is a brief summary of the results he has obtained

For Great Britain, the period of the enormous expansion of colonial conquests is that between 1860 and 1880, and it was also very considerable in the last twenty years of the nineteenth century. For France and Germany this period falls precisely in these last twenty years. We saw above that the apex of pre-monopoly capitalist

TABLE 2

Colonial Possessions (Million square miles and million inhabitants)

	Great Britain		France		Germany	
	Area	Pop.	Area	Pop.	Area	Pop.
1815–30	?	126.4	0.02	0.5	. . .	. . .
1860	2.5	145.1	0.2	3.4	. . .	. . .
1880	7.7	267.9	0.7	7.5	. . .	. . .
1899	9.3	309.0	3.7	56.4	1.0	14.7

development, of capitalism in which free competition was predominant, was reached in the sixties and seventies of the last
century. We now see that it is *precisely after that period* that the
"boom" in colonial annexations begins, and that the struggle for the
territorial division of the world becomes extraordinarily keen. It is
beyond doubt, therefore, that capitalism's transition to the stage of
monopoly capitalism, to finance capital, is *bound up* with the intensification of the struggle for the partition of the world.

Hobson, in his work on imperialism, marks the years 1884–1900
as the period of the intensification of the colonial "expansion" of the
chief European states. According to his estimate, Great Britain during these years acquired 3.7 million square miles of territory with a
population of 57 million; France acquired 3.6 million square miles
with a population of 36.5 million; Germany 1 million square miles
with a population of 16.7 million; Belgium 900,000 square miles with
30 million inhabitants; Portugal 800,000 square miles with 9 million inhabitants. The quest for colonies by all the capitalist states at the end
of the nineteenth century and particularly since the 1880s is a commonly known fact in the history of diplomacy and of foreign affairs.

When free competition in Great Britain was at its zenith, i.e., between 1840 and 1860, the leading British bourgeois politicians were
opposed to colonial policy and were of the opinion that the liberation
of the colonies and their complete separation from Britain was inevitable and desirable. M. Beer, in an article, "Modern British Imperialism," published in 1898, shows that in 1852, Disraeli, a statesman generally inclined towards imperialism, declared: "The colonies
are millstones round our necks." But at the end of the nineteenth
century the heroes of the hour in England were Cecil Rhodes and
Joseph Chamberlain, open advocates of imperialism, who applied
the imperialist policy in the most cynical manner.

It is not without interest to observe that even at that time these leading British bourgeois politicians fully appreciated the connection between what might be called the purely economic and the politico-social roots of modern imperialism. Chamberlain advocated imperialism by calling it a "true, wise and economical policy," and he pointed particularly to the German, American and Belgian competition which Great Britain was encountering in the world market. Salvation lies in monopolies, said the capitalists as they formed cartels, syndicates and trusts. Salvation lies in monopolies, echoed the political leaders of the bourgeoisie, hastening to appropriate the parts of the world not yet shared out. The journalist, Stead, relates the following remarks uttered by his close friend Cecil Rhodes, in 1895, regarding his imperialist ideas:

> *I was in the East End of London yesterday and attended a meeting of the unemployed. I listened to the wild speeches, which were just a cry for "bread," "bread," "bread," and on my way home I pondered over the scene and I became more than ever convinced of the importance of imperialism. . . . My cherished idea is a solution for the social problem, i.e., in order to save the 40 million inhabitants of the United Kingdom from a bloody civil war, we colonial statesmen must acquire new lands to settle the surplus population, to provide new markets for the goods produced by them in the factories and mines. The Empire, as I have always said, is a bread and butter question. If you want to avoid civil war, you must become imperialists.*

This is what Cecil Rhodes, millionaire, king of finance, the man who was mainly responsible for the Boer War, said in 1895. His defense of imperialism is just crude and cynical, but in substance it does not differ from the "theory" advocated by Messrs. Maslov, Südekum, Potresov, David, and the founder of Russian Marxism and others. Cecil Rhodes was a somewhat more honest social-chauvinist.

To tabulate as exactly as possible the territorial division of the world, and the changes which have occurred during the last decades, we will take the data furnished by Supan in the work already quoted on the colonial possessions of all the powers of the world. Supan examines the years 1876 and 1900; we will take the year 1876—a year aptly oolootod, for it is preclsely at that time that the pre-monopolist stage of development of West European capitalism can be said to have been completed, in the main, and we will take the year 1914, and in place of Supan's figures we will quote the more

recent statistics of Hübner's *Geographical and Statistical Tables.*
Supan gives figures only for colonies: we think it useful in order to
present a complete picture of the division of the world to add brief
figures on noncolonial and semicolonial countries like Persia, China
and Turkey. Persia is already almost completely a colony; China and
Turkey are on the way to becoming colonies. We thus get the
following summary [see Table 3].

We see from these figures how "complete" was the partition of
the world at the end of the nineteenth and beginning of the twentieth
centuries. After 1876 colonial possessions increased to an enormous
degree, more than one and a half times, from 40 million to 65 million
square kilometers in area for the six biggest powers, an increase of
25 million square kilometers, that is, one and a half times greater
than the area of the "home" countries, which have a total of 16.5
million square kilometers. In 1876 three powers had no colonies,
and a fourth, France, had scarcely any. In 1914 these four powers
had 14.1 million square kilometers of colonies, or an area one and a
half times greater than that of Europe, with a population of nearly
100 million. The unevenness in the rate of expansion of colonial
possessions is very marked. If, for instance, we compare France,
Germany and Japan, which do not differ very much in area and

TABLE 3

Colonial Possessions of the Great Powers
(Million square kilometers and million inhabitants)

	Colonies				Home Countries		Total	
	1876		1914		1914		1914	
	Area	Pop.	Area	Pop.	Area	Pop.	Area	Pop.
Great Britain	22.5	251.9	33.5	393.5	0.3	46.5	33.8	440.0
Russia	17.0	15.9	17.4	33.2	5.4	136.2	22.8	169.4
France	0.9	6.0	10.6	55.5	0.5	39.6	11.1	95.1
Germany	...	...	2.9	12.3	0.5	64.9	3.4	77.2
U.S.A.	...	...	0.3	9.7	9.4	97.0	9.7	106.7
Japan	...	...	0.3	19.2	0.4	53.0	0.7	72.2
Total	40.4	273.8	65.0	523.4	16.5	437.2	81.5	960.6
Colonies of other powers (Belgium, Holland, etc.)							9.9	45.3
Semi-colonial countries (Persia, China, Turkey)							14.5	361.2
Other countries							28.0	289.9
Total area and population of the world							133.9	1,657.0

population, we will see that the first has annexed almost three times as much colonial territory as the other two combined. In regard to finance capital, also, France, at the beginning of the period we are considering, was perhaps several times richer than Germany and Japan put together. In addition to, and on the basis of, purely economic causes, geographical conditions and other factors also affect the dimensions of colonial possessions. However strong the process of leveling the world, of leveling the economic and living conditions in different countries, may have been in the past decades as a result of the pressure of large-scale industry, exchange and finance capital, great differences still remain; and among the six powers, we see, firstly, young capitalist powers (America, Germany, Japan) which progressed very rapidly; secondly, countries with an old capitalist development (France and Great Britain), which, of late, have made much slower progress than the previously mentioned countries, and, thirdly, a country (Russia) which is economically most backward, in which modern capitalist imperialism is enmeshed, so to speak, in a particularly close network of precapitalist relations.

Alongside the colonial possessions of these great powers, we have placed the small colonies of the small states, which are, so to speak, the next possible and probable objects of a new colonial "shareout." Most of these little states are able to retain their colonies only because of the conflicting interests, frictions, etc., among the big powers, which prevent them from coming to an agreement in regard to the division of the spoils. The "semi-colonial states" provide an example of the transitional forms which are to be found in all spheres of nature and society. Finance capital is such a great, it may be said, such a decisive force in all economic and international relations, that it is capable of subordinating to itself, and actually does subordinate to itself, even states enjoying complete political independence. We shall shortly see examples of this. Naturally, however, finance capital finds it most "convenient," and is able to extract the greatest profit from a subordination which involves the loss of the political independence of the subjected countries and peoples. In this connection, the semicolonial countries provide a typical example of the "middle stage." It is natural that the struggle for these semidependent countries should have become particularly bitter during the period of finance capital, when the rest of the world had already been divided up.

Colonial policy and imperialism existed before this latest stage of capitalism, and even before capitalism. Rome, founded on slavery, pursued a colonial policy and achieved imperialism. But "general" arguments about imperialism, which ignore, or put into the background the fundamental difference of social-economic systems, inevitably degenerate into absolutely empty banalities, or into grandiloquent comparisons like "Greater Rome and Greater Britain." Even the colonial policy of capitalism in its *previous* stages is essentially different from the colonial policy of finance capital.

The principal feature of modern capitalism is the domination of monopolist combines of the big capitalists. These monopolies are most firmly established when *all* the sources of raw materials are controlled by the one group. And we have seen with what zeal the international capitalist combines exert every effort to make it impossible for their rivals to compete with them; for example, by buying up mineral lands, oil fields, etc. Colonial possession alone gives complete guarantee of success to the monopolies against all the risks of the struggle with competitors, including the risk that the latter will defend themselves by means of a law establishing a state monopoly. The more capitalism is developed, the more the need for raw materials is felt, the more bitter competition becomes, and the more feverishly the hunt for raw materials proceeds throughout the whole world, the more desperate becomes the struggle for the acquisition of colonies.

Schilder writes:

> *It may even be asserted, although it may sound paradoxical to some, that in the more or less discernible future the growth of the urban industrial population is more likely to be hindered by a shortage of raw materials for industry than by a shortage of food.*

For example, there is a growing shortage of timber—the price of which is steadily rising—of leather, and raw materials for the textile industry.

> *As instances of the efforts of associations of manufacturers to create an equilibrium between industry and agriculture in world economy as a whole, we might mention the International Federation of Cotton Spinners' Associations in the most important industrial countries, founded in 1904, and the European Federation of Flax Spinners' Associations, founded on the same model in 1910.*

The bourgeois reformists, and among them particularly the present-day adherents of Kautsky, of course, try to belittle the importance of facts of this kind by arguing that it "would be possible" to obtain raw materials in the open market without a "costly and dangerous" colonial policy; and that it would be "possible" to increase the supply of raw materials to an enormous extent "simply" by improving agriculture. But these arguments are merely an apology for imperialism, an attempt to embellish it, because they ignore the principal feature of modern capitalism: monopoly. Free markets are becoming more and more a thing of the past; monopolist syndicates and trusts are restricting them more and more every day, and "simply" improving agriculture reduces itself to improving the conditions of the masses, to raising wages and reducing profits. Where, except in the imagination of the sentimental reformists, are there any trusts capable of interesting themselves in the condition of the masses instead of the conquest of colonies?

Finance capital is not only interested in the already known sources of raw materials; it is also interested in potential sources of raw materials, because present-day technical development is extremely rapid, and because land which is useless today may be made fertile tomorrow if new methods are applied (to devise these new methods a big bank can equip a whole expedition of engineers, agricultural experts, etc.), and large amounts of capital are invested. This also applies to prospecting for minerals, to new methods of working up and utilizing raw materials, etc., etc. Hence, the inevitable striving of finance capital to extend its economic territory and even its territory in general. In the same way that the trusts capitalize their property by estimating it at two or three times its value, taking into account its "potential" (and not present) returns, and the further results of monopoly, so finance capital strives to seize the largest possible amount of land of all kinds and in any place it can, and by any means, counting on the possibilities of finding raw materials there, and fearing to be left behind in the insensate struggle for the last available scraps of undivided territory, or for the repartition of that which has been already divided.

The British capitalists are exerting every effort to develop cotton growing in *their* colony, Egypt (in 1904, out of 2.3 million hectares of land under cultivation, 600,000, or more than one-fourth, were devoted to cotton growing); the Russians are doing the same in *their* colony, Turkestan; and they are doing so because in this way they will be in a better position to defeat their foreign competitors, to monopolize the sources of raw materials and form a more economical and profitable textile trust in which *all* the processes of cotton production and manufacturing will be "combined" and concentrated in the hands of a single owner.

The necessity of exporting capital also gives an impetus to the conquest of colonies, for in the colonial market it is easier to eliminate competition, to make sure of orders, to strengthen the necessary "connections," etc., by monopolist methods (and sometimes it is the only possible way). . . .

Imperialism as a Special Stage of Capitalism

We must now try to sum up and put together what has been said above on the subject of imperialism. Imperialism emerged as the development and direct continuation of the fundamental attributes of capitalism in general. But capitalism only became capitalist imperialism at a definite and very high stage of its development, when certain of its fundamental attributes began to be transformed into their opposites, when the features of a period of transition from capitalism to a higher social and economic system began to take shape and reveal themselves along the line. Economically, the main thing in this process is the substitution of capitalist monopolies for capitalist free competition. Free competition is the fundamental attribute of capitalism, and of commodity production generally. Monopoly is exactly the opposite of free competition; but we have seen the latter being transformed into monopoly before our very eyes, creating large-scale industry and eliminating small industry, replacing large-scale industry by still larger-scale industry, finally leading to such a concentration of production and capital that monopoly has been and is the result: cartels, syndicates and trusts, and merging with them, the capital of a dozen or so banks manipulating thousands of millions. At the same time monopoly, which has grown out of free competition, does not abolish the latter, but exists over it and alongside of it, and thereby gives rise to a number of very acute, intense antagonisms, friction and conflicts. Monopoly is the transition from capitalism to a higher system.

If it were necessary to give the briefest possible definition of imperialism we should have to say that imperialism is the monopoly stage of capitalism. Such a definition would include what is most important, for, on the one hand, finance capital is the bank capital of a few big monopolist banks, merged with the capital of the monopolist combines of manufacturers; and, on the other hand, the division of the world is the transition from a colonial policy which has extended without hindrance to territories unoccupied by any capitalist power, to a colonial policy of monopolistic possession of the territory of the world which has been completely divided up.

But very brief definitions, although convenient, for they sum up the main points, are nevertheless inadequate, because very important features of the phenomenon that has to be defined have to be especially deduced. And so, without forgetting the conditional and relative value of all definitions, which can never include all the concatenations of a phenomenon in its complete development, we must give a definition of imperialism that will embrace the following five essential features:

1. The concentration of production and capital developed to such a high stage that it created monopolies which play a decisive role in economic life.
2. The merging of bank capital with industrial capital, and the creation, on the basis of this "finance capital," of a "financial oligarchy."
3. The export of capital, which has become extremely important, as distinguished from the export of commodities.
4. The formation of international capitalist monopolies which share the world among themselves.
5. The territorial division of the whole world among the greatest capitalist powers is completed.

Imperialism is capitalism in that stage of development in which the dominance of monopolies and finance capital has established itself; in which the export of capital has acquired pronounced importance; in which the division of the world among the international trusts has begun; in which the division of all territories of the globe among the great capitalist powers has been completed.

We shall see later that imperialism can and must be defined differently if consideration is to be given, not only to the basic, purely economic factors—to which the above definition is limited—but also to the historical place of this stage of capitalism in relation to capitalism in general, or to the relations between imperialism and the two main trends in the working-class movement. The point to be noted just now is that imperialism, as interpreted above, undoubtedly represents a special stage in the development of capitalism. In order to enable the reader to obtain as well-grounded an idea of imperialism as possible, we deliberately quoted largely from bourgeois economists who are obliged to admit the particularly incontrovertible facts regarding modern capitalist economy. With the same object in view, we have produced detailed statistics which reveal the extent to which bank capital, etc., has developed, showing how the transformation of quantity into quality, of developed capitalism into imperialism, has expressed itself. Needless to say, all boundaries in nature and in society are conditional and changeable, and, consequently, it would be absurd to discuss the exact year or the decade in which imperialism "definitely" became established.

In this manner of defining imperialism, however, we have to enter into controversy, primarily, with K. Kautsky, the principal Marxian theoretician of the epoch of the so-called Second International—that is, of the twenty-five years between 1889 and 1914.

Kautsky, in 1915 and even in November 1914, very emphatically attacked the fundamental ideas expressed in our definition of imperialism. Kautsky said that imperialism must not be regarded as a "phase" or stage of economy, but as a policy; a definite policy "preferred" by finance capital; that imperialism cannot be "identified" with "contemporary capitalism"; that if imperialism is to be understood to mean "all the phenomena of contemporary capitalism"—cartels, protection, the domination of the financiers and colonial policy—then the question as to whether imperialism is necessary to capitalism becomes reduced to the "flattest tautology"; because, in that case, "imperialism is naturally a vital necessity for capitalism," and so on. The best way to present Kautsky's ideas is to quote his own definition of imperialism, which is diametrically opposed to the substance of the ideas which we have set forth (for the objections coming from the camp of the German Marxists, who have been advocating such ideas for many years already, have been long known to Kautsky as the objections of a definite trend in Marxism).

Kautsky's definition is as follows:

Imperialism is a product of highly developed industrial capitalism. It consists in the striving of every industrial capitalist nation to bring under its control and to annex increasingly big agrarian *[Kautsky's emphasis] regions irrespective of what nations inhabit those regions.*

This definition is utterly worthless because it one-sidedly, i.e., arbitrarily, brings out the national question alone (although this is extremely important in itself as well as in its relation to imperialism), it arbitrarily and *inaccurately* relates this question *only* to industrial capital in the countries which annex other nations, and in an equally arbitrary and inaccurate manner brings out the annexation of agrarian regions.

Imperialism is a striving for annexations—this is what the *political* part of Kautsky's definition amounts to. It Is correct, but very incomplete, for politically, imperialism is, in general, a striving towards violence and reaction. For the moment, however, we are interested in the *economic* aspect of the question, which Kautsky *himself* introduced into *his* definition. The inaccuracy of Kautsky's definition is strikingly obvious. The characteristic feature of imperialism is *not* industrial capital, *but* finance capital. It is not an accident that in France it was precisely the extraordinarily rapid development of *finance* capital, and the weakening of industrial capital, that, from 1880 onwards, gave rise to the extreme extension of annexationist (colonial) policy. The characteristic feature of imperialism is precisely that it strives to annex *not only* agricultural regions, but even highly industrialized regions (German appetite for Belgium; French appetite for Lorraine), because (1) the fact that the world is already divided up obliges those contemplating a *new* division to reach out for *any kind* of territory; and (2) because an essential feature of imperialism is the rivalry between a number of great powers in the striving for hegemony, i e , for the conquest of territory, not so much directly for themselves as to weaken the adversary and undermine *his* hegemony. (Belgium is chiefly necessary to Germany as a base

for operations against England; England needs Bagdad as a base
for operations against Germany, etc.). . . .

The Place of Imperialism in History

We have seen that the economic quintessence of imperialism is
monopoly capitalism. This very fact determines its place in history,
for monopoly that grew up on the basis of free competition, and
precisely out of free competition, is the transition from the capitalist
system to a higher social-economic order. We must take special
note of the four principal forms of monopoly, or the four principal
manifestations of monopoly capitalism, which are characteristic of
the epoch under review.

Firstly, monopoly arose out of the concentration of production
at a very advanced stage of development. This refers to the monopolist capitalist combines, cartels, syndicates and trusts. We have
seen the important part that these play in modern economic life.
At the beginning of the twentieth century, monopolies acquired complete supremacy in the advanced countries. And although the first
steps towards the formation of the cartels were first taken by countries enjoying the protection of high tariffs (Germany, America),
Great Britain, with her system of free trade, was not far behind in
revealing the same basic phenomenon, namely, the birth of monopoly out of the concentration of production.

Secondly, monopolies have accelerated the capture of the most
important sources of raw materials, especially for the coal and iron
industries, which are the basic and most highly cartelized industries
in capitalist society. The monopoly of the most important sources
of raw materials has enormously increased the power of big capital,
and has sharpened the antagonism between cartelized and non-
cartelized industry.

Thirdly, monopoly has sprung from the banks. The banks have
developed from modest intermediary enterprises into the monop-
olists of finance capital. Some three or five of the biggest banks in
each of the foremost capitalist countries have achieved the "personal union" of industrial and bank capital, and have concentrated
in their hands the disposal of thousands upon thousands of millions
which form the greater part of the capital and income of entire
countries. A financial oligarchy, which throws a close net of rela-

tions of dependence over all the economic and political institutions of contemporary bourgeois society without exception—such is the most striking manifestation of this monopoly.

Fourthly, monopoly has grown out of colonial policy. To the numerous "old" motives of colonial policy, finance capital has added the struggle for the sources of raw materials, for the export of capital, for "spheres of influence," i.e., for spheres for profitable deals, concessions, monopolist profits and so on; in fine, for economic territory in general. When the colonies of the European powers in Africa, for instance, comprised only one-tenth of that territory (as was the case in 1876), colonial policy was able to develop by methods other than those of monopoly—by the "free grabbing" of territories, so to speak. But when nine-tenths of Africa had been seized (approximately by 1900), when the whole world had been divided up, there was inevitably ushered in a period of colonial monopoly and, consequently, a period of particularly intense struggle for the division and the redivision of the world.

The extent to which monopolist capital has intensified all the contradictions of capitalism is generally known. It is sufficient to mention the high cost of living and the oppression of the cartels. This intensification of contradictions constitutes the most powerful driving force of the transitional period of history, which began from the time of the definite victory of world finance capital.

Monopolies, oligarchy, the striving for domination instead of the striving for liberty, the exploitation of an increasing number of small or weak nations by an extremely small group of the richest or most powerful nations—all these have given birth to those distinctive characteristics of imperialism which compel us to define it as parasitic or decaying capitalism. More and more prominently there emerges, as one of the tendencies of imperialism, the creation of the "bond-holding" (rentier) state, the usurer state, in which the bourgeoisie lives on the proceeds of capital exports and by "clipping coupons." It would be a mistake to believe that this tendency to decay precludes the possibility of the rapid growth of capitalism. It does not. In the epoch of imperialism, certain branches of industry, certain strata of the bourgeoisie and certain countries betray, to a more or less degree, one or other of these tendencies. On the whole, capitalism is growing far more rapidly than before. But this growth is not only becoming more and more uneven in general; its unevenness also manifests itself, in particular, in the decay of the countries which are richest in capital (such as England).

In regard to the rapidity of Germany's economic development, Riesser, the author of the book on the big German banks, states:

> *The progress of the preceding period (1848–70), which had not been exactly slow, stood in about the same ratio to the rapidity with which the whole of Germany's national economy, and with it German banking, progressed during this period (1870–1905) as the mail coach of the Holy Roman Empire of the German nation stood to the speed of the present-day automobile . . . which in whizzing past, it must be said, often endangers not only innocent pedestrians in its path, but also the occupants of the car.*

In its turn, this finance capital which has grown so rapidly is not unwilling (precisely because it has grown so quickly) to pass on to a more "tranquil" possession of colonies which have to be seized —and not only by peaceful methods—from richer nations. In the United States, economic development in the last decades has been even more rapid than in Germany, and *for this very reason* the parasitic character of modern American capitalism has stood out with particular prominence. On the other hand, a comparison of, say, the republican American bourgeoisie with the monarchist Japanese or German bourgeoisie shows that the most pronounced political distinctions diminish to an extreme degree in the epoch of imperialism—not because they are unimportant in general, but because in all these cases we are discussing a bourgeoisie which has definite features of parasitism.

The receipt of high monopoly profits by the capitalists in one of the numerous branches of industry, in one of numerous countries, etc., makes it economically possible for them to corrupt certain sections of the working class, and for a time a fairly considerable minority, and win them to the side of the bourgeoisie of a given industry or nation against all the others. The intensification of antagonisms between imperialist nations for the division of the world increases this striving. And so there is created that bond between imperialism and opportunism, which revealed itself first and most clearly in England, owing to the fact that certain features of imperialist development were observable there much earlier than in other countries. . . .

From all that has been said in this book on the economic nature of imperialism, it follows that we must define it as capitalism in transition, or, more precisely, as moribund capitalism. It is very instructive in this respect to note that the bourgeois economists, in describing modern capitalism, frequently employ terms like "interlocking," "absence of isolation," etc.; "in conformity with their functions and course of development," banks are "not purely private business enterprises; they are more and more outgrowing the sphere of purely private business regulation." And this very Riesser, who uttered the words just quoted, declares with all seriousness that the "prophecy" of the Marxists concerning "socialization" has "not come true"! . . .

Leonard Woolf
EMPIRE AND COMMERCE

Leonard Sidney Woolf (1880–1969), the well-known author, editor, publisher (and husband of Virginia Woolf), spent seven years of his early adulthood in the Ceylon Civil Service. Returning to England shortly before World War I, he became interested in socialism and joined the Fabian Society and the Labour Party. Thereafter he was editor of the International Review, *literary editor of the British* Nation, *editor (1931–1959) of the* Political Quarterly, *and author of a variety of works on political and social subjects. Woolf argued that "imperialism," while not necessarily inevitable, had resulted in the recent past from the greed of capitalist businessmen and governments. His controversial* Empire and Commerce in Africa *is a detailed examination of the European penetration into Africa, based on a multitude of facts. Critics argue that these facts are highly selective and that the conclusions drawn from them are therefore unreliable; but Woolf argues that the facts are representative and speak for themselves.*

I have already given some proof of the assertion that Europe has almost universally accepted the principle of policy that the power

From Leonard Woolf, *Empire and Commerce in Africa: A Study in Economic Imperialism* (London, 1919?), pp. 16–19, 24–27, 31–33, 34–36. Reprinted by permission of George Allen & Unwin Ltd.

of the State should be used upon the world outside the State for the economic purposes of the world within the State. Detailed proofs will occur again and again in the pages which follow. But one word is necessary here to many persons who will immediately dissent from this interpretation of the modern statesman's and citizen's view of State action. They will accuse us of placing the cart before the horse, of confusing means with ends. Modern policy, they will say, has aimed at economic ends, but only to use them as means for other and higher ends. Thus Mr. Arthur Greenwood in an excellent little book, designed to instruct the uninitiated in the problems of international relations, writes thus of Mr. Chamberlain's twentieth-century campaign for the reintroduction of a "Colonial system":[1]

> *And much of the flood of argument was used to show the free-traders, on the one hand, that they would be better off under a protective tariff, and the protectionists on the other that they were better off with the system of free imports. But Mr. Chamberlain's motive was political. Rightly or wrongly, he believed that fiscal changes were called for in what he considered to be the best interests of the nation and the Empire. The economic results were not to him ends in themselves, but means for the realization of imperial power and prestige. The tariff was an economic instrument to be wielded for political purposes, a weapon with which to gain state ends in the sphere of international politics.*

There is in Mr. Greenwood's exposition an element of truth, but also an element of confusion. It is true that Mr. Chamberlain's motive for desiring Colonial Preference was political rather than economic, in the sense that he recommended it as a weapon or means for the realization of imperial power and prestige. But it is wrong to argue that, therefore, Mr. Chamberlain did not regard national economic interests as the ultimate ends of policy. The question is whether Mr. Chamberlain regarded "imperial power and prestige" as the ultimate ends of national policy, or whether he really looked upon them only as means for the realization of other and more important ends. Now statesmen and nations are not always logical, clear, or consistent in their desires and beliefs. It is the commonest thing for human beings to shirk or confuse the issue as to whether some-

---

[1] Joseph Chamberlain, British colonial secretary, 1895–1903, resigned that office to campaign for imperial tariff preference within the British Empire.—Ed.

thing which they desire and aim at is to them an ultimate end or merely valuable as the means for realizing some other end. The man who desires money as a means for the realization of leisure and pleasure ends as a miser who desires money because it is money. It is possible that the Chamberlain of 1904 had come to believe that "imperial power and prestige" were ends in themselves: certainly some of his fellow-imperialists in all countries, and particularly Germany, have written and spoken as if Empire was to be desired simply because it is Empire. But that was most certainly not the view of the Chamberlain of 1896, who told the leaders of the Empire's commerce assembled in London that "I believe that the toast of Empire would have carried with it all that is meant by Commerce and Empire, because, gentlemen, the Empire, to parody a celebrated expression, is commerce." Nor was it the opinion of the Chamberlain of 1894 who said to the people of Birmingham:

> Give me the demand for more goods and then I will undertake to give plenty of employment in making the goods; and the only thing, in my opinion, that the Government can do in order to meet this great difficulty that we are considering is so to arrange its policy that every inducement shall be given to the demand; that new markets shall be created, and that old markets shall be effectually developed. You are aware that some of my opponents please themselves occasionally by finding names for me, and among other names lately they have been calling me a Jingo. I am no more a Jingo than you are. But for the reasons and arguments I have put before you tonight, I am convinced that it is a necessity, as well as a duty, for us to uphold the dominion and empire which we now possess. For these reasons among others I would never lose the hold which we now have over our great Indian dependency—by far the greatest and most valuable of all the customers we have or ever shall have in this country. For the same reasons I approve of the continued occupation of Egypt; and for the same reasons I have urged upon this Government, and upon previous Governments, the necessity for using every legitimate opportunity to extend our influence and control in that great African continent which is now being opened up to civilization and to commerce.

The Chamberlain of 1894 and 1896, it will be observed, regarded imperial power and prestige as definite means to economic ends, the provision of markets and customers, because he held that commerce, not empire and prestige, was the greatest of political interests. It is possible, as I have said, that a nation or a man who begins by seeking Empire as a means to commerce may end by acquiring a taste for Empire "in itself," just as many persons who begin to drink beer as a means of quenching thirst end by acquiring a taste for beer "in itself." That, however, does not affect the truth of the generalization that the main and ultimate end of policy during the last fifty years has been economic interests, commercial, industrial, and financial. What I propose to do in this book is to examine the results of this view that the power and organization of the State should be used upon the world outside the State in order to promote the economic interests of the world inside the State. For that purpose it is unnecessary at present to say anything more about the ends of this international economic policy. In the modern world there is little, if any, difference of opinion over those ends. . . .

*   *   *

Between 1880 and 1914 the States of Britain, France, and Germany each acquired an immense colonial empire outside Europe. These empires were empires in the literal sense of the word: they were founded by conquest, sometimes openly acknowledged, and sometimes disguised under various synonyms for civilization. The territories acquired were incorporated, usually against the wishes of their inhabitants, in the European State, and the inhabitants were subjected to the autocratic rule of the European State. The territory acquired by the British State in this way was about $3^1/_4$ million square miles, and the population subjected to its rule was about 46 million. The French State acquired 4 million square miles, and a population of over 50 million; the German State 1 million square miles, and a population of 15 million. The policy which led to the acquisition of this empire by Britain was the policy of Mr. Chamberlain and his followers. The motives have been sufficiently illustrated above from the declarations of Mr. Chamberlain himself. They were purely economic. In conquering the unexploited portions of Asia and Africa we were "pegging out claims for posterity," and the claims of posterity were for more markets. And the reasons which this school of policy gave for our "never losing the hold which we now have" over "our great Indian dependency" and over Egypt were the same, namely, the provision of markets and customers for the European citizens of the British State. Now, if we turn to France, we find that in that country, too, the creation of a colonial empire was the work of a political party with definite and imperial and colonial aims. A French writer upon colonial affairs, an imperialist, and a man of sound and moderate judgments, M. E. Fallot, has pointed out that the first colonial acquisitions of France after the revolution were not the result of any conscious plan: they were fortuitous and occasional, the acts of a Government to which the people remained indifferent. But it is not the same with the colonial policy of the Republic for which Gambetta, Jules Ferry, and Barthélemy Saint-Hilaire[2] were responsible. That policy was the result of a political plan carefully studied, applied methodically in the face of great difficulties, and finally realized with complete success. Those who urged this *politique coloniale* upon the French people with such persistence and success gave as their reasons for the necessity of "expansion" precisely the same political motives as the imperialists of Britain. The ends of the French *politique coloniale* were mainly economic, and where the Englishmen made "provision for markets" in Asia and Africa the Frenchman talked of the necessity for colonies as *débouchés à nos produits.* If anything, the economic nature of the new imperialism was recognized or admitted earlier in France than in Britain. This is shown by the motives for the French Tonkin expedition which was almost the prelude to the imperial activities of the Republic and which was the first act in the partition or domination of China for economic ends by European States. Jules Ferry, the minister responsible for this expedition, at the time repeatedly defended his action by urging that the possession of Tonkin would assure to the French the navigation of the Red River, and that, thanks to that magnificent natural highway (*magnifique voie naturelle*) they would be able to penetrate into China and secure for themselves the commercial monopoly of the Western Provinces of China.

It is true that particularly between 1880 and 1890 the partisans of the *politique coloniale* put forward motives, which were not economic, for their imperialism. In those early days it was pointed out, for instance, that France had to carry out in Algeria her mission

---

[2] Léon Gambetta, as president of the Chamber of Deputies, 1879–81, and premier, 1881–82, Jules Ferry, as premier, 1880–81 and 1883–85, and Jules Barthélemy Saint-Hilaire, as minister of foreign affairs, 1880–81, inaugurated France's late-nineteenth-century expansion.—Ed.

of civilization (*remplir notre mission civilisatrice*). But the desire for and belief in Europe's mission of civilization in Asia and Africa rapidly lost its position as a motive for policy in the last decade of the century.... After 1890 it is extremely rare to find any authoritative imperialist recommending imperialism as a duty: the stress is laid upon economic necessity and commercial profit. Thus, even the Englishman, Sir F. D. Lugard, an expert in these matters—for he added an immense territory to the British Empire—writes in 1893 that "the scramble for Africa ... was due to the growing commercial rivalry, which brought home to civilized nations the vital necessity of securing the only remaining fields for industrial enterprise and expansion." "It is well then to realize," he continues, "that it is for our advantage—and not alone at the dictates of duty—that we have undertaken responsibilities in East Africa. It is in order to foster the growth of the trade of this country, and to find an outlet for our manufactures and our surplus energy, that our far-seeing statesmen and our commercial men advocate colonial expansion.... I do not believe that in these days our national policy is based on motives of philanthropy only." And Sir F. D. Lugard shows what, in his view, were the relative importance of the "dictates of duty," the motives of philanthropy, and economic motives, by saying practically nothing more about duty and philanthropy, but devoting whole chapters to the economic advantages which the inhabitants of Britain will derive from the subjection of Uganda to the British State. So, too, when a well-known French writer has to sum up in 1904 the causes of the French *mouvement colonial,* he forgets to mention the *mission civilisatrice,* and puts it all down to "vital necessity," the universal competition, and the struggle for national existence....

*   *   *

Nowhere ... is the economic nature of modern imperialism shown more clearly than in the history of Germany. The German has a brutal habit of saying what he thinks, and of calling spades spades. In German trade is not a synonym for Christianity, nor finance for civilization. Already in the seventies German writers were insisting upon the necessity of colonies for the protection and fostering of German trade. Innumerable schemes were put forward in newspapers and books and pamphlets for founding colonies in every part of the world. This was part of the same current of beliefs and desires which was also gathering strength in France and Britain, and which finally burst out into the economic imperialism of the eighties in all three countries. It was only the passion of Germans for dotting their i's and crossing their t's which made the nature of their beliefs and desires plain in those early years. This kind of propaganda culminated in Fabri's well-known book, *Bedarf Deutschland der Kolonien?* which was published in 1879. Fabri[3] answered his question in the affirmative for economic reasons, and proposed the foundation of "Handelskolonien" in Samoa, New Guinea, North Borneo, Formosa, Madagascar, and Central Africa. A strong and definite German policy of economic imperialism sprang directly from Fabri and his book. The important thing to notice is that this policy was not only pressed upon the Government for economic reasons, but, as in the case of French and British imperialism, its chief support came from certain strong financial and commercial interests.

The close connection between colonial policy and commercial interests began in Germany even before Fabri. In 1871 a proposal was put about that Samoa should be taken as a naval station and colony. The proposal was certainly not unconnected with the large Hamburg firm of Godeffroy which "was all-powerful in Samoa." At that time the Government was indisposed to imperialist adventure, and nothing came of the idea beyond the visit of German warships and the signing of treaties with the natives in 1876, 1877, and 1879. But in 1878 there was a development most significant of the future. The Godeffroy firm was in difficulties, and proposed or threatened to sell its interests to the London firm of Baring. The firm of Godeffroy was one of the earliest to realize that financial difficulties can be made the first stepping-stone towards Empire. The method of converting bankruptcy into lucrative imperialism has since become a commonplace of colonial policy, but this early example, though unsuccessful, is illuminating. Godeffroy appealed to German patriotism not to allow him to sell patriotically his interests in Samoa to a British firm. He looked to German patriots to invest five million marks in a German Trading and Plantation Company which would relieve him of his South Sea interests. But the security offered by Herr Godeffroy was insufficient to induce German patriotism to invest more than one million marks; and one million marks was insuf-

---

[3] Friedrich Fabri was a German mission administrator for over twenty years.—Ed.

ficient to induce Herr Godeffroy's patriotism to part with his interests. He then conceived the idea of appealing to the patriotism of the German Government by floating a new Company to take over his interests, and of inducing the Government to guarantee a $4\frac{1}{2}$ percent dividend for twenty years. In this way the interests of Herr Godeffroy, of German trade and finance, and of imperialism, would be all promoted, and the financial difficulties of Herr Godeffroy would become the first stepping-stone to a German colony in Samoa. At that time the German Government was Bismarck, and Bismarck was by no means favorable to "colonial policies" and economic imperialism. But no man can be more resourceful than a patriotic financier in financial difficulties. Herr Godeffroy went to a well-known financier, von Hansemann, Director of the Diskontogesellschaft, who was a friend of Geheimrat von Kusserow of the German Foreign Office, and of the banker von Bleichröder, who was Bismarck's financial adviser. Herr Godeffroy talked von Hansemann over to his scheme; von Hansemann talked over the Geheimrat and the banker; the Geheimrat and the banker talked over Bismarck. And Bismarck was talked over because Herr Godeffroy could, as it happened, offer a *quid pro quo*. At that moment Bismarck was anxious to get his protection proposals accepted among the trading interests, particularly in the Hanse towns. The firm of Godeffroy strenuously supported these proposals, and did very much to obtain for them the support of the Hanse traders and financiers. In return, the Government proposed in the Reichstag to guarantee the dividend of $4\frac{1}{2}$ percent to the new company for twenty years. Unfortunately for Herr Godeffroy he had forgotten to talk over the Reichstag, and the proposal was rejected. So, for the moment, the German Government failed to step into Samoa over the financial corpse of J. C. Godeffroy & Son by the process through which that Government between 1880 and 1890 stepped into East Africa over the financial corpse of the Deutsch-Ostafrikanische Gesellschaft, or through which the British Government stepped into East Africa and Uganda over the financial corpse of the British East Africa Company, or through which, in 1902, the French Government all but succeeded in stepping into Abyssinia over the financial corpse of the Compagnie Impériale des Chemins de Fer éthiopiens. It should, however, be remarked that the firm of J. C. Godeffroy was not as moribund as it appeared to be in 1878. It continued through its

Bismarckian manager, Theodor Weber, to be "all-powerful" in Samoa, and its influence and machinations led finally to the treaties and annexations of 1899 and 1900. . . .

In 1880 Bismarck was the German equivalent of a Little Englander. By 1885 the imperialists, explorers, and traders had forced his hand and converted him ostensibly to a policy of imperialism. His policy and his imperialism were purely economic. The causes of this conversion and the facts connected with it throw great light upon the general motives of modern imperialism. First of all, let us examine the immediate influences within Germany which were brought to bear upon Bismarck. They were commercial and financial. Bismarck's change of policy was actually shown by his extending the power and rule of the German State to four places in Africa, South-West Africa, the Cameroons, Togoland, and East Africa. Now in South-West Africa the immediate impulse came from Lüderitz, the Bremen merchant, who after a year's hard work at last in 1883 obtained official backing from the Chancellor for his enterprise. And it is significant that the financial backing of the German West African Company, which took over Lüderitz's newly acquired interests in 1885, came from the financiers Hansemann and Bleichröder, to whose connection with German colonial policy we have previously had to refer. In the Cameroons the impulse came from Woermann, the Hamburg trader and ally of Fabri, who, in 1884, laid before Bismarck, at the Chancellor's request, a memorandum suggesting steps to be taken for protecting German commercial interests in the Cameroons. This memorandum formed the basis of Bismarck's instructions to the Nachtigal expedition which acquired the Cameroons for Germany. In Togoland Woermann again was chiefly responsible, for, as soon as Bismarck's consent to the occupation of South-West Africa became known, Woermann dispatched an agent to prepare the way for similar action in Togoland, and in 1885 similar action followed. In East Africa the course of events was even more illuminating. In 1884 Dr. Peters the explorer arrived in Zanzibar with the intention of obtaining certain "concessions" on the coast. The German consul, acting on direct orders from Bismarck, refused him all Government protection or encouragement. He then turned to the business firms, and from them, e.g., Hansing & Co., he obtained every assistance. Owing to their help he succeeded in making various treaties with the natives for concessions of land. He then returned to Berlin and, now heavily backed by the commercial interests, betook himself to that same Geheimrat von Kusserow of the Foreign Office who had proved so useful to Herr Godeffroy in his financial difficulties. Peters and the German traders in East Africa found no more difficulty in talking over von Kusserow than had Herr Godeffroy in the case of Samoa. And von Kusserow once more talked over Bismarck, this time, it is said, by his glowing account of East Africa. The result was a charter for Peters' Deutsch-Ostafrikanische Gesellschaft.

Thus the immediate impulse which caused the German State to lay its hand upon islands in the Pacific, upon Togoland and the Cameroons, and South-West and East Africa, came from trade and finance, from the Godeffroys, Woermanns, Lüderitz's, and Hansings. In Germany these traders, shippers, and financiers prepared the ground by working upon public opinion through their agents, the agitators, politicians, and civil servants, like Fabri, Hohenlohe, von Maltzan, and von Kusserow; in Africa they prepared the ground by working upon the natives through their agents, the explorers, like Dr. Peters and Flegel. But the economic impulse is shown not only in these subterranean workings and interconnections: it is shown just as clearly in the words and actions by which Bismarck expressed the new policy of the German State. For the preliminary step to Bismarck's public change of policy was his circular to the senates of the Hanse towns asking for their recommendations with respect to the difficulties and interests of firms operating in Africa. In other words, the Chancellor consulted only economic interests and thought only of economic motives. And when he had determined upon his new policy and publicly announced it, he showed that it was the policy of the flag following and protecting trade, and that the center of it was the German trader (*der deutsche Kaufman*). "It is not possible," he said in 1884, "to conquer oversea territories by men-of-war or to take possession of them without further ceremony. Nevertheless the German trader wherever he has settled will be protected, and wherever he has assumed possession of territory there the Administration will follow him, as England has continually done." And in the Reichstag, on June 26, 1884, he made his policy and objects even more plain: "Our purpose is therefore to found not provinces but commercial enterprises: but it is also our purpose that these enterprises in their highest development shall acquire a sovereignty, a commercial sovereignty resting ultimately upon the support of the German Empire and standing under its protection, and that we shall protect them not only against the attacks of their immediate neighbors, but also against any harms or harassings which may come from other European Powers."...

Joseph A. Schumpeter
IMPERIALISM AS A SOCIAL ATAVISM

Born in Moravia and educated in Vienna, Joseph A. Schumpeter (1883–1950) taught economics in Austria and Germany until 1932, and in 1919–20 was Austrian Minister of Finance. He went to Harvard University in 1932 and remained there as a professor until his death. Famous in economic circles while still in his twenties, he then and later published a series of imposing economic works, among which were The Theory of Economic Development, Business Cycles, *and* Capitalism, Socialism, and Democracy. *Schumpeter's semiconservative economic system was one of stupendous scope and in no way confined to purely economic matters, as the following extract illustrates. The essay on "imperialism" was published in German in 1919 as "The Sociology of Imperialisms," but it was not widely recognized in America until its publication in English in 1951.*

The Problem

No one calls it imperialism when a state, no matter how brutally and vigorously, pursues concrete interests of its own; and when it can be expected to abandon its aggressive attitude as soon as it has attained what it was after. The word "imperialism" has been abused as a slogan to the point where it threatens to lose all meaning, but up to this point our definition is quite in keeping with common usage, even in the press. For whenever the word imperialism is used, there is always the implication—whether sincere or not—of an aggressiveness, the true reasons for which do not lie in the aims which are temporarily being pursued; of an aggressiveness that is only kindled anew by each success; of an aggressiveness for its own sake, as reflected in such terms as "hegemony," "world dominion," and so forth. And history, in truth, shows us nations and classes—most nations furnish an example at some time or other—that seek expansion for the sake of expanding, war for the sake of fighting, victory for the sake of winning, dominion for the sake of ruling. This determination cannot be explained by any of the pretexts that bring it into action, by any of the aims for which it seems to be struggling at the time. It confronts us, independent of all concrete purpose or occasion, as an enduring disposition, seizing upon one opportunity as eagerly as the next. It shines through all the arguments put forward on behalf of present aims. It values conquest not so much on account of the immediate advantages—advantages that more often than not are more than dubious, or that are heedlessly cast away with the same frequency —as because it *is* conquest, success, action. Here the theory of concrete interest in our sense fails. What needs to be explained is how the will to victory itself came into being.

Expansion for its own sake always requires, among other things, concrete objects if it is to reach the action stage and maintain itself, but this does not constitute its meaning. Such expansion is in a sense its own "object," and the truth is that it has no adequate object beyond itself. Let us therefore, in the absence of a better term, call it "objectless." It follows for that very reason that, just as such expansion cannot be explained by concrete interest, so too it is never satisfied by the fulfillment of a concrete interest, as would be the case if fulfillment were the motive, and the struggle for it merely a necessary evil—a counterargument, in fact. Hence the tendency of such expansion to transcend all bounds and tangible limits, to the point of utter exhaustion. This, then, is our definition: imperialism is the objectless disposition on the part of a state to unlimited forcible expansion.

Now it may be possible, in the final analysis, to give an "economic explanation" for this phenomenon, to end up with economic factors. Two different points present themselves in this connection: First, an attempt can be made, following the basic idea of the economic interpretation of history, to derive imperialist tendencies from the economic-structural influences that shape life in general and from the relations of production. I should like to emphasize that I do not doubt in the least that this powerful instrument of analysis will stand up here in the same sense that it has with other, similar phenomena—if only it is kept in mind that customary modes of political thought and feeling in a given age can never be mere "reflexes" of, or counterparts to, the production situation of that age. Because of the persistence of such habits, they will always, to a considerable degree, be dominated by the production context of past ages. Again, the attempt may be made to reduce imperialist phenomena to economic class *interests* of the age in question. This is precisely what neo-Marxist theory does. Briefly, it views imperialism simply as the reflex of the interests of the capitalist upper stratum, at a given stage of capitalist development. Beyond doubt this is by far the most serious contribution toward a solution of our problem. Certainly there is much truth in it. We shall deal with this theory later. But let us emphasize even here that it does not, of logical necessity, follow from the economic interpretation of history. It may be discarded without coming into conflict with that interpretation; indeed, without even departing from its premises. It is the treatment of this factor that constitutes the contribution of the present inquiry into the sociology of the *Zeitgeist*.

Our method of investigation is simple: we propose to analyze the birth and life of imperialism by means of historical examples which I regard as typical. A common basic trait emerges in every case, making a single sociological problem of imperialism in all ages, though there are substantial differences among the individual cases. Hence the plural, "imperialisms," in the title.

Imperialism as a Catch Phrase

An example will suffice. . . .

. . . The [British] election campaign of 1874—or, to fix the date exactly, Disraeli's speech in the Crystal Palace in 1872—marked the birth of imperialism as the catch phrase of domestic policy.

It was put in the form of "Imperial Federation." The colonies—of which Disraeli in 1852 had written: "These wretched colonies . . . are a millstone round our necks" (Malmesbury, *Memoirs of an Ex-Minister,* p. 343)—these same colonies were to become autonomous members in a unified empire. This empire was to form a customs union. The free soil of the colonies was to remain reserved for Englishmen. A uniform defense system was to be created. The whole structure was to be crowned by a central representative organ in London, creating a closer, living connection between the imperial government and the colonies. The appeal to national sentiment, the battle cry against "Liberal" cosmopolitanism, already emerged sharply, just as they did later on in the agitation sponsored by Chamberlain, on whom fell Disraeli's mantle. Of itself the plan showed no inherent tendency to reach out beyond the "Empire," and "the Preservation of the Empire" was and is a good description of it. If we nevertheless include the "Imperial Federation" plan under the heading of imperialism, this is because its protective tariff, its militarist sentiments, its ideology of a unified "Greater Britain" all foreshadowed vague aggressive trends that would have emerged soon enough if the plan had ever passed from the sphere of the slogan into the realm of actual policy.

That it was not without value as a slogan is shown by the very fact that a man of Chamberlain's political instinct took it up—characteristically enough in another period, when effective Conservative rallying cries were at a premium. Indeed, it never vanished again, becoming a stock weapon in the political arsenal of English Conservatism, usurped even by many Liberals. As early as the nineties it meant a great deal to the youth of Oxford and Cambridge. It played a leading part in the Conservative press and at Conservative rallies. Commercial advertising grew very fond of employing its emblems—which explains why it was so conspicuous to foreign (and usually superficial) observers, and why there was so much discussion in the foreign press about "British Imperialism," a topic, moreover, that was most welcome to many political parties on the Continent. This success is readily explained. In the first place, the plan had much to offer to a whole series of special interests—primarily a protective tariff and the prospect of lucrative opportunities for exploitation, inaccessible to industry under a system of free trade. Here was the opportunity to smother consumer resistance in a flood of patriotic enthusiasm. Later on, this advantage weighed all the more heavily in the balance, for certain English industries were beginning to grow quite sensitive to the dumping tactics employed by German and American exporters. Equally important was the fact that such a plan was calculated to divert the attention of the people from social problems at home. But the main thing, before which all arguments stemming from calculating self-interest must recede into the background, was the unfailing power of the appeal to national sentiment. No other appeal is as effective, except at a time when the people happen to be caught in the midst of flaming social struggle. All other appeals are rooted in interests that must be grasped by reason. This one alone arouses the dark powers of the subconscious, calls into play instincts that carry over from the life habits of the dim past. Driven out everywhere else, the irrational seeks refuge in nationalism—the irrational which consists of belligerence, the need to hate, a goodly quota of inchoate idealism, the most naive (and hence also the most unrestrained) egotism. This is precisely what constitutes the impact of nationalism. It satisfies the need for surrender to a concrete and familiar super-personal cause, the need for self-glorification and violent self-assertion. Whenever a vacuum arises in the mind of a people—as happens especially after exhausting social agitation, or after a war—the nationalist element comes to the fore. The idea of "Imperial Federation" gave form and direction to these trends in England. It was, in truth, a fascinating vision which was unfolded before the provincial mind. An additional factor was a vague faith in the advantages of colonial possessions, preferably to be exploited to the exclusion of all foreigners. Here we see ancient notions still at work. Once upon a time it had been feasible to treat colonies in the way that highwaymen treat their victims, and the possession of colonies unquestionably brought advantages. Trade had been possible only under immediate military protection and there could be no question that military bases were necessary. It is because of the survival of such arguments that colonialism is not yet dead, even in England today, though only in exceptional circumstances do colonies under free trade become objects of exploitation in a sense different from that in which independent countries can be exploited. And finally, there is the instinctive urge to domination. Objectively, the man in the street derives little enough satisfaction even from modern English colonial policy, but he does take pleasure in the idea, much as a card player vicariously satisfies his primitive aggressive instincts. At the time of the Boer War there was not a beggar in London who did not speak of "our" rebellious subjects. These circumstances, in all their melancholy irony, are serious factors in politics. They eliminate many courses of action that alone seem reasonable to the leaders. Here is an example: In 1815 the Ionian Islands became an English protectorate, not to be surrendered until 1863. Long before then, however, one foreign secretary after another had realized that this possession was meaningless and untenable—not in the absolute sense, but simply because no reasonable person in England would have approved of the smallest sacrifice on its behalf. Nevertheless, none dared surrender it, for it was clear that this would have appeared as a loss and a defeat, chalked up against the cabinet in question. The only thing to do was to insist that Corfu was a military base of the highest importance which must be retained. Now, during his first term as head of the government,[1] Gladstone had frequently made concessions—to Russia, to America, to others. At bottom everyone was glad that he had made them. Yet an uncomfortable feeling persisted, together with the occasion for much speech-making about national power and glory. The political genius who headed the opposition party saw all this—and *spoke* accordingly.

That this imperialism is no more than a phrase is seen from the fact that Disraeli *spoke,* but did not *act.* But this alone is not convincing. After all, he might have lacked the opportunity to act. The crucial factor is that he *did* have the opportunity. He had a majority. He was master of his people as only an English prime minister can be. The time was auspicious. The people had lost patience with Gladstone's peace-loving nature. Disraeli owed his success in part to the slogan we have been discussing. Yet he did not even try to follow through. He took not a single step in that direction. He scarcely even mentioned it in his speeches, once it had served his purpose. His foreign policy moved wholly within the framework of Conservative tradition. For this reason it was pro-Austrian and pro-Turkish. The notion that the integrity of Turkey was in the English interest was still alive, not yet overthrown by the power of Gladstone's Midlothian speeches which were to change public opinion on this point and later, under Salisbury, invade even the Conservative credo. Hence the new Earl of Beaconsfield [Disraeli] supported

[1] Between 1868 and 1885, William Gladstone and Benjamin Disraeli alternated as prime ministers of Great Britain. (Gladstone served as prime minister in 1868–74 and 1880–85; Disraeli in 1868 and 1874–80.) Disraeli was created Earl of Beaconsfield in 1876.—Ed.

Turkey, hence he tore up the Treaty of San Stefano. Yet even this, and the capture of Cyprus, were of no avail. A tide of public indignation toppled his rule soon afterward.

We can see that Beaconsfield was quite right in not taking a single step in the direction of practical imperialism and that his policy was based on good sense. The masses of the British electorate would never have sanctioned an imperialist policy, would never have made sacrifices for it. As a toy, as a political arabesque, they accepted imperialism, just so long as no one tried it in earnest. This is seen conclusively when the fate of Chamberlain's agitation is traced. Chamberlain was unquestionably serious. A man of great talent, he rallied every ounce of personal and political power, marshaled tremendous resources, organized all the interests that stood to gain, employed a consummate propaganda technique—all this to the limits of the possible. Yet England rejected him, turning over the reins to the opposition by an overwhelming majority.[2] It condemned the Boer War, did everything in its power to "undo" it, proving that it was merely a chance aberration from the general trend. So complete was the defeat of imperialism that the Conservatives under Bonar Law, in order to achieve some degree of political rehabilitation, had to strike from their program the tariffs on food imports, necessarily the basis for any policy of colonial preference.

The rejection of imperialism meant the rejection of all the interests and arguments on which the movement was based. The elements that were decisive for the formation of political will power—above all the radicals and gradually the labor representatives as well—showed little enthusiasm for the ideology of world empire. They were much more inclined to give credence to the Disraeli of 1852, who had compared colonies to millstones, than to the Disraeli of 1874, to the Chamberlain of the eighties rather than the Chamberlain of 1903. They showed not the least desire to make presents to agriculture, whether from national or other pretexts, at the expense of the general welfare. They were far too well versed in the free-trade argument—and this applies to the very lowest layers of the English electorate—to believe the gloomy prophecies of the "yellow press," which insisted that free trade was sacrificing to current consumer interests employment opportunities and the very roots of material

---

[2] In the election of 1905.—Ed.

welfare. After all, the rise of British export trade after 1900 belied this argument as plainly as could be. Nor had they any sympathy for military splendor and adventures in foreign policy. The whole struggle served only to demonstrate the utter impotence of jingoism. The question of "objective interest"—that is, whether and to what extent there is an economic interest in a policy of imperialism—remains to be discussed. Here we are concerned only with those political notions that have proved effective—whether they were false or true.

What effect the present war [World War I] will have in this respect remains to be seen. For our purposes what has still to be shown is how this anti-imperialist sentiment—and especially anti-imperialism in practice—developed in England. In the distant past England did have imperialist tendencies, just as most other nations did. The process that concerns us now begins with the moment when the struggle between the people and the crown ended differently in England from the way it did on the Continent—namely, with the victory of the people. Under the Tudors and Stuarts the absolute monarchy developed in England much as it did at the same time on the Continent. Specifically, the British Crown also succeeded in winning over part of the nobility, the "cavaliers," who subsequently sided with it against the "roundheads" and who, but for the outcome of the battles of Naseby and Marston Moor, would surely have become a military palace guard. Presumably England, too, would then have seen the rise of an arbitrary military absolutism, and the same tendencies which we shall discover elsewhere would have led to continual wars of aggression there too. . . .

Imperialism and Capitalism

Our analysis of the historical evidence has shown, first, the unquestionable fact that "objectless" tendencies toward forcible expansion, without definite, utilitarian limits—that is, nonrational and irrational, purely instinctual inclinations toward war and conquest—play a very large role in the history of mankind. It may sound paradoxical, but numberless wars—perhaps the majority of all wars—have been waged without adequate "reason"—not so much from the moral viewpoint as from that of reasoned and reasonable interest. The most herculean efforts of the nations, in other words, have faded into the empty air. Our analysis, in the second place, provides an explanation for this drive to action, this will to war—a theory by no means exhausted by mere references to an "urge" or an "instinct." The explanation lies, instead, in the vital needs of situations that molded peoples and classes into warriors—if they wanted to avoid extinction—and in the fact that psychological dispositions and social structures acquired in the dim past in such situations, once firmly established, tend to maintain themselves and to continue in effect long after they have lost their meaning and their life-preserving function. Our analysis, in the third place, has shown the existence of subsidiary factors that facilitate the survival of such dispositions and structures—factors that may be divided into two groups. The orientation toward war is mainly fostered by the domestic interests of ruling classes, but also by the influence of all those who stand to gain individually from a war policy, whether economically or socially. Both groups of factors are generally overgrown by elements of an altogether different character, not only in terms of political phraseology, but also of psychological motivation. Imperialisms differ greatly in detail, but they all have at least these traits in common, turning them into a single phenomenon in the field of sociology, as we noted in the introduction.

Imperialism thus is atavistic in character. It falls into that large group of surviving features from earlier ages that play such an important part in every concrete social situation. In other words, it is an element that stems from the living conditions, not of the present, but of the past—or, put in terms of the economic interpretation of history, from past rather than present relations of production. It is an atavism in the social structure, in individual, psychological habits of emotional reaction. Since the vital needs that created it have passed away for good, it too must gradually disappear, even though every warlike involvement, no matter how nonimperialist in character, tends to revive it. It tends to disappear as a structural element because the structure that brought it to the fore goes into a decline, giving way, in the course of social development, to other structures that have no room for it and eliminate the power factors that supported it. It tends to disappear as an element of habitual emotional reaction, because of the progressive rationalization of life and mind, a process in which old functional needs are absorbed by new tasks, in which heretofore military energies are functionally modified. If our theory is correct, cases of imperialism should decline in intensity the later they occur in the history of a people and of a culture. Our most recent examples of unmistakable, clear-cut imperialism are the absolute monarchies of the eighteenth century. They are unmistakably "more civilized" than their predecessors.

It is from absolute autocracy that the present age has taken over what imperialist tendencies it displays. And the imperialism of absolute autocracy flourished before the Industrial Revolution that created the modern world, or rather, before the consequences of that revolution began to be felt in all their aspects. These two statements are primarily meant in a historical sense, and as such they are no more than self-evident. We shall nevertheless try, within the framework of our theory, to define the significance of capitalism for our phenomenon and to examine the relationship between present-day imperialist tendencies and the autocratic imperialism of the eighteenth century.

The floodtide that burst the dams in the Industrial Revolution had its sources, of course, back in the Middle Ages. But capitalism began to shape society and impress its stamp on every page of social history only with the second half of the eighteenth century. Before that time there had been only islands of capitalist economy imbedded in an ocean of village and urban economy. True, certain political influences emanated from these islands, but they were able to assert themselves only indirectly. Not until the process we term the Industrial Revolution did the working masses, led by the entrepreneur, overcome the bonds of older life-forms—the environment of peasantry, guild, and aristocracy. . . .

*   *   *

These new types were now cast adrift from the fixed order of earlier times, from the environment that had shackled and protected people for centuries, from the old associations of village, manor house, clan fellowship, often even from families in the broader sense. They were severed from the things that had been constant year after year, from cradle to grave—tools, homes, the countryside. especially the soil. They were on their own, enmeshed in the pitiless logic of gainful employment, mere drops in the vast ocean of industrial life, exposed to the inexorable pressures of competition. They were freed from the control of ancient patterns of thought, of the grip of institutions and organs that taught and represented these outlooks in village, manor, and guild. They were removed from the old world, engaged in building a new one for themselves—a specialized, mechanized world. Thus they were all inevitably democratized, individualized, and rationalized. They were democratized, because the picture of time-honored power and privilege gave way to one of continual change, set in motion by industrial life. They were individualized, because subjective opportunities to shape their lives took the place of immutable objective factors. They were rationalized, because the instability of economic position made their survival hinge on continual, deliberately rationalistic decisions—a dependence that emerged with great sharpness. Trained to economic rationalism, these people left no sphere of life unrationalized, questioning everything about themselves, the social structure, the state, the ruling class. The marks of this process are engraved on every aspect of modern culture. It is this process that explains the basic features of that culture.

These are things that are well known today, recognized in their full significance—indeed, often exaggerated. Their application to our subject is plain. Everything that is purely instinctual, everything insofar as it is purely instinctual, is driven into the background by this development. It creates a social and psychological atmosphere in keeping with modern economic forms, where traditional habits, merely because they were traditional, could no more survive than obsolete economic forms. Just as the latter can survive only if they are continually "adapted," so instinctual tendencies can survive only when the conditions that gave rise to them continue to apply, or when the "instinct" in question derives a new purpose from new conditions. The "instinct" that is *only* "instinct," that has lost its purpose, languishes relatively quickly in the capitalist world, just as does an inefficient economic practice. We see this process of rationalization at work even in the case of the strongest impulses. We observe it, for example, in the facts of procreation. We must therefore anticipate finding it in the case of the imperialist impulse as well; we must expect to see this impulse, which rests on the primitive contingencies of physical combat, gradually disappear, washed away by new exigencies of daily life. There is another factor too. The competitive system absorbs the full energies of most of the people at all economic levels. Constant application, attention, and concentration of energy are the conditions of survival within it, primarily in the specifically economic professions, but also in other activities organized on their model. There is much less excess energy to be vented in war and conquest than in any precapitalist society. What excess energy there is flows largely into industry itself, accounts for its shining figures—the type of the captain of industry—and for the rest is applied to art, science, and the social struggle. In a purely capitalist world, what was once energy for war becomes simply energy for labor of every kind. Wars of conquest and adventurism in foreign policy in general are bound to be regarded as troublesome distractions, destructive of life's meaning, a diversion from the accustomed and therefore "true" task.

A purely capitalist world therefore can offer no fertile soil to imperialist impulses. That does not mean that it cannot still maintain an interest in imperialist expansion. We shall discuss this immediately. The point is that its people are likely to be essentially of an unwarlike disposition. Hence we must expect that anti-imperialist tendencies will show themselves wherever capitalism penetrates the economy and, through the economy, the mind of modern nations—most strongly, of course, where capitalism itself is strongest, where it has advanced furthest, encountered the least resistance, and preeminently where its types and hence democracy—in the "bourgeois" sense—come closest to political dominion. We must further expect that the types formed by capitalism will actually be the carriers of these tendencies. Is such the case? The facts that follow are cited to show that this expectation, which flows from our theory, is in fact justified.

1. Throughout the world of capitalism, and specifically among the elements formed by capitalism in modern social life, there has arisen a fundamental opposition to war, expansion, cabinet diplomacy, armaments, and socially entrenched professional armies. This opposition had its origin in the country that first turned capitalist—England—and arose coincidentally with that country's capitalist development. "Philosophical radicalism" was the first politically influential intellectual movement to represent this trend successfully, linking it up, as was to be expected, with economic freedom in general and free trade in particular. Molesworth became a cabinet member, even though he had publicly declared—on the occasion of the Canadian revolution—that he prayed for the defeat of his country's arms. In step with the advance of capitalism, the movement

also gained adherents elsewhere—though at first only adherents without influence. It found support in Paris—indeed, in a circle oriented toward capitalist enterprise (for example, Frédéric Passy). True, pacifism as a matter of principle had existed before, though only among a few small religious sects. But modern pacifism, in its political foundations if not its derivation, is unquestionably a phenomenon of the capitalist world.

2. Wherever capitalism penetrated, peace parties of such strength arose that virtually every war meant a political struggle on the domestic scene. The exceptions are rare—Germany in the Franco-Prussian war of 1870–1871, both belligerents in the Russo-Turkish war of 1877–1878. That is why every war is carefully justified as a defensive war by the governments involved, and by all the political parties, in their official utterances—indicating a realization that a war of a different nature would scarcely be tenable in a political sense. (Here too the Russo-Turkish war is an exception, but a significant one.) In former times this would not have been necessary. Reference to an interest or pretense at moral justification was customary as early as the eighteenth century, but only in the nineteenth century did the assertion of attack, or the threat of attack, become the only avowed occasion for war. In the distant past, imperialism had needed no disguise whatever, and in the absolute autocracies only a very transparent one; but today imperialism is carefully hidden from public view—even though there may still be an unofficial appeal to warlike instincts. No people and no ruling class today can openly afford to regard war as a normal state of affairs or a normal element in the life of nations. No one doubts that today it must be characterized as an abnormality and a disaster. True, war is still glorified. But glorification in the style of King Tuglâtî-palisharra is rare and unleashes such a storm of indignation that every practical politician carefully dissociates himself from such things. Everywhere there is official acknowledgment that peace is an end in itself—though not necessarily an end overshadowing all purposes that can be realized by means of war. Every expansionist urge must be carefully related to a concrete goal. All this is primarily a matter of political phraseology, to be sure. But the necessity for this phraseology is a symptom of the popular attitude. And that attitude makes a policy of imperialism more and more difficult—indeed, the very word imperialism is applied only to the enemy, in a reproachful

sense, being carefully avoided with reference to the speaker's own policies.

3. The type of industrial worker created by capitalism is always vigorously anti-imperialist. In the individual case, skillful agitation may persuade the working masses to approve or remain neutral—a concrete goal or interest in self-defense always playing the main part—but no initiative for a forcible policy of expansion ever emanates from this quarter. On this point official socialism unquestionably formulates not merely the interests but also the conscious will of the workers. Even less than peasant imperialism is there any such thing as socialist or other working-class imperialism.

4. Despite manifest resistance on the part of powerful elements, the capitalist age has seen the development of methods for preventing war, for the peaceful settlement of disputes among states. The very fact of resistance means that the trend can be explained only from the mentality of capitalism as a mode of life. It definitely limits the opportunities imperialism needs if it is to be a powerful force. True, the methods in question often fail, but even more often they are successful. I am thinking not merely of the Hague Court of Arbitration but of the practice of submitting controversial issues to conferences of the major powers or at least those powers directly concerned—a course of action that has become less and less avoidable. True, here too the individual case may become a farce. But the serious setbacks of today must not blind us to the real importance or sociological significance of these things.

5. Among all capitalist economies, that of the United States is least burdened with precapitalist elements, survivals, reminiscences, and power factors. Certainly we cannot expect to find imperialist tendencies altogether lacking even in the United States, for the immigrants came from Europe with their convictions fully formed, and the environment certainly favored the revival of instincts of pugnacity. But we can conjecture that among all countries the United States is likely to exhibit the weakest imperialist trend. This turns out to be the truth. The case is particularly instructive, because the United States has seen a particularly strong emergence of capitalist interests in an imperialist direction—those very interests to which the phenomenon of imperialism has so often been reduced, a subject we shall yet touch on. Nevertheless the United States was the first advocate of disarmament and arbitration. It was the first to conclude

treaties concerning arms limitations (1817) and arbitral courts (first attempt in 1797)—doing so most zealously, by the way, when economic interest in expansion was at its greatest. Since 1908 such treaties have been concluded with twenty-two states. In the course of the nineteenth century, the United States had numerous occasions for war, including instances that were well calculated to test its patience. It made almost no use of such occasions. Leading industrial and financial circles in the United States had and still have an evident interest in incorporating Mexico into the Union. There was more than enough opportunity for such annexation—but Mexico remained unconquered. Racial catch phrases and working-class interests pointed to Japan as a possible danger. Hence possession of the Philippines was not a matter of indifference—yet surrender of this possession is being discussed. Canada was an almost defenseless prize—but Canada remained independent. Even in the United States, of course, politicians need slogans—especially slogans calculated to divert attention from domestic issues. Theodore Roosevelt and certain magnates of the press actually resorted to imperialism—and the result, in that world of high capitalism, was utter defeat, a defeat that would have been even more abject, if other slogans, notably those appealing to anti-trust sentiment, had not met with better success.

These facts are scarcely in dispute. And since they fit into the picture of the mode of life which we have recognized to be the necessary product of capitalism, since we can grasp them adequately from the necessities of that mode of life and industry, it follows that capitalism is by nature anti-imperialist. Hence we cannot readily derive from it such imperialist tendencies as actually exist, but must evidently see them only as alien elements, carried into the world of capitalism from the outside, supported by non-capitalist factors in modern life. The survival of interest in a policy of forcible expansion does not, by itself, alter these facts—not even, it must be steadily emphasized, from the viewpoint of the economic interpretation of history. . . .

*   *   *

. . . The character of capitalism leads to large-scale production but with few exceptions large-scale production does not lead to the kind of unlimited concentration that would leave but one or only a few firms in each industry. On the contrary, any plant runs up against limits to its growth in a given location; and the growth of combinations which would make sense under a system of free trade encounters limits of organizational efficiency. Beyond these limits there is no tendency toward combination inherent in the competitive system. In particular, the rise of trusts and cartels—a phenomenon quite different from the trend to large-scale production with which it is often confused—can never be explained by the automatism of the competitive system. This follows from the very fact that trusts and cartels can attain their primary purpose—to pursue a monopoly policy—only behind protective tariffs, without which they would lose their essential significance. But protective tariffs do not automatically grow from the competitive system. They are the fruit of political action—*a type of action that by no means reflects the objective interests of all those concerned* but that, on the contrary, becomes impossible as soon as the majority of those whose consent is necessary realize their true interests. To some extent it is obvious, and for the rest it will be presently shown, that the interests of the minority, quite appropriately expressed in support of a protective tariff, do not stem from capitalism as such. It follows that *it is a basic fallacy to describe imperialism as a necessary phase of capitalism, or even to speak of the development of capitalism into imperialism.* We have seen before that the mode of life of the capitalist world does not favor imperialist attitudes. We now see that the alignment of interests in a capitalist economy—even the interests of its upper strata—by no means points unequivocally in the direction of imperialism. We now come to the final step in our line of reasoning.

Since we cannot derive even export monopolism from any tendencies of the competitive system toward big enterprise, we must find some other explanation. A glance at the original purpose of tariffs provides what we need. Tariffs sprang from the financial interests of the monarchy. They were a method of exploiting the trader which differed from the method of the robber baron in the same way that the royal chase differed from the method of the poacher. They were in line with the royal prerogatives of safe conduct, of protection for the Jews, of the granting of market rights, and so forth. From the thirteenth century onward this method was progressively refined in the autocratic state, less and less emphasis being placed on the direct monetary yield of customs revenues, and more and more on their indirect effect in creating productive taxable objects. In other words, while the protective value of a tariff counted, it counted only from the viewpoint of the ultimate monetary advantage of the sovereign. It does not matter, for our purposes, that occasionally this policy, under the influence of lay notions of economics, blundered badly in the choice of its methods. (From the viewpoint of autocratic interest, incidentally, such measures were not nearly so self-defeating as they were from the viewpoint of the national economy.) Every customs house, every privilege conferring the right to produce, market, or store, thus created a new economic situation which deflected trade and industry into "unnatural" channels. All tariffs, rights, and the like became the seed bed for economic growth that could have neither sprung up nor maintained itself without them. Further, all such economic institutions dictated by autocratic interest were surrounded by manifold interests of people who were dependent on them and now began to demand their continuance—a wholly paradoxical though at the same time quite understandable situation. The trading and manufacturing bourgeoisie was all the more aware of its dependence on the sovereign, since it needed his protection against the remaining feudal powers; and the uncertainties of the times, together with the lack of great consuming centers, impeded the rise of free economic competition. Insofar as commerce and manufacturing came into being at all, therefore, they arose under the sign of monopolistic interest. Thus the bourgeoisie willingly allowed itself to be molded into one of the power instruments of the monarchy, both in a territorial and in a national sense. It is even true that the bourgeoisie, because of the character of its interests and the kind of economic outlook that corresponded to those interests, made an essential contribution to the emergence of modern nationalism. Another factor that worked in the same direction was the financial relation between the great merchant houses and the sovereign. This theory of the nature of the relationship between the autocratic state and the bourgeoisie is not refuted by pointing out that it was precisely the mercantile republics of the Middle Ages and the early modern period that initially pursued a policy of mercantilism. They were no more than enclaves in a world pervaded by the struggle among feudal powers. The Hanseatic League and Venice, for example, could maintain themselves only as military powers, could pursue their business only by means of fortified bases, warehousing privileges, protective treaties. This forced the people to stand shoulder to shoulder, made the exploitation of political gains more important than domestic competition, infused them with a corporate and monopolistic spirit. Wherever autocratic power vanished at an early date—as in the Netherlands and later in England—and the protective interest receded into the background, they swiftly discovered that trade must be free—"free to the nethermost recesses of hell."

Trade and industry of the early capitalist period thus remained strongly pervaded with precapitalist methods, bore the stamp of autocracy, and served its interests, either willingly or by force. With its traditional habits of feeling, thinking, and acting molded along such lines, the bourgeoisie entered the Industrial Revolution. It was shaped, in other words, by the needs and interests of an environment that was essentially noncapitalist, or at least precapitalist—needs stemming not from the nature of the capitalist economy as such but from the fact of the coexistence of early capitalism with another and at first overwhelmingly powerful mode of life and business. Established habits of thought and action tend to persist, and hence the spirit of guild and monopoly at first maintained itself, and was only slowly undermined, even where capitalism was in sole possession of the field. Actually capitalism did not fully prevail *anywhere* on the Continent. Existing economic interests, "artificially" shaped by the autocratic state, remained dependent on the "protection" of the state. The industrial organism, such as it was, would not have been able to withstand free competition. Even where the old barriers crumbled in the autocratic state, the people did not all at once flock to the clear track. They were creatures of mercantilism and even earlier periods, and many of them huddled together and protested against the affront of being forced to depend on their own ability. They cried for paternalism, for protection, for forcible restraint of strangers, and above all for tariffs. They met with partial success, particularly because capitalism failed to take radical action in the agrarian field. Capitalism did bring about many changes on the land, springing in part from its automatic mechanisms, in part from the political trends it engendered—abolition of serfdom, freeing the soil from feudal entanglements, and so on—but initially it did not alter the basic outlines of the social structure of the countryside. Even less did it affect the spirit of the people, and least of all their political goals. This explains why the features and trends of autocracy—including imperialism—proved so resistant, why they exerted such a powerful influence on capitalist development, why the old export monopolism could live on and merge into the new.

These are facts of fundamental significance to an understanding of the soul of modern Europe. Had the ruling class of the Middle Ages—the war-oriented nobility—changed its profession and function and become the ruling class of the capitalist world; or had developing capitalism swept it away, put it out of business, instead of merely clashing head-on with it in the agrarian sphere—then much would have been different in the life of modern peoples. But as things actually were, neither eventuality occurred; or, more correctly, both are taking place, only at a very slow pace. . . .

*   *   *

Here we find that we have penetrated to the historical as well as the sociological sources of modern imperialism. It does not *coincide* with nationalism and militarism, though it *fuses* with them by supporting them as it is supported by them. It too is—not only historically, but also sociologically—a heritage of the autocratic state, of its structural elements, organizational forms, interest alignments, and human attitudes, the outcome of precapitalist forces which the autocratic state has reorganized, in part by the methods of early capitalism. It would never have been evolved by the "inner logic" of capitalism itself. This is true even of mere export monopolism. It too has its sources in absolutist policy and the action habits of an essentially precapitalist environment. That it was able to develop to its present dimensions is owing to the momentum of a situation once created, which continued to engender ever new "artificial" economic structures, that is, those which maintain themselves by political power alone. In most of the countries addicted to export monopolism it is also owing to the fact that the old autocratic state and the old attitude of the bourgeoisie toward it were so vigorously maintained. But export monopolism, to go a step further, is not yet imperialism. And even if it had been able to arise without protective tariffs, it would never have developed into imperialism in the hands of an unwarlike bourgeoisie. If this did happen, it was only because the heritage included the war machine, together with its socio-psychological aura and aggressive bent, and because a class oriented toward war maintained itself in a ruling position. This class clung to its domestic interest in war, and the pro-military interests among the bourgeoisie were able to ally themselves with it. This alliance kept alive war instincts and ideas of overlordship, male supremacy, and triumphant glory—ideas that would have otherwise long since died. It led to social conditions that, while they ultimately stem from the conditions of production, cannot be explained from capitalist production methods alone. . . .

William L. Langer
A CRITIQUE OF IMPERIALISM

William L. Langer (b. 1896), while maintaining an eminent reputation as a historian at Harvard, served with distinction in a variety of nonhistorical capacities as well, including Chief of Research and Analysis Branch, Office of Strategic Services, 1942–45; assistant director of the Central Intelligence Agency, 1950–52; and director of Harvard's Russian Research Center and the Center for Middle Eastern Studies, after 1954. Langer's international historical reputation was established in the early 1930s with two companion volumes on nineteenth-century diplomacy, European Alliances and Alignments, 1871–1890 (1931) *and* The Diplomacy of Imperialism, 1890–1902 (1935), *of which the essay below is a widely read by-product. A "middle-of-the-roader" in historical interpretation and an historian of great erudition, Langer was well suited both by temperament and scholarship to evaluate the different theories of nineteenth-century European expansion.*

It is now roughly fifty years since the beginning of that great outburst of expansive activity on the part of the Great Powers of Europe which we have come to call "imperialism." And it is about a generation since J. A. Hobson published his "Imperialism: A Study," a book which has served as the starting point for most later discussions and which has proved a perennial inspiration for writers of the most diverse schools. A reappraisal of it is therefore decidedly in order. The wonder is that it has not been undertaken sooner.

From William L. Langer, "A Critique of Imperialism," *Foreign Affairs* 14 (October 1935): 102–114. Reproduced by special permission from *Foreign Affairs,* October 1935. Copyright by the Council on Foreign Relations, Inc., New York.

Since before the outbreak of the World War the theoretical writing on imperialism has been very largely monopolized by the so-called Neo-Marxians, that is, by those who, following in the footsteps of the master, have carried on his historical analysis from the critique of capitalism to the study of this further phase, imperialism, the significance of which Marx himself did not appreciate and the very existence of which he barely adumbrated. The Neo-Marxians, beginning with Rudolf Hilferding and Rosa Luxemburg, have by this time elaborated a complete theory, which has recently been expounded in several ponderous German works. The theory hinges upon the idea of the accumulation of capital, its adherents holding that imperialism is nothing more nor less than the last stage in the development of capitalism—the stage in which the surplus capital resulting from the system of production is obliged by ever diminishing returns at home to seek new fields for investment abroad. When this surplus capital has transformed the whole world and remade even the most backward areas in the image of capitalism, the whole economic-social system will inevitably die of congestion.

That the classical writers of the socialistic school derived this basic idea from Hobson's book there can be no doubt. Lenin himself admitted, in his "Imperialism, the Latest Stage of Capitalism," that Hobson gave "a very good and accurate description of the fundamental economic and political traits of imperialism," and that Hobson and Hilferding had said the essentials on the subject. This, then, has been the most fruitful contribution of Hobson's essay. When we examine his ideas on this subject we refer indirectly to the larger part of the writing on imperialism since his day.

As a matter of pure economic theory it is most difficult to break down the logic of the accumulation theory. It is a fact that since the middle of the last century certain countries—first England, then France, Germany and the United States—have exported large amounts of capital, and that the financial returns from these investments in many instances came to overshadow completely the income derived by the lending countries from foreign trade. It is also indisputable that industry embarked upon the road to concentration and monopoly, that increased efficiency in production led to larger profits and to the amassing of ever greater surpluses of capital. We must recognize further that, as a general rule, the return from investments abroad was distinctly above the return on reinvestment in home industry. In other words, the postulates of the socialist theory undoubtedly existed. There is no mentionable reason why the development of the capitalist system should not have had the results attributed to it.

But, as it happens, the actual course of history refutes the thesis. The course of British investment abroad shows that there was a very considerable export of capital before 1875, that is, during the climax of anti-imperialism in England. Between 1875 and 1895, while the tide of imperialism was coming to the full, there was a marked falling off of foreign investment. Capital export was then resumed on a large scale in the years before the war, though England was, in this period, already somewhat disillusioned by the outcome of the South African adventure and rather inclined to be skeptical about imperialism. Similar observations hold true of the United States. If the promulgation of the Monroe Doctrine was an act of imperialism, where was the export of capital which ought to have been its condition? Let us concede that the war with Spain was an imperialist episode. At that time the United States was still a debtor nation, importing rather than exporting capital. In Russia, too, the heyday of imperialism coincided with a period of heavy borrowing rather than of lending.

There is this further objection to be raised against the view of Hobson and his Neo-Marxian followers, that the export of capital seems to have little direct connection with territorial expansion. France, before the war, had plenty of capital to export, and some of her earliest and most vigorous imperialists, like Jules Ferry, declared that she required colonies in order to have adequate fields for the placement of this capital. But when France had secured colonies, she did not send her capital to them. By far the larger part of her exported funds went to Russia, Rumania, Spain and Portugal, Egypt and the Ottoman Empire. In 1902 only two or two and a half billion francs out of a total foreign investment of some 30 or 35 billion francs was placed in the colonies. In 1913 Britain had more money invested in the United States than in any colony or other foreign country. Less than half of her total export of capital had been to other parts of the Empire. The United States put more capital into the development of Canada than did England; and when, after the war, the United States became a creditor nation, 43 percent of her investment was in Latin America, 27 percent in Canada and Newfoundland, and 22 percent in European countries. What she sent to her colonies was insignificant. Or let us take Germany, which in 1914 had about 25 billion marks placed abroad. Of this total only 3 percent was invested in Asia and Africa, and of that 3 percent only a small part in her colonies. Prewar Russia was a great imperialist power, but Russia had to borrow from France the money invested in her Far Eastern projects. In our own day two of the most outspokenly imperialist powers, Japan and Italy, are both nations poor in capital. Whatever the urge that drives them to expansion, it cannot be the need for the export of capital.

At the height of the imperialist tide, let us say from 1885 to 1914, there was much less talk among the advocates of expansion about the need for foreign investment fields than about the need for new markets and for the safeguarding of markets from the tariff restrictions of competitors. It is certain that in the opinion of contemporaries that was the mainspring of the whole movement. But this economic explanation, like the other, has not been borne out by the actual developments. Very few colonies have done even half of their trading with the mother country and many have done less. Taken in the large it can be proved statistically that the colonial trade has always played a relatively unimportant part in the total foreign commerce of the great industrial nations. These nations have always been each other's best customers and no amount of rivalry and competition has prevented their trade from following, not the flag, but the price-list. The position of Canada within the British Empire did not prevent her from levying tariffs against British goods, nor from developing exceedingly close economic relations with the United States. In the prewar period German commerce with the British possessions was expanding at a relatively higher rate than was Britain's.

If one must have an economic interpretation of imperialism, one will probably find its historical evolution to have been something like this: In the days of England's industrial preeminence she was, by the very nature of the case, interested in free trade. In the palmiest days of Cobdenism she exported manufactured goods to the four corners of the earth, but she exported also machinery and other producers' goods, thereby preparing the way for the industrialization of the continental nations and latterly of other regions of the world. In order to protect their infant industries from British competition, these new industrial Powers threw over the teachings of the Manchester school and began to set up tariffs. The result was that the national markets were set aside, to a large extent, for home industry. British trade was driven to seek new markets, where the process was repeated. But the introduction of protective tariffs had this further effect, that it made possible the organization of cartels and trusts, that is, the concentration of industry, the increase of production and the lowering of costs. Surplus goods and low prices caused the other industrial Powers likewise to look abroad for additional markets, and, while this development was taking place, technological improvements were making transportation and communication safer and more expeditious. The exploration of Africa at that time was probably a pure coincidence, but it contributed to the movement toward trade and expansion and the growth of a world market. Fear that the newly opened areas of the world might be taken over by others and then enclosed in tariff walls led directly to the scramble for territory in Asia and Africa.

The socialist writers would have us believe that concentration in industry made for monopoly and that the banks, undergoing the same process of evolution, were, through their connection with industry, enabled to take over control of the whole capitalist system. They were the repositories of the surplus capital accumulated by a monopolistic system and they were therefore the prime movers in the drive for imperial expansion, their problem being to find fields for the investment of capital. This is an argument which does violence to the facts as they appear historically. The socialist writers almost to a man argue chiefly from the example of Germany, where cartelization came early and where the concentration of banking and the control of industry by the banks went further than in most countries. But even in Germany the movement towards overseas expansion came before the growth of monopoly and the amalgamation of the banks. In England, the imperialist country *par excellence,* there was no obvious connection between the two phenomena. The trust movement came late and never went as far as in Germany. The same was true of the consolidation of the banking system. One of the perennial complaints in England was the lack of proper coordination between the banks and industry. To a certain extent the English exported capital because the machinery for foreign investment was better than the organization for home investment. In the

United States, to be sure, there was already a pronounced concentration of industry when the great outburst of imperialism came in the last years of the past century, but in general the trust movement ran parallel to the movement for territorial expansion. In any event, it would be hard to disprove the contention that the growth of world trade and the world market brought on the tendency toward better organization and concentration in industry, rather than the reverse. It is obvious not only that one large unit can manufacture more cheaply than many small ones, but that it can act more efficiently in competition with others in the world market.

But this much is clear—that territorial control of extra-European territory solved neither the trade problem nor the question of surplus capital. The white colonies, which were the best customers, followed their own economic interests and not even tariff restrictions could prevent them from doing so. In the backward, colored, tropical colonies, which could be more easily controlled and exploited, it proved difficult to develop a market, because of the low purchasing power of the natives. The question of raw materials, of which so much has always been made, also remained open. The great industrial countries got but a fraction of their raw materials from the colonies, and the colonies themselves continued to show a tendency to sell their products in the best market. As for the export of capital, that continued to flow in an ever broader stream, not because the opportunities for investment at home were exhausted, but because the return from foreign investment was apt to be better and because, in many cases, foreign investment was the easier course. Capital flowed from the great industrial countries of Europe, but it did not flow to their colonies. The United States and Canada, Latin America (especially the Argentine) and even old countries like Austria-Hungary and Russia, got the bulk of it. The export of capital necessarily took the form of the extension of credit, which in turn implied the transfer of goods. Not infrequently the granting of loans was made conditional on trade concessions by the borrowing country. So we come back to the question of trade and tariffs. In a sense the export of capital was nothing but a device to stimulate trade and to circumvent tariff barriers, which brings us back to the coincidence of the movement for protection and the movement toward imperialism.

This may seem like an oversimplified explanation and it probably is. Some may argue that imperialism is more than a movement toward territorial expansion and that financial imperialism in particular lays the iron hand of control on many countries supposedly independent. But if you try to divorce imperialism from territorial control you will get nowhere. Practically all writers on the subject have been driven to the conclusion that the problem cannot be handled at all unless you restrict it in this way. When Hobson wrote on imperialism, he had reference to the great spectacle of a few Powers taking over tremendous areas in Africa and Asia. Imperialism is, in a sense, synonymous with the appropriation by the Western nations of the largest part of the rest of the world. If you take it to be anything else, you will soon be lost in nebulous concepts and bloodless abstractions. If imperialism is to mean any vague interference of traders and bankers in the affairs of other countries, you may as well extend it to cover any form of influence. You will have to admit cultural imperialism, religious imperialism, and whatnot. Personally I prefer to stick by a measurable, manageable concept.

But even though Hobson's idea, that imperialism "is the endeavor of the great controllers of industry to broaden the channel for the flow of their surplus wealth by seeking foreign markets and foreign investments to take off the goods and capital they cannot sell or use at home," proved to be the most stimulating and fertile of his arguments, he had the very correct idea that imperialism was also a "medley of aims and feelings." He had many other contributory explanations of the phenomenon. For example, he was keenly aware of the relationship between democracy and imperialism. The enfranchisement of the working classes and the introduction of free education had brought the rank and file of the population into the political arena. One result of this epoch-making change was the rise of the so-called yellow press, which catered to the common man's love of excitement and sensationalism. Northcliffe was one of the first to sense the value of imperialism as a "talking point." Colonial adventure and far-away conflict satisfied the craving for excitement of the industrial and white-collar classes which had to find some outlet for their "spectatorial lust." The upper crust of the working class, as Lenin admitted, was easily converted to the teaching of imperialism and took pride in the extension of empire.

No doubt this aspect of the problem is important. The mechanization of humanity in an industrial society is a phenomenon with which we have became all too familiar, and every thoughtful person now recognizes the tremendous dangers inherent in the powers which the demagogue can exercise through the press, the motion picture and the radio. In Hobson's day propaganda was still carried on primarily through the press, but later developments were already foreshadowed in the activities of a Northcliffe or a Hearst. Hobson himself was able to show how, during the war in South Africa, the English press took its information from the South African press, which had been brought very largely under the control of Rhodes and his associates. Even at that time Hobson and others were pointing out how imperialistic capital was influencing not only the press, but the pulpit and the universities. Indeed, Hobson went so far as to claim that the great inert mass of the population, who saw the tangled maze of world movements through dim and bewildered eyes, were the inevitable dupes of able, organized interests who could lure or scare or drive them into any convenient course.

Recognizing as we do that control of the public mind involves the most urgent political problems of the day, it is nevertheless important to point out that there is nothing inexorable about the connection of propaganda and imperialism. Even if you admit that a generation ago moneyed interests believed that imperialism was to their advantage, that these interests exercised a far-reaching control over public opinion, and that they used this control to dupe the common man into support of imperial ventures, it is obvious that at some other time these same interests might have different ideas with regard to their own welfare, just as it is evident that public opinion may be controlled by some other agency—the modern dictator, for example.

But the same thing is not true of another influence upon which Hobson laid great stress, namely the biological conception of politics and international relations. During the last years of the nineteenth century the ideas of "social Darwinism," as it was called, carried everything before them. Darwin's catchwords—the struggle for existence and the survival of the fittest—which he himself always refused to apply to the social organism, were snapped up by others who were less scrupulous, and soon became an integral part of popular and even official thought on foreign affairs. It not only served to justify the ruthless treatment of the "backward" races and the carving up *in spe* of the Portuguese, Spanish, Ottoman and Chinese

Empires and of other "dying nations," as Lord Salisbury called them, but it put the necessary imprimatur on the ideas of conflict between the great imperialistic Powers themselves, and supplied a divine sanction for expansion. It was currently believed, in the days of exuberant imperialism, that the world would soon be the preserve of the great states—the British, the American and the Russian—and it was deduced from this belief that survival in the struggle for existence was in itself adequate evidence of superiority and supernatural appointment. The British therefore looked upon their empire as a work of the divine will, while the Americans and Russians were filled with the idea of a manifest destiny. It will be at once apparent that glorification of war and joy in the conflict was intimately connected with the evolutionary mentality. Hobson, the most determined of anti-imperialists, was finally driven to define the whole movement as "a depraved choice of national life, imposed by self-seeking interests which appeal to the lusts of quantitative acquisitiveness and of forceful domination surviving in a nation from early centuries of animal struggle for existence."[1]

The last phrases of this quotation will serve to lead us to the consideration of what has proved to be another fruitful thought of Hobson. He speaks, in one place, of imperialism as a sociological atavism, a remnant of the roving instinct, just as hunting and sport are leftovers of the physical struggle for existence. This idea of the roving instinct has made but little appeal to later writers, but the basic interpretation of imperialism as an atavism underlies the ingenious and highly intelligent essay of Joseph Schumpeter, "Zur Soziologie der Imperialismen," the only work from the bourgeois side which has had anything like the influence exerted by the writers of the socialist school. Schumpeter, who is an eminent economist, worked out a most convincing argument to prove that imperialism has nothing to do with capitalism, and that it is certainly not a development of capitalism. Capitalism, he holds, is by nature opposed to expansion, war, armaments and professional militarism, and imperialism is nothing but an atavism, one of those elements of the social structure which cannot be explained from existing conditions, but only from the conditions of the past. It is, in other words, a hangover from a preceding economic order. Imperialism antedates capi-

[1] In the last paragraph of his *Imperialism: A Study.*—Ed.

talism, going back at least to the time of the Assyrians and Egyptians. It is, according to Schumpeter, the disposition of a state to forceful expansion without any special object and without a definable limit. Conquests are desired not so much because of their advantages, which are often questionable, but merely for the sake of conquest, success and activity.

Schumpeter's theory is in some ways extravagant, but it has served as the starting point for some very interesting speculation, especially among German scholars of the liberal persuasion. It is now fairly clear, I think, that the Neo-Marxian critics have paid far too little attention to the imponderable, psychological ingredients of imperialism. The movement may, without much exaggeration, be interpreted not only as an atavism, as a remnant of the days of absolute monarchy and mercantilism, when it was to the interest of the prince to increase his territory and the number of his subjects, but also as an aberration, to be classed with the extravagances of nationalism. Just as nationalism can drive individuals to the point of sacrificing their very lives for the purposes of the state, so imperialism has driven them to the utmost exertions and the extreme sacrifice, even though the stake might be only some little-known and at bottom valueless part of Africa or Asia. In the days when communication and economic interdependence have made the world one in so many ways, men still interpret international relations in terms of the old cabinet policies, they are still swayed by outmoded, feudalistic ideas of honor and prestige.

In a sense, then, you can say that there is, in every people, a certain indefinable national energy, which may find expression in a variety of ways.

As a general rule great domestic crises and outbursts of expansion follow each other in the history of the world. In many of the continental countries of Europe, and for that matter in our own country, great internal problems were fought out in the period before 1870. The energies which, in Germany and Italy, went into the victory of the national cause, soon began to project themselves beyond the frontiers. While the continental nations were settling great issues between them, England sat "like a bloated Quaker, rubbing his hands at the roaring trade" he was carrying on. In those days the British cared very little for their empire. Many of them would have felt relieved if the colonies had broken away without a fuss. But, says Egerton, the best-known historian of British colonial policy, when the Germans and the French began to show an interest in colonial expansion, then the British began to think that there must be some value as yet undiscovered in the colonies. They not only started a movement to bind the colonies and the mother country more closely together, but they stretched out their hands for more. In the end they, who had the largest empire to begin with, got easily the lion's share of the yet unappropriated parts of the world. Some thought they were engaged in the fulfillment of a divine mission to abolish slavery, to spread the gospel, to clothe and educate the heathen. Others thought they were protecting the new markets from dangerous competitors, securing their supply of raw materials, or finding new fields for investment. But underlying the whole imperial outlook there was certainly more than a little misapprehension of economics, much self-delusion and self-righteousness, much mis-application of evolutionary teaching and above all much of the hoary tradition of honor, prestige, power and even plain combativeness. Imperialism always carries with it the connotation of the *Imperator* and of the tradition of rule. It is bound up with conscious or sub-conscious ideas of force, of brutality, of ruthlessness. It was these traits and tendencies that were so vividly expressed in the poetry and stories of Kipling, and it was his almost uncanny ability to sense the emotions of his time and people that made him the greatest apostle of imperialism.

We shall not go far wrong, then, if we stress the psychological and political factors in imperialism as well as its economic and intellectual elements. It was, of course, connected closely with the great changes in the social structure of the Western world, but it was also a projection of nationalism beyond the boundaries of Europe, a projection on a world scale of the time-honored struggle for power and for a balance of power as it had existed on the Continent for centuries. The most casual perusal of the literature of imperialism will reveal the continued potency of these atavistic motives. In a recent number of this very journal a leading Italian diplomat, explaining the policy of the Duce, recurred [sic] again and again to the failure of the other countries to appreciate the fact that Italy is a young and active country "animated by new spiritual values." By the much-decried Corfu episode of 1923, Mus-solini, to give a concrete example, "called Europe's attention to the respect due to the new Italy and to the reawakened energies of the Italian people." In the present Ethiopian crisis there is not very much suggestion of economic or civilizing motives on the part of the Italians; rather the Duce holds before his followers the prospect of revenge for the defeat at Adua (reminiscent of Britain's thirst to avenge Gordon) and promises them a glorious future. Not long ago he spoke to a group of veterans among the ruins of ancient Rome and told them that every stone surrounding them should remind them that Rome once dominated the world by the wisdom of her rule and the might of her arms and that "nothing forbids us to believe that what was our destiny yesterday may again become our destiny tomorrow." In much the same spirit an eminent Japanese statesman expressed himself recently in *Foreign Affairs:* "As soon as the Meiji Restoration lifted the ban on foreign intercourse, the long-pent-up energy of our race was released, and with fresh outlook and enthusiasm the nation has made swift progress. When you know this historical background and understand this overflowing vitality of our race, you will see the impossibility of compelling us to stay still within the confines of our little island home. We are destined to grow and expand overseas." It is the same emphasis given by the Italian diplomat to the need for an outlet for surplus energies.

It is, of course, true that both Italy and Japan have a serious population problem and that Japan, at any rate, has an economic argument to back her imperialistic enterprises in Manchuria and China. But it has been shown long ago that the acquisition of new territory has no direct bearing on the population problem and that emigrants go where their interest calls them, not where their governments would like to have them go. As for Japan's economic needs, it may at least be questioned whether she would not be better off if she avoided political and military commitments in China. Her cheap goods have made very extensive inroads in all the markets of the world, and her eventual conquest of the whole Chinese market is perhaps inevitable. Far from having gained much from her recent policy, she has had to face boycotts and other forms of hostility. In this case, certainly, one might debate whether the game is worth the candle.

Baron Wakatsuki,[2] whose statement is quoted above, was careful

---

[2] Baron Wakatsuki was premier of Japan, 1926–27.—Ed.

to avoid mention of a factor in Japanese imperialism which, as every well-informed person knows, is probably the real explanation of Japanese policy. After the Meiji Restoration it was more the exuberance and bellicosity of the military caste in Japan than the enthusiasm of the country at large which determined the policy of the government. If one reads modern Japanese history aright one will find that from 1870 onward the military classes were constantly pressing upon the government for action in Korea. Only with the greatest difficulty did the civil authorities stave off this pressure. In 1894 the Tokyo government more or less rushed into the war with China in order to avoid a dangerous domestic crisis. In other words, the ideas of honor and patriotism were appealed to in order to divert attention from the parliamentary conflict which was then raging. After the Japanese victory it was the military men who, against the better judgment of men like Count Ito and Baron Mutsu, insisted on the cession of the Liao-tung Peninsula, which netted Japan nothing but the intervention of Russia, Germany, and France. We need not pursue this subject in all its minute details. The point I want to make is that in the case of Japan, as in the case of many other countries, it is easier to show that the military and official classes are a driving force behind the movement for expansion than to show that a clique of nefarious bankers or industrialists is the determining factor. Business interests may have an interest in the acquisition of territory, or they may not. But military and official classes almost always have. War is, for the soldiers, a profession, and it is no mere chance that war and imperialism are so commonly lumped together. For officials, expansion means new territories to govern and new jobs to be filled. . . .

Carlton J. H. Hayes
BASES OF A NEW NATIONAL IMPERIALISM

Carlton J. H. Hayes (1882–1964) was associated with Columbia University from 1900, when he entered the college as an undergraduate, until 1950, when he retired as Seth Low Professor of History. He was a gifted and prolific historian. During his career he served as a visiting professor to a number of universities and, from 1942 to 1945, as the United States ambassador to Spain. His best-known works, including some distinguished texts, were in the fields of nationalism and of general European history. A Generation of Materialism, 1871–1900, one of The Rise of Modern Europe series, edited by W. L. Langer, combined these two interests in both scope and approach. It was one of Hayes' most highly regarded and most controversial books.

Synchronizing with the revival of protective tariffs and the extension of socializing legislation toward the close of the 1870s, was a tremendous outburst of imperialistic interest and activity. The outburst was common to all great powers of Europe (except Austria-Hungary); and it was so potent that during the next three decades greater progress was made toward subjecting the world to European domination than had been made during three centuries previous.

This may seem odd in view of the fact that the immediately preceding era of Liberal ascendancy, say from the 1840s into the 1870s, had witnessed a marked decline of European imperialism. There had been, to be sure, some spasmodic additions to British India, some scattered efforts of Napoleon III to resuscitate a colonial empire for France, some continuing Russian expansion in central and northeastern Asia. Although China and Japan had been forcefully opened to European (and American) trade, the opening had been for practically everybody on free and equal terms and had been unattended by any considerable expropriation of territory. The surviving far-flung British Empire had ceased to be an exclusive preserve for British merchants since the 1840s, and in 1861 France had freely admitted to her colonies the commerce of all nations. In

1870–1871 European colonialism appeared to be approaching its nadir. Gladstone was prime minister of Great Britain, and he was notoriously a "Little Englander." The provisional French government so slightly esteemed the colonies it had inherited that it offered them all to Bismarck at the end of the Franco-Prussian War if only he would spare Alsace-Lorraine. Bismarck spurned the offer, as he had recently refused Portugal's offer to sell him Mozambique. A colonial policy for Germany, he said, "would be just like the silken sables of Polish noble families who have no shirts."

A favorite explanation of why European imperialism turned abruptly within a decade from nadir to apogee, has been the economic. It was advanced originally by publicists and statesmen to win the support of business interests for imperialistic policies, and it received classical treatment, at the time of the Boer War, by John A. Hobson. Latterly it has been taken up by Marxian writers and integrated with their dogma of materialistic determinism, so that the argument now runs in this wise: Imperialism is an inevitable phase in the evolution of capitalism, a phase in which surplus capital, accumulated by the exploitation of domestic labor, is obliged by diminishing returns at home to find new outlets for investment abroad. Hence it seeks nonindustrialized areas ever farther afield where it may dispose of surplus manufactures, obtain needed raw materials, invest surplus capital, and exploit cheap native labor. The resulting "new imperialism," unlike the old, is not primarily a colonizing or a simply commercial imperialism, but rather an investing one in regions ill-adapted to European settlement. Conditions are alleged to have been ripe for it about 1880, when tariff protection restricted customary markets of European capitalists and impelled them to seek new ones.

Doubtless large-scale mechanized industry, with accompanying improvement of transportation facilities, did immensely stimulate an ever-widening quest for markets where surplus manufactures might be disposed of, necessary raw materials procured, and lucrative investments made. Nor can there be any doubt that by the 1870s, when industrialization on the Continent was beginning seriously to vie with England's, the quest was being as eagerly pursued by commercial and banking houses of Hamburg and Bremen, Marseilles and Paris, as by those of London and Liverpool. In Germany, for example, at the very time when Bismarck was disdaining the French proffer of colonies, his banking friends, Bleichröder and Hansemann, were helping to finance distant trade ventures of various Hanseatic firms—O'Swald's in East Africa, Woermann's in West Africa, Godeffroy's in Samoa and other South Sea islands. In 1880 some 335,000 marks' worth of German goods were shipped to West Africa alone, while 6,735,000 marks' worth of African products entered the port of Hamburg.

Yet the only novel feature of all this was a relatively greater importation of tropical and subtropical products and hence a special concern with Africa, southern Asia, the Indies, and Oceania. Surplus manufactures from industrialized countries of Europe, even after the imposition of protective tariffs, still found export markets principally within that Continent or in temperate zones outside, notably in America, Australasia, northern India, and the Far East. What actually started the economic push into the "Dark Continent" and the sun-baked islands of the Pacific was not so much an overproduction of factory goods in Europe as an undersupply of raw materials. Cotton grew finer in Egypt than in the United States, and with the partial cutting off of the latter's copious supply by the American Civil War it was but natural that dealers in raw cotton should enter the Egyptian field and raise its yield ninefold during the next twenty years. Rubber was now needed also, and it could be got from the Congo and from Malaysia more cheaply and plentifully than from Brazil. Copra, with its useful oil, was to be had in the South Sea islands, and the Godeffroy firm at Hamburg made a specialty of going for it. Tin was essential for the new canning industry, and gold, for measuring the new industrial wealth; rich supplies of the former were obtainable in the East Indies, and of the latter in Guinea and the Transvaal. Sugar cane and coffee, cocoa and tea, bananas and dates, if not directly serviceable to industrial machinery, were very palatable to the enlarging European multitude that tended it.

But commercial expansion into the tropics was a novelty of degree rather than of kind and hardly suffices to explain the political imperialism of the seventies and eighties. This was inaugurated prior to any general resort to tariff protectionism in Europe, and prior also to any universal export of capital. Neither Russia nor Italy had surplus manufactures to dispose of or surplus wealth to invest; yet both engaged in the scramble for imperial dominion, the one with striking success and the other not. Germany exported little capital until after she had acquired an extensive colonial empire, and France secured a far more extensive one while her industrial development lagged behind Germany's. Great Britain had long had all the supposed economic motives for imperialism—export of manufactured goods, demand for raw materials, supply of surplus capital—and yet these did not move her in the sixties as much as they did in the seventies.[1] On the other hand, Norway, whose ocean-borne commerce was exceeded only by Great Britain's and Germany's, remained consistently aloof from overseas imperialism.

Apparently the flag of a European nation did not have to follow its trade—or its financial investments. But once flag raising became common and competitive in Africa and on the Pacific, economic considerations undoubtedly spurred most of the European participants to greater efforts and keener competition in those regions. Then the tariff protectionism of Continental nations was applied, in one form or another, to their respective colonies, and the more colonies each one had the greater were its opportunities for favorable trade and investment and the closer it approached to the ideal of all-around self-sufficiency. And to prevent too much of the world from being thus monopolized by France, Germany, Italy, or any other protectionist power, Great Britain moved mightily to gather the lion's share into her own free-trade empire. In other words, neo-mercantilism, once established, had very important imperialistic consequences.

The fact remains, nevertheless, that the founding of new colonial empires and the fortifying of old ones antedated the establishment of neo-mercantilism, and that the economic arguments adduced in support of imperialism seem to have been a rationalization *ex post facto*. In the main, it was not Liberal parties, with their super-abundance of industrialists and bankers, who sponsored the outward imperialistic thrusts of the seventies and early eighties. Instead, it was Conservative parties, with a preponderantly agricultural cli-

---

[1] It should be remarked, however, that the depression which began in 1873, by limiting opportunities for profitable investment in countries already largely industrialized, probably stimulated investment in "backward" regions and may thus have contributed to a revival of imperialistic interests and ambitions. Nevertheless, this was truer of Great Britain than of any nation on the Continent, and it scarcely suffices to explain why with almost all the great powers (and only with them) political imperialism preceded any substantial financial investment in particular regions appropriated.

entele notoriously suspicious of moneylenders and big business, and, above all, it was patriotic professors and publicists regardless of political affiliation and unmindful of personal economic interest. These put forth the economic arguments which eventually drew bankers and traders and industrialists into the imperialist camp.

Basically the new imperialism was a nationalistic phenomenon. It followed hard upon the national wars which created an all-powerful Germany and a united Italy, which carried Russia within sight of Constantinople, and which left England fearful and France eclipsed. It expressed a resulting psychological reaction, an ardent desire to maintain or recover national prestige. France sought compensation for European loss in oversea gain. England would offset her European isolation by enlarging and glorifying the British Empire. Russia, halted in the Balkans, would turn anew to Asia, and before long Germany and Italy would show the world that the prestige they had won by might inside Europe they were entitled to enhance by imperial exploits outside. The lesser powers, with no great prestige at stake, managed to get on without any new imperialism, though Portugal and Holland displayed a revived pride in the empires they already possessed and the latter's was administered with renewed vigor.

Public agitation for extending overseas the political dominion of European national states certainly began with patriotic intellectuals. As early as 1867 Lothar Bucher, one of Bismarck's associates in the Prussian foreign office, published in the influential *Norddeutsche Allgemeine Zeitung* a series of articles endorsing and advertising the hitherto neglected counsels of Friedrich List: "Companies should be founded in the German seaports to buy lands in foreign countries and settle them with German colonies; also companies for commerce and navigation whose object would be to open new markets abroad for German manufacturers and to establish steamship lines. . . . Colonies are the best means of developing manufactures, export and import trade, and finally a respectable navy."

The next year Otto Kersten, traveler and explorer, founded at Berlin a "Central Society for Commercial Geography and German Interests Abroad," with an official journal, *Der Export*. Simultaneously the "Royal Colonial Institute" was founded at London; and a brilliant young English gentleman, Sir Charles Dilke, returning from a trip around the world, published his patriotic and immensely popular

Greater Britain. Two years later, in the midst of the Franco-Prussian War, the redoubtable Froude scored his fellow Englishmen in the pages of *Fraser's Magazine* for their blindness to imperial glories. In 1872 Disraeli practically committed the Conservative party in Britain to a program of imperialism, and in 1874 Paul Leroy-Beaulieu, dean of political economists in France and implacable foe of tariff protection, plumped for French imperialism in a "scientific" treatise, *De la Colonisation chez les peuples modernes.*

These were foretastes. Heartier fare was served immediately after the Russo-Turkish War and the Congress of Berlin. In 1879 Friedrich Fabri, a pious promoter of Christian foreign missions, asked rhetorically "Does Germany need Colonies?" and answered with a resounding "Yes!" Germany's surplus population, he argued, should have places where it could go and still buy German goods and share in the other blessings of German *Kultur.* Fabri was eloquently seconded in 1881 by Hübbe-Schleiden, a lawyer and sometime explorer in equatorial Africa, who now insisted that through imperialistic endeavors "a country exhibits before the world its strength or weakness as a nation." In like vein the historian Treitschke edified his student audiences at the University of Berlin with the moral that "every virile people has established colonial power."

In 1882 a frankly propagandist "Colonial Society" was formed in Germany through the joint efforts of a naturalist, a geographer, and a politician, while in France Professor Leroy-Beaulieu brought out a new edition of his classic with the dogmatic addendum that "colonization is for France a question of life and death: either France will become a great African power, or in a century or two she will be no more than a secondary European power; she will count for about as much in the world as Greece and Rumania in Europe." The following year Professor John Seeley published his celebrated Cambridge lectures on the *Expansion of England.* The book took the British public by storm. It sold 80,000 copies within a brief time and won for its author the warm discipleship of Lord Rosebery[2] and a knighthood.

In 1883 the stridently imperialistic "Primrose League" was

---

[2] Rosebery was Liberal foreign secretary, 1886, 1892–94, and prime minister, 1894–95. —Ed.

launched by Tory Democrats and soon afterwards the more sedate "Imperial Federation League" by nationalistic Liberals. In 1883, also, was founded a "Society for German Colonization." And capping the academic contributions to the imperialist cause, Froude published *Oceana* in 1885, while Alfred Rambaud, historian of Russia and first occupant of the chair in contemporary history at the Sorbonne, edited in 1886 a cooperative work on *La France coloniale.*

Already, statesmen were following the professors and proclaiming that commerce and investments should follow the flag. If Gladstone hesitated, Disraeli and Salisbury did not; nor did such "new" Liberals as Rosebery, Chamberlain, and Grey. Jules Ferry surely did not hesitate. Replying to parliamentary critics of his aggressive policy in Tunis and Tonkin, he marshaled in speeches from 1881 to 1885 all the professorial arguments: that superior races have a civilizing mission to inferior races; that an industrial nation needs colonial markets; that coaling stations are requisite for navy and mercantile marine; and that if France refrained from imperialism, she would "descend from the first rank to the third or fourth." Bismarck seemed to hesitate more than he actually did. He privately expressed sympathy with imperialist ambitions in 1876 and publicly backed them, at least in the case of Samoa, in 1879. By 1884–85 he was persuading the Reichstag that colonies were vital to national economy. "Colonies would mean the winning of new markets for German industries, the expansion of trade, and a new field for German activity, civilization, and capital."

Most simply, the sequence of imperialism after 1870 appears to have been, first, pleas for colonies on the ground of national prestige; second, getting them; third, disarming critics by economic argument; and fourth, carrying this into effect and relating the results to the neo-mercantilism of tariff protection and social legislation at home.

There were, of course, complexities in the imperialistic movement. Insofar as it was economic, it did not affect the "capitalist class" as a whole, but only particular business interests: exporters and manufacturers of certain commodities such as calico and cheap alcoholic beverages; importers of rubber, raw cotton, coffee, copra, etc.; shipping magnates; some bankers, though a very small percentage of all; and those "parasites of imperialism," the makers of arms and uniforms, the producers of telegraph and railway material, etc. But these last did not "cause" imperialism; they merely throve on it.

Christian missions provided an important adjunct to imperialism. They spread and multiplied in the second half of the nineteenth century as never before, in part as a reaction, we have suggested elsewhere, to the prevalent materialism in Europe, and in larger part because of the immensely improved means of travel and communication throughout the world. A missionary might have gone his way, like a merchant, the one conveying spiritual and the other material goods to heathen peoples, without any thought of raising a national flag over them or subjecting them to European rule. Actually, however, missionaries like merchants lived in a nationalistic age, and many of them were quite willing, on occasion, to invoke the naval or military protection of their respective national states. Not a few of Europe's footholds in other continents were obtained as penalties for the persecution of Christian missionaries. Even where missionaries did not directly prompt the extension of European dominion, they frequently paved the way for adventurers who did; and stories published back home by them or about them stimulated popular interest in, and support of, imperial undertakings. About David Livingstone, for example, something like a cult grew up in England, so that when he died in the wilds of Africa on May Day, 1873, his body was borne with hierophantic solemnity all the way to Zanzibar and thence under naval escort to England, where finally it was deposited amid Britain's national heroes in Westminster Abbey on April 18, 1874. The year was that of Disraeli's accession to the premiership, and for the popular favor accorded his subsequent imperial activities, he should have thanked the dead Livingstone more than any live merchant or banker.

It was a time, too, when evolutionary biology was beginning to occupy a central place in European thought, when hundreds of naturalists, emulating Darwin, engaged in scientific expeditions to strange distant regions and furnished millions of ordinary stay-at-homes with fascinating descriptions of the extraordinary flora and fauna they had observed. Already in 1861 the Franco-American Du Chaillu had reported from Gabun in equatorial Africa his amazing discovery of the gorilla, which was readily imagined to be the "missing link" between ape and man. In 1867 he published an account of a race of pygmies he had found, and for years afterwards his pen poured out popular tales of African adventure. Meanwhile, in the early seventies, Faidherbe was exploring upper Egypt, Nachtigal was visiting Khartum, De Brazza was following Du Chaillu into the hinterland of Gabun, Skobelev with notebook in hand was investigating the borders of Turkestan, Evelyn Baring (the later Lord Cromer) was describing the natural wonders of India, and Henry Morton Stanley was "finding" Livingstone for the New York *Herald* and an avid public, and then heading an Anglo-American scientific expedition into the vast Congo basin. Presently George Goldie was exploring the Niger country, Joseph Thomson was leading an expedition into east-central Africa, Harry Johnston was traversing Angola and meeting Stanley on the Congo, and Frederick Lugard, a young veteran of the Afghan War, was penetrating Nyasaland and Uganda.

Of these explorers, the majority had military training. Faidherbe was a French general, former governor of Senegal, and Skobelev a Russian general who was to win laurels in the Russo-Turkish War. Nachtigal was a German army surgeon, De Brazza a French naval officer. Cromer and Goldie and Lugard had all been British soldiers. As a group they were intensely patriotic, and they nicely combined with scientific interests a zeal to serve the political, economic, and military interests of their respective nations. They were prime promoters of imperialism, and most of them remained as pro-consuls of provinces they charted and helped to appropriate.

Sheer love of adventure was a potent lure to imperialism. Africa in particular, by reason of the widespread advertising its marvels and dangers received at the beginning of the seventies, beckoned to bold and venturesome spirits in Europe, and some of the boldest became empire-builders in the grand style, in a few cases acquiring fabulous personal wealth, in all cases experiencing that sense of power which comes from great achievement. Stanley was patently an adventurer. He had no surplus goods to sell, no surplus capital to invest. He was a self-made man, if ever there was one. A Welshman by birth, with the original name of Rowlands, he ran away from home and school at an early age to find work in Liverpool, first in a haberdasher's shop, then with a butcher. When this grew tedious he worked his way across the Atlantic to New Orleans and fell in with a merchant by the name of Stanley, who adopted him. At the outbreak of the American Civil War he enlisted in the Confederate army, only to be taken prisoner at the battle of Shiloh; then, "with ready versatility he joined the Union army to fight against his former comrades-in-arms. Toward the close of the war he discovered a latent talent for journalism, which, when peace returned, led him to Salt Lake City to describe the extraordinary customs of the Mormons, then to Asia Minor in search of thrilling adventure, then with General Hancock against the Indians, with the British against Abyssinia, and to Crete, and Spain." He went to central Africa in 1871 because he was sent, but he remained to build a huge empire for another and the queerest kind of adventurer—a man who was not self-made and who never set foot in Africa, but who was as hypnotized by African dreams as by female realities—Leopold of the Belgians, Leopold of the Congo Free State.

But the adventurer-imperialist *par excellence* was Cecil Rhodes, and his extraordinary career began by accident. A sickly youth, son of an Anglican clergyman and intended for the church, he was bundled off in 1870, for purposes of health, to an elder brother's farm in southern Africa. He arrived just when diamonds were discovered in the nearby Kimberley fields. He joined other diggers, dug more industriously and successfully, and within a year found himself wealthy and healthy. He returned to England for study at Oxford, but the study was desultory and he was soon back permanently in South Africa, adding gold mines to diamond mines, running Cape politics, projecting British sway the entire length of the continent up to Cairo, and doing much to realize it.

The star German adventurer was Carl Peters. Son of a Lutheran clergyman and graduate of the University of Berlin, he contracted imperialist fever on a visit to England and set out in 1884 in disguise and under an alias—he was still in his twenties—to build an empire in East Africa. His method was simple, and the results startling, even to Bismarck. By a judicious distribution of toys plus injudicious application of grog, he got twelve big black chieftains, within ten days, to make their X's on documents conveying to Germany a total of 60,000 square miles. But that was only a start. Peters kept right on enlarging German East Africa until an Anglo-German convention of 1890 set bounds to his activity.

Explorers and adventurers gave rise to a peculiar species of organizer and administrator, despotic and ruthless and most devotedly imperialistic. Peters and Rhodes were transmuted by the

African environment into this species, and so too were Cromer in Egypt and Milner at the Cape. For the glory of themselves and their countries, such local potentates carried on without too much regard for merely economic considerations or for the international engagements of their distant home governments. They were on the spot and knew better than London or Berlin or any other capital what had to be done, and they usually did it in an expansive way.

The actual course of empire—the order in which distant areas were appropriated by European powers—was determined less by design than by chance. Murder of a missionary or trader and consequent forceful intervention might occur anywhere. In some instances, curiously frequent in Moslem countries, native rulers practically invited intervention by living far beyond their means and contracting debts which they were unable to repay. Such was the basis of European imperialism in Egypt, Tunis, Persia, and to a large extent in Turkey. For example, the Khedive Ismail of Egypt, a squat, red-bearded gentleman with a passion for ostentation and the externals of European culture, spent half a billion dollars in the twelve years after his accession in 1863, running up the Egyptian public debt from 16 million to 342 million and continuing to borrow money from European bankers at ever more onerous rates. In 1875 he could get only a quarter of the face value of short-term bonds bearing 20 percent interest. In 1876 he sold his shares of Suez Canal Company stock to England, and consented to joint supervision of his finances by representatives of England, France, Italy, and Austria. Soon this control was narrowed to England and France, and in 1882 to England alone. No doubt bankers and investors egged on both the khedive to spend and the English government to collect, but a less prodigal khedive, and one more intelligently concerned with the welfare of his subjects, might have staved off foreign rule. The contemporary Mikado of Japan did.

Especially active in directing the course of empire after 1870 were the European colonists already settled in Algeria, South Africa, and Australasia. These performed the same function in the latter part of the nineteenth century as their prototypes in the America of the eighteenth century. French settlers in Algeria were more eager than the government at Paris to make all adjacent African lands French. British and Dutch settlers in South Africa had almost a psychosis about others getting anywhere near them, and from the former, rather than from London, came the main drive for British expansion northward. Australians and New Zealanders were continually pressing the home government to forestall alien seizure of South Sea islands.

In many instances European flags were hoisted as a sport—a competitive sport—with about the same indifference to economic motives as characterized the later planting of American and other flags on cakes of ice around the North or South Pole. As one reads of successive French flag raisings in oases of the Sahara and on coral reefs of the Pacific, one gets a lively impression that it was all *pour le sport.*

Some capitalists undoubtedly promoted imperialism, and more profited by it. But in the last analysis it was the nationalistic masses who made it possible and who most vociferously applauded and most constantly backed it. Disraeli and Joseph Chamberlain were good politicians as well as patriots, and with a clairvoyance greater than Gladstone's, they perceived that in a country where the masses were patriotic, literate, and in possession of the ballot, a political party which frankly espoused imperialism would have magnetic attraction for them. So it proved. An unwonted popularity attended the Conservative parties of Britain and Germany during the eighties and nineties. The masses, of course, had no immediate economic interest in the matter, and it would have required an extraordinary act of faith on their part to believe the predictions of imperialistic intellectuals that somehow, sometime, everybody would be enriched from the Congo or the Niger or Tahiti. Rather, the masses were thrilled and stirred by front-page news in the popular press of far-off things and battles still to come. They devoured the yarns of a Rider Haggard—he had been secretary to the governor of Natal in the seventies and he *knew* his Africa. They learned by heart the vulgar verses of a Rudyard Kipling—he had lived in India and been a chum of doughty, swearing British soldiers. And the sporting impulse which drew crowds to prize fights and to football and cricket matches, evoked a whole nation's lusty cheers for its "team" in the mammoth competitive game of imperialism.

Into the imperial-mindedness of the masses, scarcely less than into that of Rhodes or Peters, Ferry or Chamberlain, fitted neatly the preaching of Darwinian sociology, that human progress depends upon struggle between races and nations and survival of the fittest.

Obviously most eligible for the "fittest" were the white peoples of Europe, who therefore owed it to science as well as to civilization (and religion) to establish their supremacy over inferior populations in all other continents. Which of them would ultimately be adjudged the absolutely fittest would depend on the outcome of conflict among themselves as well as with lesser breeds. This preaching justified competitive imperialism and cloaked attendant ruthlessness in the mantle of idealistic devotion to duty. It was summarized by Kipling at the close of the generation (1899) in his famous lines:

> *Take up the White Man's Burden—*
> *Send forth the best ye breed—*
> *Go bind your sons to exile*
> *To serve your captives' need;*
> *To wait in heavy harness,*
> *On fluttered fold and wild—*
> *Your new-caught, sullen peoples*
> *Half-devil and half-child.*

Nicholas Mansergh
DIPLOMATIC REASONS FOR EXPANSION

Nicholas Mansergh (b. 1910), Master of St. John's College, Cambridge, was Smuts Professor of the History of the British Commonwealth at Cambridge from 1953 to 1969 and the author or editor of many works dealing with Commonwealth affairs, including Ireland in the Age of Reform and Revolution *(1940),* The Commonwealth and the Nations *(1948),* Survey of British Commonwealth Affairs *(2 vols.; 1952, 1958), and* The Commonwealth Experience *(1969).* The Coming of the First World War *(1949), based on a series of lectures given in 1944, is a reinterpretative essay on pre-World War I Europe. International relations are at the core of Mansergh's historical analysis in this work.*

The opening up of Africa was the work not of governments but of individuals possessed of great courage and remarkable powers of endurance. There is something very revealing in that description by a companion, of Livingstone "tramping along with the steady, heavy tread which kept one in mind that he had walked across Africa." But where individuals had pioneered, governments soon intervened, and it is only with the motives that prompted their intervention that this book is concerned. The political and economic importance of Africa was popularly overestimated. In Western Europe it was commonly believed that the acquisition of colonies was the high road to rapid economic development. Many writers, principally, though not only, German, failed, as Mr. Taylor has written, "to grasp the truth about the British Empire—that it had come into being as the result of British commercial enterprise and industrial success; and they asserted the reverse, that the prosperity and wealth of Great Britain were due to the existence of her Empire. The German campaign for colonies rested on the simple dogma— give Germany colonies and the Germans will then be as prosperous as the English."[1] Such popular beliefs may have influenced the minds even of autocratic governments, but they were not the direct-

From Nicholas Mansergh, *The Coming of the First World War: A Study in the European Balance, 1878–1914* (London, 1949), pp. 43–45, 46–52, 56–58, 61–62. Copyright 1949. By permission of Longmans, Green and Co. Ltd.

[1] A. J. P. Taylor: *Germany's First Bid for Colonies 1884–5* (London, 1938), p. 4.

ing force in overseas colonial expansion. The rulers of Europe thought primarily in terms of political not economic advantage and it was on the struggle for power in Europe that their eyes were always fixed. Expansion overseas was for the Continental States, not an end, but a means to an end.

Bismarck was a late and always a skeptical convert to "colonialism." His indifference was a source of strength. In the colonial field he could play the hand that best suited his purpose in Europe. For it was on the European scene that his eye was always riveted. And not his alone. "If you were to bring me all the empires of Asia and Africa...," said General Garnier des Garets, "they wouldn't in my eyes be worth an acre of the earth where I fought in 1870, and where the *Cuirassiers* of Reichshoffen and the Zouaves of Froeschwiller lie." But the balance of forces in Europe left France after 1870 with the alternatives of enlarging her Empire overseas or a policy of resignation. Alsace-Lorraine could only be a question "reserved for the future." In the meantime, was it not folly to sit by idly nursing wrongs while other Powers extended their control over large parts of Africa and Asia? "*Au nom d'un chauvinisme exalté et à courtes vues,*" exclaimed Jules Ferry, the protagonist of Republican imperialism, "*devrions-nous acculer la politique française dans une impasse et, les yeux fixés sur la ligne bleue des Vosges, laisser tout faire, tout s'engager, tout se résoudre, sans nous, autour de nous, contre nous?*" [2] This was the reasoning produced by the psychological reaction to defeat and reinforced by a revival of France's traditional belief in mercantilist economics that led her, a country with a declining population, to embark, with direct encouragement from Bismarck, on an active policy of colonial expansion in North and Central Africa, in Madagascar and in Indo-China.

Bismarck's sympathetic interest in French imperialism was an experiment on his side, in the possibilities of Franco-German reconciliation. That France should remain ostracized in Europe was his settled policy, but clearly it was not in the interests of Germany that she should be driven to despair. An outlet for her energies, preoccupation in colonial fields in which Germany had no interest,

---

[2] "Must we, in the name of an excessive and short-sighted chauvinism, drive French policy into an impasse and, with our eyes fixed on the blue line of the Vosges, let everything be done, everything be undertaken, everything be decided—without us, around us, against us?"–Ed.

except for bargaining purposes, had everything to recommend it. The fact that, incidentally, French expansion in North Africa, and particularly in Tunis, would bring her into conflict with Italy, enhanced the attractions of this policy, even if it were not its primary purpose. To the French Ambassador, in January 1879, the Chancellor gave effusive encouragement. "Now indeed, I believe," observed Bismarck, "that the Tunisian pear is ripe and that the time has come for you to pluck it. The effrontery of the Bey has been like the August sun for this African fruit, which might very well have been spoilt or stolen by somebody else if you had let it remain too long on the bough. I don't know what you intend to do or whether it tempts you, but I take the opportunity of repeating . . . my desire to give you proofs of my good will on questions which concern you and in which there are no German interests in opposition to yours." That Italy had already received German encouragement to seize Tunis must have heightened the Chancellor's satisfaction with French reactions. For his advice was heeded, and by the end of 1881 this former province of the Turkish Empire was securely French and Italy estranged.

Not only France and Italy but also England had traditional interests in North Africa. If it was the anxiety of the Third Republic to restore French self-respect after 1870; of a united Italy to raise herself to the level of a first-class Power by the acquisition of colonies on the southern shore of the Mediterranean; it was England's concern for imperial communications that led her with some reluctance to intervene in Egypt and so come into conflict with France. The Suez Canal of which control had been dramatically acquired by Disraeli was, as Bismarck admitted, "of vital importance" to her Empire, being "like the spinal cord which connects the backbone with the brain." It was that fact that left England no freedom of choice. After "Dual Control" had been established in Egypt in the interests of British and French bond-holders in 1876, Lord Salisbury summed up the alternatives before his country. "You may," he said, "renounce, or monopolize or share. Renouncing would have been to place France across our road to India. Monopolizing would have been very near the risk of war. So we resolved to share." . . .

England's task in Egypt was undertaken with German goodwill, which soon evaporated. Where Bismarck had once acknowledged comparative German indifference in the affairs of Egypt, he felt by the end of 1883 that the time had come when a less passive attitude would better serve his ends. "We are uncommonly grateful to Prince Bismarck," Lord Granville had said to Count Herbert Bismarck in January 1883, "for the friendly attitude of German policy this summer was of great service to us. Our being left with a free hand in Egypt we owe, when all is said, to Germany's goodwill. We are all aware that at a particular moment Prince Bismarck could have upset the coach if he had chosen to, and we realize with much thankfulness that he refrained from doing so." The price however had still to be paid, and in Egypt pressure was easy to apply. For the Gladstone Government, reluctant to contemplate annexation on principle, were left with no practicable alternative to acting as the nominal mandatory of the Powers. That left Britain in a weak and vulnerable position, for, of the Powers, France burned with resentment at her exclusion from Egypt, and Russia, without any direct interest in the Nile Valley, was hostile to the consolidation of Britain's position in the Eastern Mediterranean. This was a situation from which Bismarck was not slow to profit. The situation in Egypt made England, as Baring[3] frankly recognized, dependent on German goodwill.

It seems clear now that Bismarck's colonial policy was more the incidental offshoot of tactical moves in Europe than a departure undertaken on its own merits. The price that Bismarck was most concerned to exact from England in return for German goodwill in Egypt, was some form of guarantee in Europe which would reinsure Germany in the West against French aggression. When it was made plain that this was a price that England was not prepared to pay he decided to explore again the possibility of friendship with France, founded on Franco-German hostility to England in the colonial field. That he was also influenced by internal political considerations is hardly to be denied. A forward colonial policy was well calculated to enhance the Chancellor's popularity at home.

While early in 1884 the German Ambassador in London, Count Münster, was happily contemplating the friendly acquisition of Heligoland, encouraged at once by the Chancellor's interest, and the remark of the Colonial Secretary, Lord Derby, who said "this perfectly useless piece of rock in the North Sea, the smallest of

---

[3] Sir Evelyn Baring, later first Earl of Cromer, was British agent and consul general in Egypt from 1883 to 1907.—Ed.

our Colonies, gives me the most trouble of any," a far-ranging area
of Anglo-German colonial friction loomed on the horizon. The Chancellor took up the grievances of German traders in Fiji; he then
turned a more formidable gaze on South-West Africa. The Ambassador was instructed "to cease to mention the question of
Heligoland" because it might make German colonial claims seem
of secondary importance. If Germany failed to obtain satisfaction
for her claims overseas, the Chancellor declared that "she must try
to gain closer touch with seafaring Powers, France included." But
in actual fact the colonial grievances had been put forward largely
because they might make closer cooperation with France possible.
It was on the foundation of joint hostility to Great Britain overseas
that Bismarck hoped to build up friendship with France.

From 1883 to 1885 the new policy was put into practice. The weak
but well-meaning Foreign Secretary, Lord Granville, noticed with
dismay the abrupt change in the temper of Anglo-German relations.
An atmosphere of friendly cooperation was transformed by a recital
of German grievances in many parts of the world, which lost nothing
in the telling by the Chancellor's arrogant son, Count Herbert Bismarck. Of all the disputes which followed, the most protracted was
concerned with the fate of Angra Pequeña on the west coast of
Africa some 200 miles north of the frontier of the Cape Province.
There a German trader, named Lüderitz, established himself and
asked for protection. Could the British Government give protection?
inquired Herbert Bismarck, for "if not, the German Government will
do their best to extend to it the same measure of protection which
they could give to their subjects in remote parts of the world—but
without having the least desire to establish any footing in South
Africa." In replying to his inquiry there was unpardonable delay due
partly, as Lord Granville explained, to the need of consulting the
Cape. "We cannot," he observed, "act except in agreement with the
Government of the Colony which has an independent Ministry and
Parliament." To Bismarck this sounded singularly unconvincing. But
there was a difference of view between London and the Cape. To a
German settlement in South-West Africa, London might be com-
paratively indifferent, but the Cape was resolutely opposed. And in
the event, what began as an inquiry about protection at Angra Pequeña developed, against their wishes, into German South-West

Africa. The reasons are to be found in the weakness of the British position in Egypt, which made dependence on German goodwill inevitable, and strained relations with Russia which made the more desirable friendly cooperation with the Triple Alliance.

By the end of 1885 Bismarck's new policy had laid the foundation of the German Colonial Empire, for by then she had secured her position in the Cameroons and in New Guinea as well as in South-West Africa together with a foothold in East Africa. Where the British Colonial Empire had been founded largely by the private enterprise of the chartered companies, Germany's was created through the impetus of a deliberate policy of state. If that policy met a weak and dilatory response in London, that was due to misunderstanding of its aim and not to unfriendliness. For it was generally accepted that it was right and just that Germany should have her "place in the Sun." Owing to earlier indifference and her late start, her African territories compared unfavorably with those of France or of the Belgians in the Congo Basin, or of the British. But, judged by her subsequent policy, her interest in colonial expansion remained very secondary to her interests in Europe. By 1914 the total number of German colonial settlers was no more than 23,000. While the number of European emigrants is in itself no criterion of the quality of colonial government, these trifling numbers are at least an indication that colonies did not serve as an outlet for surplus population in Germany.

While Germany was acquiring a Colonial Empire in Africa and the Pacific, France, assured of German goodwill, extended her empire chiefly in North and West Africa but also by the acquisition of Madagascar, a convenient stepping-stone to Indo-China, between 1883 and 1885, and after a protracted struggle in Tonkin and Annam. It was the losses and setbacks in Tonkin that brought about the fall of the second Ferry Ministry, and with it the end of an active imperialist policy leaning on German goodwill. "The patronage of Bismarck," noted Lord Lyons, British Ambassador in Paris, "overthrew the Freycinet Cabinet; it is not strengthening Jules Ferry.... The *revanche* is still at the bottom of every French heart." With the fall of Ferry, that was no longer to be disguised. Bismarck's colonial policy, insofar as it was an experiment in Franco-German reconciliation, had failed.

The years 1885–89 witnessed the height of the scramble for Africa. But unlike the preceding years they were marked by a revival of Anglo-German cooperation under the aegis of Bismarck and Salisbury. If Bismarck, in laying the foundations of a German Colonial Empire, had not effected a reconciliation with France, he had at least succeeded in his other objectives. France and Italy were estranged over Tunis and Italy was compelled to seek alliance with the Central Powers: England and France were divided by Egypt; and England, partly because of her concern for the security of the Nile Valley, which was the cardinal consideration in determining her colonial policy in Africa, and partly because of the advance of Russia to the Afghan frontier, was also impelled towards more friendly relations with the Central Powers. This had two consequences. The first was the Mediterranean Agreement of 1887 by which England reached an understanding, first with Italy, later extended to Austria, to preserve the status quo in the Mediterranean. Highly satisfying to Bismarck, under whose auspices it was negotiated, the agreement brought England, even if loosely, into the orbit of the Triple Alliance Powers. The other consequence was to be found in the general Anglo-German colonial settlement in Africa, concluded in 1890 after Bismarck's fall, and made possible by the cession of Heligoland. In the first instance it was hoped by the Germans that South-West Africa might be surrendered for Heligoland. Count Herbert Bismarck, very unfavorably impressed by a visit to South-West Africa, sponsored this proposal. "I think," he wrote on 27 March 1889, "the deal would be very advantageous to us and enormously popular in Germany. Our South-West African Company is stagnant, bankrupt and hopeless. . . . In the colonial area we have not in fact a single soul who would qualify as a German citizen." But the negotiations proceeded slowly, largely because Bismarck was once more concerned with the possibility of negotiating a wider agreement with England which would carry European commitments, and partly because he felt it was the course of prudence to go slow lest it might be suspected in London how much importance Germany attached to an island which commanded the entrance to the Kiel Canal, then being built. When agreement was finally reached, the *quid pro quo* for England was not in South-West but mainly in East Africa. The Sultanate of Zanzibar became a British Protectorate and German penetration in East Africa was barred by the delineation of the boundaries of British East Africa.

Russian Expansion in Asia

If German support for French imperial ambitions was an experiment which was tried, failed and abandoned, there was a remarkable consistency about Germany's attitude to Russian expansion in Asia. It was something to be encouraged. About that there were no doubts. It had almost everything to recommend it. It would distract Russia's attention from Europe, thereby lessening the risk of an Austro-Russian conflict in the Balkans; it would keep Russian forces harmlessly occupied; it would, above all, keep alive Anglo-Russian tension by playing on English fears of a Russian invasion of India. "Germany," Bismarck advised his Emperor, "has no interest in preventing Russia if she looks for the occupation which is necessary for her army in Asia rather than in Europe. If the Russian Army is unoccupied it becomes a danger to the internal security of the Empire and the dynasty, and if occupation fails in Asia it must necessarily be sought on the Western front. . . . It is therefore an aim of German policy today to bring about hostile rather than too intimate relations between Russia and England." With the Penjdeh incident in 1885, hostility nearly brought the two countries to war, much to Germany's satisfaction, before a settlement of the Afghan frontier was reached. In more flamboyant language and by more direct methods the Kaiser Wilhelm II pursued, in this respect at least, the same policies as the Chancellor he had deposed from office. "Clearly," he wrote to the Tsar Nicholas II in April 1895, "it is the great task of the future for Russia to cultivate the Asian continent and to defend Europa from the inroads of the great Yellow Race. In this you will always find me ready to help you as best I can. You have well understood the call of Providence. . . ." But though German policy was consistent, Russia, unlike France, was not a defeated country and her expansion in Central Asia owed little or nothing to German encouragement or German goodwill. Like the British in India, the frontiers of the Russian Empire in Central Asia moved steadily forward because the vacuum in power that existed in the Trans-Caspian regions left her with little alternative. . . .

The Jameson Raid and the South African War

It was Lord Salisbury who remarked that Gladstone's impassioned fight for Irish Home Rule had aroused the slumbering genius of Imperialism. It is doubtful, however, if the blatant and boastful temper of the *fin de siècle* deserves so kindly a description. One of its most notable consequences was to estrange Britain from Europe at a moment when her isolation placed her in a position whose perils were better understood in retrospect than at the time.

It was in January 1895 that President Kruger,[4] as the guest of the German Club in Pretoria on the Kaiser's birthday, spoke of Germany as "a grown-up power that would stop England from kicking the child Republic." On instructions from London the British Ambassador protested against the German encouragement of Boer hostility to Britain, of which Kruger's speech was regarded as a provocative expression. The Kaiser later maintained that the Ambassador had gone so far as to mention the "astounding word, 'war'." "For a few square miles full of niggers and palm trees England had threatened her one true friend, the German Emperor, grandson of Her Majesty the Queen of Great Britain and Ireland, with war!" According to his own highly colored narrative the Kaiser retorted with the "clear warning" that England could only escape from her existing isolation "by a frank and outspoken attitude either for or against the Triple Alliance." As things were England's attitude, her policy "of selfishness and bullying" were forcing Germany to make "common cause with France and Russia, each of whom had about a million men ready to pour in over my frontier. . . ." Into this atmosphere of artificial tension came with explosive effect the news of the Jameson Raid. Ill-judged, ill-considered, wholly indefensible, even in its limited Anglo-South African context, it played straight into the hands of the most dangerous forces at work in Germany. The Kaiser responded with a telegram to President Kruger, dated 3 January 1896. "I express my sincere congratulations that, supported by your people, without appealing for the help of friendly Powers, you have succeeded by your own energetic action against armed bands which invaded your country as disturbers of the peace, and have thus been enabled to restore peace and safeguard the

[4] Paul Kruger was president of the Transvaal from 1883 to 1900.—Ed.

independence of the country against attacks from the outside." If the telegram was designed to embody every phrase best calculated to inflame sentiment in a country whose first reaction to the news of the Raid was one of profound misgiving, it could not have been better drafted. At once opinion hardened against the Boer Republics. President Kruger was no longer felt to be the much-wronged defender of his people's rights, but a collaborator with the Kaiser challenging British rule in South Africa. Self-respect was restored and internal divisions papered over.

To send a telegram was one thing; to intervene effectively in South Africa was another. Germany had no fleet. What course was open to her? Holstein[5] supplied the answer. The Triple Alliance and the Dual Alliance should forget their rivalry and cooperate against Britain. There was a wide field for common action and many colonial ambitions that could be achieved in concert. France should receive the Congo Free State, Germany further concessions in China, Russia, Korea; Italy would become the Protector of Abyssinia. This superficially was a tempting prospect for one and all. But behind it there were subtle reservations, soon suspected. The ultimate German intention was not the final estrangement of Britain but a practical demonstration of the dangers of isolation and of the need to cooperate with the Triple Alliance. That was why there was no mention of Egypt. In the sequel it was in Paris that this grandiose plan received its death sentence. It was Egypt alone by which France might have been momentarily deluded into a dangerous partnership and Egypt was not on offer. Moreover, the immediate background to this continental League lay in the Transvaal, and the Transvaal was of no interest to France, however much its people might sympathize with the Boer cause. There must be, commented *Le Temps,* "no unnatural alliance" arising out of Anglo-German disputes in South Africa.

Holstein's project of European Alliance was stillborn, and it is interesting to notice that when the South African War broke out in 1899, Germany's policy was very different. In 1900 it was Russia who proposed mediation and Germany who declined it, the Kaiser improving the occasion by informing the Queen and the Prince of Wales of his refusal. The Prince paid ironic tribute to this gesture

---

[5] Baron von Holstein: German diplomat and statesman, in power 1890–1906.—Ed.

thanking the Kaiser in March 1900—"You have no idea, my dear William, how all of us in England appreciate the loyal friendship you manifest towards us on every occasion." But if the political response was more judicious the lesson deduced in Berlin from the Raid and the South African War was always the same—sea power is the condition of world power. That was the most significant legacy of the Jameson Raid and the South African War to Europe. . . .

The Legacy of Imperial Expansion

Though on more than one occasion colonial rivalries brought the Great Powers within sight of war, it is not for that reason to be concluded that colonial rivalry was a fundamental cause of war. On the contrary the colonial policies of the Continental states were formulated in the light of the European balance of power and designed to serve European ends. When they no longer served those ends the colonial scene slips unobtrusively into the background. From 1900 onwards there were no important colonial disputes between Germany and England because of the preoccupation of the Powers in the Far East between 1900–1904; and after 1904 because the Anglo-French Entente had removed the possibility of attaining the political ends which German colonial policy in the eighties had been designed to promote. . . .

Hannah Arendt

THE ALLIANCE BETWEEN MOB AND CAPITAL

Hannah Arendt (b. 1906) studied at Heidelberg with the philosopher Karl Jaspers and came to the United States in 1941 as a political refugee, after residing for a number of years in France. She has been an editor, author, lecturer, and professor. In 1951 she published the much-discussed The Origins of Totalitarianism *and followed it in 1958 with* The Human Condition— *both books involving a synthesis of history, philosophy, and political science. Her later works, including* On Revolution *(1963),* Eichmann in Jerusalem *(1963), and* Crises of the Republic *(1972) have added to her reputation as one of the most original, erudite, and provocative of contemporary social and political philosophers.* The Origins of Totalitarianism, *from which this selection is drawn, discusses communism and fascism and their relations to nineteenth-century racialism and "imperialism."*

"Expansion is everything," said Cecil Rhodes, and fell into despair, for every night he saw overhead "these stars . . . these vast worlds which we can never reach. I would annex the planets if I could." He had discovered the moving principle of the new, the imperialist era . . . and yet in a flash of wisdom Rhodes recognized at the same moment its inherent insanity and its contradiction to the human condition. Naturally, neither insight nor sadness changed his policies. He had no use for the flashes of wisdom that led him so far beyond the normal capacities of an ambitious businessman with a marked tendency toward megalomania.

"World politics is for a nation what megalomania is for an individual," said Eugen Richter (leader of the German progressive party) at about the same historical moment. But his opposition in the Reichstag to Bismarck's proposal to support private companies in the foundation of trading and maritime stations, showed clearly that he understood the economic needs of a nation in his time even less than Bismarck himself. It looked as though those who opposed or ignored imperialism—like Eugen Richter in Germany, or Gladstone in England, or Clemenceau in France—had lost touch with

From Hannah Arendt, *The Origins of Totalitarianism* (Second Enlarged Edition; New York, 1958), pp. 124–125, 126–127, 147–148, 150–155. By permission of Hannah Arendt.

reality and did not realize that trade and economics had already involved every nation in world politics. The national principle was leading into provincial ignorance and the battle fought by sanity was lost.

Moderation and confusion were the only rewards of any statesman's consistent opposition to imperialist expansion. Thus Bismarck, in 1871, rejected the offer of French possessions in Africa in exchange for Alsace-Lorraine, and twenty years later acquired Heligoland from Great Britain in return for Uganda, Zanzibar, and Vitu—two kingdoms for a bathtub, as the German imperialists told him, not without justice. Thus in the eighties Clemenceau opposed the imperialist party in France when they wanted to send an expeditionary force to Egypt against the British, and thirty years later he surrendered the Mosul oil fields to England for the sake of a French-British alliance. Thus Gladstone was being denounced by Cromer in Egypt as "not a man to whom the destinies of the British Empire could safely be entrusted."

That statesmen, who thought primarily in terms of the established national territory, were suspicious of imperialism was justified enough, except that more was involved than what they called "overseas adventures." They knew by instinct rather than by insight that this new expansion movement, in which "patriotism ... is best expressed in money-making" (Huebbe-Schleiden) and the national flag is a "commercial asset" (Rhodes), could only destroy the political body of the nation-state. Conquest as well as empire-building had fallen into disrepute for very good reasons. They had been carried out successfully only by governments which, like the Roman Republic, were based primarily on law, so that conquest could be followed by integration of the most heterogeneous peoples by imposing upon them a common law. The nation-state, however, based upon a homogeneous population's active consent to its government (*"le plébiscite de tous les jours"*), lacked such a unifying principle and would, in the case of conquest, have to assimilate rather than to integrate, to enforce consent rather than justice, that is, to degenerate into tyranny. Robespierre was already well aware of this when he exclaimed: *"Périssent les colonies si elles nous en coûtent l'honneur, la liberté."* ["Perish the colonies if they cost us honor and liberty."]

Expansion as a permanent and supreme aim of politics is the

central political idea of imperialism. Since it implies neither temporary looting nor the more lasting assimilation of conquest, it is an entirely new concept in the long history of political thought and action. The reason for this surprising originality—surprising because entirely new concepts are very rare in politics—is simply that this concept is not really political at all, but has its origin in the realm of business speculation, where expansion meant the permanent broadening of industrial production and economic transactions characteristic of the nineteenth century. . . .

In contrast to the economic structure, the political structure cannot be expanded indefinitely, because it is not based upon the productivity of man, which is, indeed, unlimited. Of all forms of government and organizations of people, the nation-state is least suited for unlimited growth because the genuine consent at its base cannot be stretched indefinitely, and is only rarely, and with difficulty, won from conquered peoples. No nation-state could with a clear conscience ever try to conquer foreign peoples, since such a conscience comes only from the conviction of the conquering nation that it is imposing a superior law upon barbarians. The nation, however, conceived of its law as an outgrowth of a unique national substance which was not valid beyond its own people and the boundaries of its own territory. . . .

*   *   *

When imperialism entered the scene of politics with the scramble for Africa in the eighties, it was promoted by businessmen, opposed fiercely by the governments in power, and welcomed by a surprisingly large section of the educated classes. To the last it seemed to be God-sent, a cure for all evils, an easy panacea for all conflicts. And it is true that imperialism in a sense did not disappoint these hopes. It gave a new lease on life to political and social structures which were quite obviously threatened by new social and political forces and which, under other circumstances, without the interference of imperialist developments, would hardly have needed two world wars to disappear.

As matters stood, imperialism spirited away all troubles and produced that deceptive feeling of security, so universal in pre-war Europe, which deceived all but the most sensitive minds. Péguy in France and Chesterton in England knew instinctively that they lived in a world of hollow pretense and that its stability was the greatest pretense of all. Until everything began to crumble, the stability of obviously outdated political structures was a fact, and their stubborn unconcerned longevity seemed to give the lie to those who felt the ground tremble under their feet. The solution of the riddle was imperialism. The answer to the fateful question: why did the European comity of nations allow this evil to spread until everything was destroyed, the good as well as the bad, is that all governments knew very well that their countries were secretly disintegrating, that the body politic was being destroyed from within, and that they lived on borrowed time.

Innocently enough, expansion appeared first as the outlet for excess capital production and offered a remedy, capital export. The tremendously increased wealth produced by capitalist production under a social system based on maldistribution had resulted in "oversaving"—that is, the accumulation of capital which was condemned to idleness within the existing national capacity for production and consumption. This money was actually superfluous, needed by nobody though owned by a growing class of somebodies. . . .

Older than the superfluous wealth was another by-product of capitalist production: the human debris that every crisis, following invariably upon each period of industrial growth, eliminated permanently from producing society. Men who had become permanently idle were as superfluous to the community as the owners of superfluous wealth. That they were an actual menace to society had been recognized throughout the nineteenth century and their export had helped to populate the dominions of Canada and Australia as well as the United States. The new fact in the imperialist era is that these two superfluous forces, superfluous capital and superfluous working power, joined hands and left the country together. The concept of expansion, the export of government power and annexation of every territory in which nationals had invested either their wealth or their work, seemed the only alternative to increasing losses in wealth and population. Imperialism and its idea of unlimited expansion seemed to offer a permanent remedy for a permanent evil.

Ironically enough, the first country in which superfluous wealth and superfluous men were brought together was itself becoming superfluous. South Africa had been in British possession since the beginning of the century because it assured the maritime road to

India. The opening of the Suez Canal, however, and the subsequent administrative conquest of Egypt, lessened considerably the importance of the old trade station on the Cape. The British would, in all probability, have withdrawn from Africa just as all European nations had done whenever their possessions and trade interests in India were liquidated.

The particular irony and, in a sense, symbolical circumstance in the unexpected development of South Africa into the "culture-bed of Imperialism" lies in the very nature of its sudden attractiveness when it had lost all value for the Empire proper: diamond fields were discovered in the seventies and large gold mines in the eighties. The new desire for profit-at-any-price converged for the first time with the old fortune hunt. Prospectors, adventurers, and the scum of the big cities emigrated to the Dark Continent along with capital from industrially developed countries. From now on, the mob, begotten by the monstrous accumulation of capital, accompanied its begetter on those voyages of discovery where nothing was discovered but new possibilities for investment. The owners of superfluous wealth were the only men who could use the superfluous men who came from the four corners of the earth. Together they established the first paradise of parasites whose lifeblood was gold. Imperialism, the product of superfluous money and superfluous men, began its startling career by producing the most superfluous and unreal goods.

It may still be doubtful whether the panacea of expansion would have become so great a temptation for nonimperialists if it had offered its dangerous solutions only for those superfluous forces which, in any case, were already outside the nation's body corporate. The complicity of all parliamentary parties in imperialist programs is a matter of record. The history of the British Labour Party in this respect is an almost unbroken chain of justifications of Cecil Rhodes's early prediction: "The workmen find that although the Americans are exceedingly fond of them, and are just now exchanging the most brotherly sentiments with them yet are shutting out their goods. The workmen also find that Russia, France and Germany locally are doing the same, and the workmen see that if they do not look out they will have no place in the world to trade at all. And so the workmen have become Imperialist and the Liberal Party are following." In Germany, the liberals (and not the Conservative

Party) were the actual promoters of that famous naval policy which contributed so heavily to the outbreak of the First World War. The Socialist Party wavered between active support of the imperialist naval policy (it repeatedly voted funds for the building of a German navy after 1906) and complete neglect of all questions of foreign policy. Occasional warnings against the *Lumpenproletariat,* and the possible bribing of sections of the working class with crumbs from the imperialist table, did not lead to a deeper understanding of the great appeal which the imperialist programs had to the rank and file of the party. In Marxist terms the new phenomenon of an alliance between mob and capital seemed so unnatural, so obviously in conflict with the doctrine of class struggle, that the actual dangers of the imperialist attempt—to divide mankind into master races and slave races, into higher and lower breeds, into colored peoples and white men, all of which were attempts to unify the people on the basis of the mob—were completely overlooked. Even the breakdown of international solidarity at the outbreak of the First World War did not disturb the complacency of the socialists and their faith in the proletariat as such. Socialists were still probing the economic laws of imperialism when imperialists had long since stopped obeying them, when in overseas countries these laws had been sacrificed to the "imperial factor" or to the "race factor," and when only a few elderly gentlemen in high finance still believed in the inalienable rights of the profit rate.

The curious weakness of popular opposition to imperialism, the numerous inconsistencies and outright broken promises of liberal statesmen, frequently ascribed to opportunism or bribery, have other and deeper causes. Neither opportunism nor bribery could have persuaded a man like Gladstone to break his promise, as the leader of the Liberal Party, to evacuate Egypt when he became Prime Minister. Half consciously and hardly articulately, these men shared with the people the conviction that the national body itself was so deeply split into classes, that class struggle was so universal a characteristic of modern political life, that the very cohesion of the nation was jeopardized. Expansion again appeared as a lifesaver, if and insofar as it could provide a common interest for the nation as a whole, and it is mainly for this reason that imperialists were allowed to become 'parasites upon patriotism."

Partly, of course, such hopes still belonged with the old vicious practice of "healing" domestic conflicts with foreign adventures. The difference, however, is marked. Adventures are by their very nature limited in time and space; they may succeed temporarily in overcoming conflicts, although as a rule they fail and tend rather to sharpen them. From the very beginning the imperialist adventure of expansion appeared to be an eternal solution, because expansion was conceived as unlimited. Furthermore, imperialism was not an adventure in the usual sense, because it depended less on nationalist slogans than on the seemingly solid basis of economic interests. In a society of clashing interests, where the common good was identified with the sum total of individual interests, expansion as such appeared to be a possible common interest of the nation as a whole. Since the owning and dominant classes had convinced everybody that economic interest and the passion for ownership are a sound basis for the body politic, even nonimperialist statesmen were easily persuaded to yield when a common economic interest appeared on the horizon.

These then are the reasons why nationalism developed so clear a tendency toward imperialism, the inner contradiction of the two principles notwithstanding. The more ill-fitted nations were for the incorporation of foreign peoples (which contradicted the constitution of their own body politic), the more they were tempted to oppress them. In theory, there is an abyss between nationalism and imperialism; in practice, it can and has been bridged by tribal nationalism and outright racism. From the beginning, imperialists in all countries preached and boasted of their being "beyond the parties," and the only ones to speak for the nation as a whole. This was especially true of the Central and Eastern European countries with few or no overseas holdings; there the alliance between mob and capital took place at home and resented even more bitterly (and attacked much more violently) the national institutions and all national parties.

The contemptuous indifference of imperialist politicians to domestic issues was marked everywhere, however, and especially in England. While "parties above parties" like the Primrose League[1] were of secondary influence, imperialism was the chief cause of the degeneration of the two-party system into the Front Bench system, which lead to a "diminution of the power of opposition" in Parlia-

---

[1] An organization of conservatives dedicated to the principles of Disraeli, founded 1883.—Ed.

ment and to a growth of "power of the Cabinet as against the House of Commons." Of course this was also carried through as a policy beyond the strife of parties and particular interests, and by men who claimed to speak for the nation as a whole. Such language was bound to attract and delude precisely those persons who still retained a spark of political idealism. The cry for unity resembled exactly the battle cries which had always led peoples to war; and yet, nobody detected in the universal and permanent instrument of unity the germ of universal and permanent war.

Government officials engaged more actively than any other group in the nationalist brand of imperialism and were chiefly responsible for the confusion of imperialism with nationalism. The nation-states had created and depended upon the civil services as a permanent body of officials who served regardless of class interest and governmental changes. Their professional honor and self-respect—especially in England and Germany—derived from their being servants of the nation as a whole. They were the only group with a direct interest in supporting the state's fundamental claim to independence of classes and factions. That the authority of the nation-state itself depended largely on the economic independence and political neutrality of its civil servants becomes obvious in our time; the decline of nations has invariably started with the corruption of its permanent administration and the general conviction that civil servants are in the pay, not of the state, but of the owning classes. At the close of the century the owning classes had become so dominant that it was almost ridiculous for a state employee to keep up the pretense of serving the nation. Division into classes left them outside the social body and forced them to form a clique of their own. In the colonial services they escaped the actual disintegration of the national body. In ruling foreign peoples in faraway countries, they could much better pretend to be heroic servants of the nation, "who by their services had glorified the British race," than if they had stayed at home. The colonies were no longer simply "a vast system of outdoor relief for the upper classes" as James Mill could still describe them; they were to become the very backbone of British nationalism, which discovered in the domination of distant countries and the rule over strange peoples the only way to serve British, and nothing but British, interests. The services actually believed that "the peculiar genius of each nation shows itself nowhere more clearly than in their system of dealing with subject races."

The truth was that only far from home could a citizen of England, Germany, or France be nothing but an Englishman or German or Frenchman. In his own country he was so entangled in economic interests or social loyalties that he felt closer to a member of his class in a foreign country than to a man of another class in his own. Expansion gave nationalism a new lease on life and therefore was accepted as an instrument of national politics. The members of the new colonial societies and imperialist leagues felt "far removed from the strife of parties," and the farther away they moved the stronger their belief that they "represented only a national purpose." This shows the desperate state of the European nations before imperialism, how fragile their institutions had become, how outdated their social system proved in the face of man's growing capacity to produce. The means for preservation were desperate too, and in the end the remedy proved worse than the evil—which, incidentally, it did not cure.

The alliance between capital and mob is to be found at the genesis of every consistently imperialist policy. In some countries, particularly in Great Britain, this new alliance between the much-too-rich and the much-too-poor was and remained confined to overseas possessions. The so-called hypocrisy of British policies was the result of the good sense of English statesmen who drew a sharp line between colonial methods and normal domestic policies, thereby avoiding with considerable success the feared boomerang effect of imperialism upon the homeland. In other countries, particularly in Germany and Austria, the alliance took effect at home in the form of pan-movements, and to a lesser extent in France, in a so-called colonial policy. The aim of these "movements" was, so to speak, to imperialize the whole nation (and not only the "superfluous" part of it), to combine domestic and foreign policy in such a way as to organize the nation for the looting of foreign territories and the permanent degradation of alien peoples.

Ronald Robinson and John Gallagher

THE "ROBINSON AND GALLAGHER THESIS"

Professors Ronald Edward Robinson (b. 1920) and John Anderson Gallagher (b. 1919) have each taught at Oxford and at Cambridge. Robinson moved from Cambridge to Oxford in 1971 to take Gallagher's position as Beit Professor of the History of the British Commonwealth, while Gallagher went to Cambridge to become Harmsworth Professor of Imperial and Naval History. They are known primarily for their joint works on European expansion: "The Imperialism of Free Trade," Economic History Review *(1953), concerned with the changing nature of British economic and political expansion in the nineteenth century;* Africa and the Victorians *(with Alice Denny, Robinson's wife) (1961), which focussed on the relation between British decision-making and the partition of Africa; and a chapter, "The Partition of Africa," in* The New Cambridge Modern History, *vol. XI (1962). Selections from the first two of these works are published below.*

THE IMPERIALISM OF FREE TRADE

I

It ought to be a commonplace that Great Britain during the nineteenth century expanded overseas by means of "informal empire" as much as by acquiring dominion in the strict constitutional sense. For purposes of economic analysis it would clearly be unreal to define imperial history exclusively as the history of those colonies colored red on the map. Nevertheless, almost all imperial history has been written on the assumption that the empire of formal dominion is historically comprehensible in itself and can be cut out of its context in British expansion and world politics. The conventional interpretation of the nineteenth-century empire continues to rest upon study of the formal empire alone, which is rather like judging the size and character of icebergs solely from the parts above the water-line.

From John Gallagher and Ronald Robinson, "The Imperialism of Free Trade," *The Economic History Review,* 2nd ser., VI, no. 1 (1953), pp. 1–15 (with omissions). By permission of the Economic History Society.

The imperial historian, in fact, is very much at the mercy of his own particular concept of empire. By that, he decides what facts are of "imperial" significance; his data are limited in the same way as his concept, and his final interpretation itself depends largely upon the scope of his hypothesis. Different hypotheses have led to conflicting conclusions. Since imperial historians are writing about different empires and since they are generalizing from eccentric or isolated aspects of them, it is hardly surprising that these historians sometimes contradict each other.

The orthodox view of nineteenth-century imperial history remains that laid down from the standpoint of the racial and legalistic concept which inspired the Imperial Federation movement. Historians such as Seeley and Egerton looked on events in the formal empire as the only test of imperial activity; and they regarded the empire of kinship and constitutional dependence as an organism with its own laws of growth. In this way the nineteenth century was divided into periods of imperialism and anti-imperialism, according to the extension or contraction of the formal empire and the degree of belief in the value of British rule overseas.

Ironically enough, the alternative interpretation of "imperialism," which began as part of the radical polemic against the Federationists, has in effect only confirmed their analysis. Those who have seen imperialism as the high stage of capitalism and the inevitable result of foreign investment agree that it applied historically only to the period after 1880. As a result they have been led into a similar preoccupation with formal manifestations of imperialism because the late-Victorian age was one of spectacular extension of British rule. Consequently, Hobson and Lenin, Professor [Parker T.] Moon and Mr. Woolf have confirmed from the opposite point of view their opponents' contention that late-Victorian imperialism was a qualitative change in the nature of British expansion and a sharp deviation from the innocent and static liberalism of the middle of the century. This alleged change, welcomed by one school, condemned by the other, was accepted by both.

For all their disagreement these two doctrines pointed to one interpretation; that mid-Victorian "indifference" and late-Victorian "enthusiasm" for empire were directly related to the rise and decline in free-trade beliefs. Thus Lenin wrote: "When free competition in Great Britain was at its height, i.e. between 1840 and 1860, the leading British bourgeois politicians were ... of the opinion that the liberation of the colonies and their complete separation from Great Britain was inevitable and desirable." Professor [Robert L.] Schuyler extends this to the decade from 1861 to 1870: "... for it was during those years that tendencies toward the disruption of the empire reached their climax. The doctrines of the Manchester school were at the height of their influence."

In the last quarter of the century, Professor Langer finds that "there was an obvious danger that the British (export) market would be steadily restricted. Hence the emergence and sudden flowering of the movement for expansion. ... Manchester doctrine had been belied by the facts. It was an outworn theory to be thrown into the discard." Their argument may be summarized in this way: the mid-Victorian formal empire did not expand, indeed it seemed to be dis-integrating, therefore the period was anti-imperialist; the later-Victorian formal empire expanded rapidly, therefore this was an era of imperialism; the change was caused by the obsolescence of free trade.

The trouble with this argument is that it leaves out too many of the facts which it claims to explain. Consider the results of a decade of "indifference" to empire. Between 1841 and 1851 Great Britain occupied or annexed New Zealand, the Gold Coast, Labuan, Natal, the Punjab, Sind and Hong Kong. In the next twenty years British control was asserted over Berar, Oudh, Lower Burma and Kowloon, over Lagos and the neighborhood of Sierra Leone, over Basutoland, Griqualand and the Transvaal; and new colonies were established in Queensland and British Columbia. Unless this expansion can be explained by "fits of absence of mind," we are faced with the para-dox that it occurred despite the determination of the imperial au-thorities to avoid extending their rule.

This contradiction arises even if we confine our attention to the formal empire, as the orthodox viewpoint would force us to do. But if we look beyond into the regions of informal empire, then the difficulties become overwhelming. The normal account of South African policy in the middle of the century is that Britain abandoned any idea of controlling the interior. But in fact what looked like with-drawal from the Orange River Sovereignty and the Transvaal was based not on any *a priori* theories about the inconveniences of colo-nies but upon hard facts of strategy and commerce in a wider field.

Great Britain was in South Africa primarily to safeguard the routes to the East, by preventing foreign powers from acquiring bases on the flank of those routes. In one way or another this imperial interest demanded some kind of hold upon Africa south of the Limpopo River, and although between 1852 and 1877 the Boer Republics were not controlled formally for this purpose by Britain, they were effectually dominated by informal paramountcy and by their dependence on British ports. If we refuse to narrow our view to that of formal empire, we can see how steadily and successfully the main imperial interest was pursued by maintaining supremacy over the whole region, and that it was pursued as steadily throughout the so-called anti-imperialist era as in the late-Victorian period. But it was done by shutting in the Boer Republics from the Indian Ocean: by the annexation of Natal in 1843, by keeping the Boers out of Delagoa Bay in 1860 and 1868, out of St. Lucia Bay in 1861 and 1866, and by British intervention to block the union of the two Republics under Pretorius in 1860. Strangely enough it was the first Gladstone Government which Schuyler regards as the climax of anti-imperialism, which annexed Basutoland in 1868 and Griqualand West in 1871 in order to ensure "the safety of our South African Possessions." By informal means if possible, or by formal annexations when necessary, British paramountcy was steadily upheld.

Are these the actions of ministers anxious to preside over the liquidation of the British Empire? Do they look like "indifference" to an empire rendered superfluous by free trade? On the contrary, here is a continuity of policy which the conventional interpretation misses because it takes account only of formal methods of control. It also misses the continuous grasp of the West African coast and of the South Pacific which British seapower was able to maintain. Refusals to annex are no proof of reluctance to control. As Lord Aberdeen put it in 1845: ". . . it is unnecessary to add that Her Majesty's Government will not view with indifference the assumption by another Power of a Protectorate which they, with due regard for the true interests of those [Pacific] islands, have refused." . . .

To sum up: the conventional view of Victorian imperial history leaves us with a series of awkward questions. In the age of "anti-imperialism" why were all colonies retained? Why were so many more obtained? Why were so many new spheres of influence set up? Or again, in the age of "imperialism," as we shall see later, why was there such reluctance to annex further territory? Why did decentralization, begun under the impetus of anti-imperialism, continue? In the age of laissez-faire, why was the Indian economy developed by the state?

These paradoxes are too radical to explain as merely exceptions which prove the rule or by concluding that imperial policy was largely irrational and inconsistent, the product of a series of accidents and chances. The contradictions, it may be suspected, arise not from the historical reality but from the historians' approach to it. A hypothesis which fits more of the facts might be that of a fundamental continuity in British expansion throughout the nineteenth century.

II

The hypothesis which is needed must include informal as well as formal expansion, and must allow for the continuity of the process. The most striking fact about British history in the nineteenth century, as Seeley pointed out, is that it is the history of an expanding society. The exports of capital and manufactures, the migration of citizens, the dissemination of the English language, ideas and constitutional forms, were all of them radiations of the social energies of the British peoples. Between 1812 and 1914 over twenty million persons emigrated from the British Isles, and nearly 70 percent of them went outside the Empire. Between 1815 and 1880, it is estimated, £1.187 billion in credit had accumulated abroad, but no more than one-sixth was placed in the formal empire. Even by 1913, something less than half of the £3.975 billion of foreign investment lay inside the Empire. Similarly, in no year of the century did the Empire buy much more than one-third of Britain's exports. The basic fact is that British industrialization caused an ever-extending and intensifying development of overseas regions. Whether they were formally British or not, was a secondary consideration.

Imperialism, perhaps, may be defined as a sufficient political function of this process of integrating new regions into the expanding economy; its character is largely decided by the various and changing relationships between the political and economic elements of expansion in any particular region and time. . . .

On this hypothesis the phasing of British expansion or imperialism is not likely to be chronological. Not all regions will reach the same level of economic integration at any one time; neither will all regions need the same type of political control at any one time. As the British industrial revolution grew, so new markets and sources of supply were linked to it at different times, and the degree of imperialist action accompanying that process varied accordingly. Thus mercantilist techniques of formal empire were being employed to develop India in the mid-Victorian age at the same time as informal techniques of free trade were being used in Latin America for the same purpose. It is for this reason that attempts to make phases of imperialism correspond directly to phases in the economic growth of the metropolitan economy are likely to prove in vain. The fundamental continuity of British expansion is only obscured by arguing that changes in the terms of trade or in the character of British exports necessitated a sharp change in the process.

From this vantage point the many-sided expansion of British industrial society can be viewed as a whole of which both the formal and informal empires are only parts. Both of them then appear as variable political functions of the extending pattern of overseas trade, investment, migration and culture. If this is accepted, it follows that formal and informal empire are essentially interconnected and to some extent interchangeable. Then not only is the old, legalistic, narrow idea of empire unsatisfactory, but so is the old idea of informal empire as a separate, nonpolitical category of expansion. A concept of informal empire which fails to bring out the underlying unity between it and the formal empire is sterile. Only within the total framework of expansion is nineteenth-century empire intelligible. So we are faced with the task of re-fashioning the interpretations resulting from defective concepts of organic constitutional empire on the one hand and Hobsonian "imperialism" on the other.

The economic importance—even the preeminence—of informal empire in this period has been stressed often enough. What was overlooked was the interrelation of its economic and political arms; how political action aided the growth of commercial supremacy, and how this supremacy in turn strengthened political influence. In other words, it is the politics as well as the economics of the informal empire which we have to include in the account. . . .

III

Let us now attempt, tentatively, to use the concept of the totality of British expansion described above to restate the main themes of the history of modern British expansion. We have seen that interpretation of this process fall into contradictions when based upon formal political criteria alone. If expansion both formal and informal is examined as a single process, will these contradictions disappear?

The growth of British industry made new demands upon British policy. It necessitated linking undeveloped areas with British foreign trade and, in so doing, moved the political arm to force an entry into markets closed by the power of foreign monopolies.

British policy, as Professor [Vincent T.] Harlow has shown, was active in this way before the American colonies had been lost, but its greatest opportunities came during the Napoleonic Wars. The seizure of the French and Spanish West Indies, the filibustering expedition to Buenos Aires in 1806, the taking of Java in 1811, were all efforts to break into new regions and to tap new resources by means of political action. But the policy went further than simple house-breaking, for once the door was opened and British imports with their political implications were pouring in, they might stop the door from being shut again. Raffles, for example, temporarily broke the Dutch monopoly of the spice trade in Java and opened the island to free trade. Later, he began the informal British paramountcy over the Malacca trade routes and the Malay peninsula by founding Singapore. In South America, at the same time, British policy was aiming at indirect political hegemony over new regions for the purposes of trade. The British navy carried the Portuguese royal family to Brazil after the breach with Napoleon, and the British representative there extorted from his grateful clients the trade treaty of 1810 which left British imports paying a lower tariff than the goods of the mother country. The thoughtful stipulation was added "that the Present Treaty shall be unlimited in point of duration, and that the obligations and conditions expressed or implied in it shall be perpetual and immutable."

From 1810 onwards this policy had even better chances in Latin America, and they were taken. British governments sought to exploit the colonial revolutions to shatter the Spanish trade monopoly, and to gain informal supremacy and the good will which would all favor British commercial penetration. As Canning put it in 1824, when he had clinched the policy of recognition: "Spanish America is free and if we do not mismanage our affairs sadly she is *English*." Canning's underlying object was to clear the way for a prodigious British expansion by creating a new and informal empire, not only to redress the Old World balance of power but to restore British influence in the New. He wrote triumphantly: "The thing is done ... the Yankees will shout in triumph: but it is they who lose most by our decision ... the United States have gotten the start of us in vain; and we link once more America to Europe." It would be hard to imagine a more spectacular example of a policy of commercial hegemony in the interests of high politics, or of the use of informal political supremacy in the interests of commercial enterprise. Characteristically, the British recognition of Buenos Aires, Mexico and Colombia took the form of signing commercial treaties with them.

In both the formal and informal dependencies in the mid-Victorian age there was much effort to open the continental interiors and to extend the British influence inland from the ports and to develop the hinterlands. The general strategy of this development was to convert these areas into complementary satellite economies, which would provide raw materials and food for Great Britain, and also provide widening markets for its manufactures. This was the period, the orthodox interpretation would have us believe, in which the political arm of expansion was dormant or even withered. In fact, that alleged inactivity is seen to be a delusion if we take into account the development in the informal aspect. Once entry had been forced into Latin America, China and the Balkans, the task was to encourage stable governments as good investment risks, just as in weaker or unsatisfactory states it was considered necessary to coerce them into more cooperative attitudes. . . .

The types of informal empire and the situations it attempted to exploit were as various as the success which it achieved. Although commercial and capital penetration tended to lead to political cooperation and hegemony, there are striking exceptions. In the United States, for example, British business turned the cotton South into a colonial economy, and the British investor hoped to do the same with the Midwest. But the political strength of the country stood in his way. It was impossible to stop American industrialization, and the industrialized sections successfully campaigned for tariffs, despite the opposition of those sections which depended on the British trade connection. In the same way, American political strength thwarted British attempts to establish Texas, Mexico and Central America as informal dependencies.

Conversely, British expansion sometimes failed, if it gained political supremacy without effecting a successful commercial penetration. There were spectacular exertions of British policy in China, but they did little to produce new customers. Britain's political hold upon China failed to break down Chinese economic self-sufficiency. The Opium War of 1840, the renewal of war in 1857, widened the inlets for British trade but they did not get Chinese exports moving. Their main effect was an unfortunate one from the British point of view, for such foreign pressures put Chinese society under great strains as the Taiping Rebellion unmistakably showed. It is important to note that this weakness was regarded in London as an embarrassment, and not as a lever for extracting further concessions. In fact, the British worked to prop up the tottering Pekin regime, for as Lord Clarendon[1] put it in 1870, "British interests in China are strictly commercial, or at all events only so far political as they may be for the protection of commerce." The value of this self-denial became clear in the following decades when the Peking government, threatened with a scramble for China, leaned more and more on the diplomatic support of the honest British broker.

The simple recital of these cases of economic expansion, aided and abetted by political action in one form or other, is enough to expose the inadequacy of the conventional theory that free trade could dispense with empire. We have seen that it did not do so. Economic expansion in the mid-Victorian age was matched by a corresponding political expansion which has been overlooked because it could not be seen by that study of maps which, it has been said, drives sane men mad. It is absurd to deduce from the harmony between London and the colonies of white settlement in the mid-Victorian age any British reluctance to intervene in the fields of British interest. The warships at Canton are as much a part of the

---

[1] Lord Clarendon was British foreign secretary in 1853–58, 1865–66, and 1868–70. —Ed.

period as responsible government for Canada; the battlefields of the Punjab are as real as the abolition of suttee.

Far from being an era of "indifference," the mid-Victorian years were the decisive stage in the history of British expansion overseas, in that the combination of commercial penetration and political influence allowed the United Kingdom to command those economies which could be made to fit best into her own. A variety of techniques adapted to diverse conditions and beginning at different dates were employed to effect this domination. A paramountcy was set up in Malaya centered on Singapore; a suzerainty over much of West Africa reached out from the port of Lagos and was backed up by the African squadron. On the east coast of Africa British influence at Zanzibar, dominant thanks to the exertions of Consul Kirk, placed the heritage of Arab command on the mainland at British disposal.

But perhaps the most common political technique of British expansion was the treaty of free trade and friendship made with or imposed upon a weaker state. The treaties with Persia of 1836 and 1857, the Turkish treaties of 1838 and 1861, the Japanese treaty of 1858, the favors extracted from Zanzibar, Siam and Morocco, the hundreds of anti-slavery treaties signed with crosses by African chiefs—all these treaties enabled the British government to carry forward trade with these regions.

Even a valuable trade with one region might give place to a similar trade with another which could be more easily coerced politically. The Russian grain trade, for example, was extremely useful to Great Britain. But the Russians' refusal to hear of free trade, and the British inability to force them into it, caused efforts to develop the grain of the Ottoman empire instead, since British pressure at Constantinople had been able to hustle the Turk into a liberal trade policy. The dependence of the commercial thrust upon the political arm resulted in a general tendency for British trade to follow the invisible flag of informal empire.

Since the mid-Victorian age now appears as a time of large-scale expansion, it is necessary to revise our estimate of the so-called "imperialist" era as well. Those who accept the concept of "economic imperialism" would have us believe that the annexations at the end of the century represented a sharp break in policy, due to the decline of free trade, the need to protect foreign investment, and the conversion of statesmen to the need for unlimited land-grabbing. All these explanations are questionable. In the first place, the tariff policy of Great Britain did not change. Again, British foreign investment was no new thing and most of it was still flowing into regions outside the formal empire. Finally the statesmens' conversion to the policy of extensive annexation was partial, to say the most of it. Until 1887, and only occasionally after that date, party leaders showed little more enthusiasm for extending British rule than the mid-Victorians. Salisbury was infuriated by the "superficial philanthropy" and "roguery" of the "fanatics" who advocated expansion. When pressed to aid the missions in Nyasaland in 1888, he retorted: "It is not our duty to do it. We should be risking tremendous sacrifices for a very doubtful gain." After 1888, Salisbury, Rosebery and Chamberlain accepted the scramble for Africa as a painful but unavoidable necessity which arose from a threat of foreign expansion and the irrepressible tendency of trade to overflow the bounds of empire, dragging the government into new and irksome commitments. But it was not until 1898 that they were sufficiently confident to undertake the reconquest of so vital a region as the Sudan.

Faced with the prospect of foreign acquisitions of tropical territory hitherto opened to British merchants, the men in London resorted to one expedient after another to evade the need of formal expansion and still uphold British paramountcy in those regions. British policy in the late-, as in the mid-Victorian period preferred informal means of extending imperial supremacy rather than direct rule. Throughout the two alleged periods the extension of British rule was a last resort—and it is this preference which has given rise to the many "anti-expansionist" remarks made by Victorian ministers. What these much-quoted expressions obscure, is that in practice mid-Victorian as well as late-Victorian policy-makers did not refuse to extend the protection of formal rule over British interests when informal methods had failed to give security. The fact that informal techniques were more often sufficient for this purpose in the circumstances of the mid-century than in the later period when the foreign challenge to British supremacy intensified, should not be allowed to disguise the basic continuity of policy. Throughout, British governments worked to establish and maintain British paramountcy by whatever means best suited the circumstances of their diverse regions of interest. The aims of the mid-Victorians were no more "anti-imperialist" than their successors', though they were more often able to achieve them informally; and the late-Victorians were no more "imperialist" than their predecessors, even though they were driven to annex more often. British policy followed the principle of extending control informally if possible and formally if necessary. To label the one method "anti-imperialist" and the other "imperialist," is to ignore the fact that whatever the method British interests were steadily safeguarded and extended. The usual summing up of the policy of the free trade empire as "trade not rule" should read "trade with informal control if possible; trade with rule when necessary." This statement of the continuity of policy disposes of the oversimplified explanation of involuntary expansion inherent in the orthodox interpretation based on the discontinuity between the two periods. . . .

One principle then emerges plainly: it is only when and where informal political means failed to provide the framework of security for British enterprise (whether commercial, or philanthropic or simply strategic) that the question of establishing formal empire arose. In satellite regions peopled by European stock, in Latin America or Canada, for instance, strong governmental structures grew up; in totally non-European areas, on the other hand, expansion unleashed such disruptive forces upon the indigenous structures that they tended to wear out and even collapse with use. This tendency in many cases accounts for the extension of informal British responsibility and eventually for the change from indirect to direct control. . . .

IV

Thus the mid-Victorian period now appears as an era of large-scale expansion, and the late-Victorian age does not seem to introduce any significant novelty into that process of expansion. The annexations of vast undeveloped territories, which have been taken as proof that this period alone was the great age of expansion, now pale in significance, at least if our analysis is anywhere near the truth. That the area of direct imperial rule was extended is true, but is it the most important or characteristic development of expansion during this period? The simple historical fact that Africa was the last field of European penetration is not to say that it was the most important; this would be a truism were it not that the main case of the Hobson school is founded on African examples. On the other hand, it is our main contention that the process of expansion had reached its most valuable targets long before the exploitation of so peripheral and marginal a field as tropical Africa. Consequently arguments, founded on the technique adopted in scrambling for Africa, would seem to be of secondary importance.

Therefore, the historian who is seeking to find the deepest meaning of the expansion at the end of the nineteenth century should look not at the mere pegging out of claims in African jungles and bush, but at the successful exploitation of the empire, both formal and informal, which was then coming to fruition in India, in Latin America, in Canada and elsewhere. The main work of imperialism in the so-called expansionist era was in the more intensive development of areas already linked with the world economy, rather than in the extensive annexations of the remaining marginal regions of Africa. The best finds and prizes had already been made; in tropical Africa the imperialists were merely scraping the bottom of the barrel.

THE PARTITION OF AFRICA

Thus stood Africa in Victorian estimation in the 1870s. All the powerful processes of social expansion, except that of philanthropy, were passing that continent by. The local enterprises nibbling at its fringes—palm oil traders on the west coast, missionaries and explorers on the east, republican Boers in the south, investors in Egyptian bonds—had been making weak efforts at imperial expansion locally for half a century. But only the white pastoralists had been able to make headway, without the imperial arm to break the paths. The Home government had consistently refused to extend colonial rule. Africa remained peripheral to the Mediterranean, the

From *Africa and the Victorians: The Official Mind of Imperialism,* by Ronald Robinson and John Gallagher, with Alice Denny (London, 1961), pp. 17–21, 462–64, 464–67, 471–72. Reprinted by permission of Macmillan, London and Basingstoke, and St. Martins Press, Inc., New York.

Indian empire and the routes to the East. And therefore paramount influence over coasts and the Canal had sufficed. A far-reaching experience of colonization, commerce, influence and dominion confirmed the conclusion: it was just feasible that the south might one day turn into another Canada or Australia; but no more Indias were wanted in northern or tropical Africa.

Nevertheless the Victorians after 1882 saw an almost unbelievable revolution in their political relations with Africa, as if their former calm and rational courses had run into some freakish whirlwind in the dark. As Lord Salisbury observed: "I do not exactly know the cause of this sudden revolution. But there it is." Against all precept and prejudice, against the experience and trends of previous expansion, the British occupied Egypt and staked out a huge tropical African empire. What was more, they were ready by the end of the century to fight major wars for Sudanese deserts and South African *Kopjes*. Why, after centuries of neglect, the British and other European governments should have scrambled to appropriate nine-tenths of the African continent within sixteen years, is an old problem, still awaiting an answer.

At the center of late-Victorian imperialism in Africa lies an apparent paradox. The main streams of British trade, investment and migration continued to leave tropical Africa practically untouched; and yet it was tropical Africa that was now bundled into the empire. There is a striking discrepancy of direction here between the economic and imperial arms. The flag was not following trade and capital; nor were trade and capital as yet following the flag. The late-Victorians seemed to be concentrating their imperial effort in the continent of least importance to their prosperity.

What were the causes and incentives? Which of them were merely contributory and which decisive? The question of the motives for African empire may be opened afresh. There are several well-known elements in the problem. Perhaps the late-Victorians were more enthusiastic imperialists than their fathers. Possibly businessmen were driven to bring the unopened continent into production and so relieve surfeit and depression. The custom was once to account for the partition in such terms. Or it may be that heightened rivalries between the Powers in Europe made them seek relief in Africa from their tensions nearer home. For any or all of these reasons, the forces of imperialism in Britain and in Europe may have intensified dramatically in the last quarter of the century and caught up all Africa as they did so.

But in the British case at least, there are other possible elements which have sometimes been neglected. It cannot be taken for granted that positive impulses from European society or the European economy were alone in starting up imperial rivalries. The collapse of African governments under the strain of previous Western influences may have played a part, even a predominant part in the process. The British advances may have been the culmination of the destructive workings of earlier exercises of informal empire over the coastal regimes. Hence crises in Africa, no less than imperial ambitions and international rivalries in Europe, have to be taken into account. Allowance has also to be made for the diversity of interest and circumstance in the different regions of Africa. It seems unlikely that the motives in regions as dissimilar as Egypt, the Niger and South Africa can be fitted easily into a single, simple formula of "imperialism."

Another factor must be included. Victorian expansion by the 1880s had long historical roots and worldwide ramifications. Its manifold workings tended sometimes to build up, and sometimes to break down the societies drawn under its influence. While in some countries, British agencies helped to create vortices of disorder and nationalist reaction, in others they helped local communities to grow until they became expansive in their own right. In these ways the processes of expansion were soon receding out of metropolitan control. Some satellites tended to break up; others were beginning to throw off galaxies of their own. It is not unlikely that both these tendencies helped to drag British ministries into African empire. Lastly, it is quite possible that they did not acquire a new empire for its intrinsic value, but because Africa's relationship to their total strategy in Europe, the Mediterranean, or the East had altered.

The elements in the problem might seem so numerous and disparate as to make it insoluble. Some unified field of study has to be found where all possible incentives to African empire may be assembled without becoming indistinguishable in their several effects. Historically, only the government in London registered and balanced all the contingencies making for British expansion in Africa. In following the occasions and motives, all roads lead ineluctably to Downing Street. The files and red boxes which passed between ministers and officials at the time contain the problem in its contemporary proportions.

The collective mind of government assembled and weighed all the factors making for and against advances. Party leaders and Whips anxiously consulted the tone of the Commons and the trend of the by-elections. Secretaries for India, the Colonies and Foreign Affairs, along with the Chancellor of the Exchequer and the Service ministers, gauged the pressures: the condition of domestic and European politics, the state of the economy, the expansive demands from India and the white colonies, the risks and crises in Africa and in the whole world. Furnished with intelligences from distant ambassadors, governors and consuls, they took the rival theses of their departments to the Cabinet; and there, the Prime Minister and his colleagues argued out the differences and balanced the considerations of profit and power.

A first task in analyzing the late-Victorians' share in the partition is to understand the motives of the ministers who directed it, and the study of official thinking is indispensable to this. Policy-making was a flow of deliberation and argument, of calculation and mediation between differing impulses. Secondly, it was a reading of the long-run national interest which stayed much the same from ministry to ministry, regardless of the ideological stock in trade of the Party in power. Ministers in their private calculations used a complex political arithmetic to decide whether to advance or not. Their thinking included analogues for the expansive pressures coming from business enterprise and Home politics, from foreign rivals and British agents on the spot.

By trying to reconstruct the calculations behind the higher decisions, the interplay of these elements as they worked at different levels may begin to emerge. The study of government's own reasoning is the obvious yardstick for measuring the urgency of incentives and contingencies at the point of action. Policy-making, in other words, is the unified historical field in which all the conditions for expansion were brought together.

This is not to say that ministers and their advisers were fully aware of the forces at work, or that they knew to a nicety where they were going. Neither is it to say that they were in control of the process of expansion and could start and stop it at will. Again, their recorded arguments for this course or for that did not always bring out fully their unconscious assumptions. What is more, there are many things too well understood between colleagues to be written down. There is no denying these limitations to the study of policy. But for all its shortcomings, official calculations throw most light on the deeper reasons for imperial expansion into Africa. They offer the unique method for making a first approximation to the relative strength of the different drives.

But the study of policy-making may not only advance the subject of motives, it may in addition help toward a break-through into the crucial problem—the objective causes of the partition of Africa. Once the weights in the balance of decision have been recorded, it may still be necessary to check the scales themselves. The official mind has to be taken along with the other elements in the problem as a possible cause in its own right.

Statesmen did more than respond to pressures and calculate interests; their decisions were not mere mechanical choices of expedients. Judgments and actions in fact were heavily prejudiced by their beliefs about morals and politics, about the duties of government, the ordering of society and international relations. And their attitudes to such questions tended to be specialized and idiosyncratic because they felt that their unique function and responsibility set them apart. If official thinking was in one sense a microcosm of past and present experience of expansion, in another sense, it was consciously above and outside those processes. The aristocrat by right, the official by *expertise,* both felt socially superior and functionally detached from those who pushed trade and built empires. It was their high calling to mediate between jarring and selfish interests and to keep the state from being used as the tool of any of them. As governors, their profession was to take the long and the broad, not the short and narrow view, to reconcile one principle with another in action—and, in a hard-headed way, even to do right and eschew wrong. Whether a man entered the ruling circle through patronage, which was still usual, or through examination, which was becoming less rare, aristocratic traditions of duty to the whole nation and disdain for its parts persisted, as did the legalism with which they approached their problems. Those who governed still thought of themselves as arbiters above the tumult, slightly contemptuous of the short-sighted businessman, the impractical philanthropist and the ignorant populace alike.

But the London policy-makers' detachment from their problems overseas was physical as well as professional. In Africa they were usually dealing with countries which they had never seen, with questions apprehended intellectually from reports and recommendations on paper. Their solutions and purposes on the other hand, were charged with the experience and beliefs of the society in which they lived and worked. Inevitably, the official idea and the African reality, the analysis of Whitehall and the local significance of Arabi or Kruger, of Goldie or Rhodes, were worlds apart. Yet in the end it was the idea and the analysis of African situations in Whitehall, and not the realities in Africa as such which moved Victorian statesmen to act or not to act. The working of their minds is therefore of the utmost importance in establishing the motives of imperialism. Because those who finally decided the issue of African empire were partly insulated from pressures at Home, and remote from reality in Africa, their historical notions, their ideas of international legality and the codes of honor shared by the aristocratic castes of Europe had unusually wide scope in their decisions.

The possibility that official thinking in itself was a cause of late-Victorian imperialism, although once brilliantly suggested by an economist [i.e., Schumpeter], has usually been neglected by historians. England's rulers had inherited not only a world empire but the experience gained in bringing it together, and the assumptions and prejudices accumulated from past successes and failures inevitably influenced their behavior in the partition. . . .

*   *   *

Did new, sustained or compelling impulses towards African empire arise in British politics or business during the 1880s? The evidence seems unconvincing. The late-Victorians seem to have been no keener to rule and develop Africa than their fathers. The businessman saw no greater future there, except in the south; the politician was as reluctant to expand and administer a tropical African empire as the mid-Victorians had been; and plainly Parliament was no more eager to pay for it. British opinion restrained rather than prompted ministers to act in Africa. Hence they had to rely on private companies or colonial governments to act for them. It is true that African lobbies and a minority of imperialists did what they could to persuade government to advance. Yet they were usually too weak to be decisive. Measured by the yardstick of official thinking, there was no strong political or commercial movement in Britain in favor of African acquisitions.

The priorities of policy in tropical Africa confirm this impression. West Africa seemed to offer better prospects of markets and raw materials than East Africa and the Upper Nile; yet it was upon these poorer countries that the British government concentrated its efforts. These regions of Africa which interested the British investor and merchant least, concerned ministers the most. No expansion of commerce prompted the territorial claims to Uganda, the east coast and the Nile Valley. As Mackinnon's failure showed, private enterprise was not moving in to develop them; and they were no more useful or necessary to the British industrial economy between 1880 and 1900 than they had been earlier in the century. Territorial claims here reached out far in advance of the expanding economy. Notions of pegging out colonial estates for posterity hardly entered into British calculations until the late 1890s, when it was almost too late to affect the outcome. Nor were ministers gulled by the romantic glories of ruling desert and bush. Imperialism in the wide sense of empire for empire's sake was not their motive. Their territorial claims were not made for the sake of African empire or commerce as such. They were little more than by-products of an enforced search for better security in the Mediterranean and the East. It was not the pomps or profits of governing Africa which moved the ruling elite, but the cold rules for national safety handed on from Pitt, Palmerston and Disraeli.

According to the grammar of the policy-makers, their advances in Africa were prompted by different interests and circumstances in different regions. Egypt was occupied because of the collapse of the Khedivial regime. The occupation went on because the internal crisis remained unsolved and because of French hostility which the occupation itself provoked. Britain's insistent claims in East Africa and the Nile Valley and her yielding of so much in West Africa were largely contingent upon the Egyptian occupation and the way it affected European relations. In southern Africa, imperial intervention against the Transvaal was designed above all to uphold and restore the imperial influence which economic growth, Afrikaner nationalism and the Jameson fiasco had overthrown. Imperial claims in the Rhodesias, and to a lesser extent in Nyasaland, were contingent in turn upon Cape colonial expansion and imperial attempts to offset the rise of the Transvaal. The times and circumstances in which almost all these claims and occupations were made suggest strongly that they were called forth by crises in Egypt and South Africa, rather than by positive impulses to African empire arising in Europe.

To be sure, a variety of different interests in London—some religious and humanitarian, others strictly commercial or financial, and yet others imperialist—pressed for territorial advances and were sometimes used as their agents. In West Africa, the traders called for government protection; in Uganda and Nyasaland, the missionaries and the antislavery groups called for annexation; in Egypt, the bondholders asked government to rescue their investments; in South Africa, philanthropists and imperialists called for more government from Whitehall, while British traders and investors were divided about the best way of looking after their interests. Ministers usually listened to their pleas only when it suited their purpose; but commercial and philanthropic agitation seldom decided which territories should be claimed or occupied or when this should be done, although their slogans were frequently used by government in its public justifications.

It is the private calculations and actions of ministers far more than their speeches which reveal the primary motives behind their advances. For all the different situations in which territory was claimed, and all the different reasons which were given to justify it, one consideration, and one alone entered into all the major decisions. In all regions north of Rhodesia, the broad imperative which decided which territory to reserve and which to renounce, was the safety of the routes to the East. It did not, of course, prompt the claiming of Nyasaland or the lower Niger. Here a reluctant government acted to protect existing fields of trading and missionary enterprise from foreign annexations. In southern Africa the extension of empire seems to have been dictated by a somewhat different imperative. Here the London government felt bound as a rule to satisfy the demands for more territory which their self-governing colonials pressed on them. Ministers did this in the hope of conserving imperial influence. Nevertheless, the safety of the routes to India also figured prominently in the decision to uphold British supremacy in South Africa. It was the same imperative which after impelling the occupation of Egypt, prolonged it, and forced Britain to go into East

Africa and the Upper Nile, while yielding in most of West Africa. As soon as territory anywhere in Africa became involved, however indirectly, in this cardinal interest, ministries passed swiftly from inaction to intervention. If the papers left by the policy-makers are to be believed, they moved into Africa, not to build a new African empire, but to protect the old empire in India. . . .

An essentially negative objective, it had been attained hitherto without large African possessions. Mere influence and cooperation with other Powers had been enough to safeguard strategic points in North Africa; while in South Africa control of coastal regions had sufficed. The ambition of late-Victorian ministers reached no higher than to uphold these mid-Victorian systems of security in Egypt and South Africa. They were distinguished from their predecessors only in this: that their security by influence was breaking down. In attempting to restore it by intervention and diplomacy, they incidentally marked out the ground on which a vastly extended African empire was later to arise. Nearly all the interventions appear to have been consequences, direct or indirect, of internal Egyptian or South African crises which endangered British influence and security in the world. Such an interpretation alone seems to fit the actual calculations of policy. Ministers felt frankly that they were making the best of a bad job. They were doing no more than protecting old interests in worsening circumstances. To many, the flare-up of European rivalry in Africa seemed unreasonable and even absurd; yet most of them felt driven to take part because of tantalizing circumstances beyond their control. They went forward as a measure of precaution, or as a way back to the saner mid-Victorian systems of informal influence. Gloomily, they were fumbling to adjust their old strategy to a changing Africa. And the necessity arose much more from altered circumstances in Africa than from any revolution in the nature, strength or direction of British expansion.

Hence the question of motive should be formulated afresh. It is no longer the winning of a new empire which has to be explained. The question is simpler: Why could the late-Victorians after 1880 no longer rely upon influence to protect traditional interests? What forced them in the end into imperial solutions? The answer is to be found first in the nationalist crises in Africa itself, which were the work of intensifying European influences during previous decades; and only secondarily in the interlocking of these crises in Africa with rivalries in Europe. Together the two drove Britain step by step to regain by territorial claims and occupation that security which could no longer be had by influence alone. The compelling conditions for British advances in tropical Africa were first called into being, not by the German victory of 1871, nor by Leopold's interest in the Congo, nor by the petty rivalry of missionaries and merchants, nor by a rising imperialist spirit, nor even by the French occupation of Tunis in 1881—but by the collapse of the Khedivial regime in Egypt.

From start to finish the partition of tropical Africa was driven by the persistent crisis in Egypt. When the British entered Egypt on their own, the Scramble began; and as long as they stayed in Cairo, it continued until there was no more of Africa left to divide. Since chance and miscalculation had much to do with the way that Britain went into Egypt, it was to some extent an accident that the partition took place when it did. But once it had begun, Britain's overriding purpose in Africa was security in Egypt, the Mediterranean and the Orient. The achievement of this security became at the same time vital and more difficult, once the occupation of Egypt had increased the tension between the Powers and had dragged Africa into their rivalry. In this way the crisis in Egypt set off the Scramble, and sustained it until the end of the century.

British advances in tropical Africa have all the appearances of involuntary responses to emergencies arising from the decline of Turkish authority from the Straits to the Nile. These advances were decided by a relatively close official circle. They were largely the work of men striving in more desperate times to keep to the grand conceptions of world policy and the high standards of imperial security inherited from the mid-Victorian preponderance. Their purposes in Africa were usually esoteric; and their actions were usually inspired by notions of the world situation and calculations of its dangers, which were peculiar to the official mind.

So much for the subjective views which swayed the British partitioners. Plainly their preconceptions and purposes were one of the many objective causes of the partition itself. There remain the ultimate questions: how important a cause were these considerations of government? What were the other causes?

The answers are necessarily complicated, because they can be found only in the interplay between government's subjective appreciations and the objective emergencies. The moving causes appear to arise from chains of diverse circumstances in Britain, Europe, the Mediterranean, Asia and Africa itself, which interlocked in a set of unique relationships. These disparate situations, appraised by the official mind as a connected whole, were the products of different historical evolutions, some arising from national growth or decay, others from European expansion stretching as far back as the Mercantilist era. All of them were changing at different levels at different speeds. But although their paths were separate, they were destined to cross. There were structural changes taking place in European industry cutting down Britain's lead in commerce. The European balance of power was altering. Not only the emergence of Germany, but the alignment of France with Russia, the century-old opponent of British expansion, lessened the margins of imperial safety. National and racial feelings in Europe, in Egypt and South Africa were becoming more heated, and liberalism everywhere was on the decline. All these movements played some part in the African drama. But it seems that they were only brought to the point of imperialist action by the idiosyncratic reactions of British statesmen to internal crises in Africa. Along the Mediterranean shores, Muslim states were breaking down under European penetration. In the south, economic growth and colonial expansion were escaping from imperial control. These processes of growth or decay were moving on time scales different from that of the European expansion which was bringing them about.

By 1882 the Egyptian Khedivate had corroded and cracked after decades of European paramountcy. But economic expansion was certainly not the sufficient cause of the occupation. Hitherto, commerce and investment had gone on without the help of outright political control. The thrusts of the industrial economy into Egypt had come to a stop with Ismail's bankruptcy, and little new enterprise was to accompany British control. Although the expanding economy had helped to make a revolutionary situation in Egypt, it was not the moving interest behind the British invasion. Nor does it seem that Anglo-French rivalry or the state of the European balance precipitated the invasion. It was rather the internal nationalist reaction against a decaying government which split Britain from France and switched European rivalries into Africa. . . .

Both the crises of expansion and the official mind which attempted to control them had their origins in an historical process which had begun to unfold long before the partition of Africa began. That movement was not the manifestation of some revolutionary urge to empire. Its deeper causes do not lie in the last two decades of the century. The British advance at least, was not an isolated African episode. It was the climax of a longer process of growth and decay in Africa. The new African empire was improvised by the official mind, as events made nonsense of its old historiography and hustled government into strange deviations from old lines of policy. In the widest sense, it was an offshoot of the total processes of British expansion throughout the world and throughout the century.

How large then does the new African empire bulk in this setting? There are good reasons for regarding the mid-Victorian period as the golden age of British expansion, and the late-Victorian as an age which saw the beginnings of contraction and decline. The Palmerstonians were no more "anti-imperialist" than their successors, though they were more often able to achieve their purposes informally; and the late-Victorians were no more "imperialist" than their predecessors, though they were driven to extend imperial claims more often. To label them thus is to ignore the fact that whatever their method, they were both of set purpose engineering the expansion of Britain. Both preferred to promote trade and security without the expense of empire; but neither shrank from forward policies wherever they seemed necessary.

But their circumstances were very different. During the first three-quarters of the century, Britain enjoyed an almost effortless supremacy in the world outside Europe, thanks to her sea power and her industrial strength, and because she had little foreign rivalry to face. Thus Canning and Palmerston had a very wide freedom of action. On the one hand, they had little need to bring economically valueless regions such as tropical Africa into their formal empire for the sake of strategic security; and on the other, they were free to extend their influence and power to develop those regions best suited to contribute to Britain's strength. Until the 1880s, British political expansion had been positive, in the sense that it went on bringing valuable areas into her orbit. That of the late-Victorians in the so-called "Age of Imperialism" was by comparison negative, both in purpose and achievement. It was largely concerned with defending the maturing inheritance of the mid-Victorian imperialism of free trade, not with opening fresh fields of substantial importance to the economy. Whereas the earlier Victorians could afford to concentrate on the extension of free trade, their successors were compelled to look above all to the preservation of what they held, since they were coming to suspect that Britain's power was not what it once had been. The early Victorians had been playing from strength. The supremacy they had built in the world had been the work of confidence and faith in the future. The African empire of their successors was the product of fear lest this great heritage should be lost in the time of troubles ahead.

Because it went far ahead of commercial expansion and imperial ambition, because its aims were essentially defensive and strategic, the movement into Africa remained superficial. The partition of tropical Africa might seem impressive on the wall maps of the Foreign Office. Yet it was at the time an empty and theoretical expansion. That British governments before 1900 did very little to pacify, administer and develop their spheres of influence and protectorates, shows once again the weakness of any commercial and imperial motives for claiming them. The partition did not accompany, it preceded the invasion of tropical Africa by the trader, the planter and the official. It was the prelude to European occupation; it was not that occupation itself. The sequence illuminates the true nature of the British movement into tropical Africa. So far from commercial expansion requiring the extension of territorial claims, it was the extension of territorial claims which in time required commercial expansion. The arguments of the so-called new imperialism were *ex post facto* justifications of advances, they were not the original reasons for making them. Ministers had publicly justified their improvisations in tropical Africa with appeals to imperial sentiment and promises of African progress. After 1900, something had to be done to fulfill these aspirations, when the spheres allotted on the map had to be made good on the ground. The same fabulous artificers who had galvanized America, Australia and Asia, had come to the last continent.

Geoffrey Barraclough

INDUSTRIALISM AND IMPERIALISM
AS REVOLUTIONARY FORCES

Geoffrey Barraclough (b. 1908), professor of modern history at Oxford, is one of England's leading historians. He has written widely, on topics that range from medieval history (particularly medieval Germany) to modern international affairs. Among his works are The Origins of Modern Germany *(1946),* The Medieval Empire *(1950),* History in A Changing World *(1955), and shared authorship of three volumes of the* Survey of International Affairs. *The book from which this selection is drawn,* An Introduction to Contemporary History *(1964), argues that one of the great periodical revolutions of history took place in roughly the years 1890–1960, as the world moved from its "Modern" to its "Contemporary" period. Part of the evidence for this position Barraclough finds in the second industrial revolution and the European expansion at the end of the nineteenth century.*

When we seek to pinpoint the structural changes which lie at the roots of contemporary society, we are carried back to the last decade of the nineteenth century; and there we come to a halt. Even the most resolute upholder of the theory of historical continuity cannot fail to be struck by the extent of the differences between the world in 1870 and the world in 1900. In England, where the industrial revolution had begun early and advanced in a steady progression, the fundamental nature of the changes after 1870 is less apparent than elsewhere; but once we extend our vision to cover the whole world, their revolutionary character is beyond dispute. Even in continental Europe, with perhaps the sole exception of Belgium, industrialization was a product of the last quarter rather than of the first two-thirds of the nineteenth century; it was a consequence, rather than a concomitant, of the "railway age," which by 1870 had provided the Continent with a new system of communications. Across the Atlantic the Civil War had proved a major stimulus to industrialization; but it was after the ending of the Civil War in 1865 and the uneasy postwar interlude spanned by the presidencies of General Grant (1868–76) that the great industrial expansion be-

From *An Introduction to Contemporary History* by Geoffrey Barraclough (C. A. Watts & Co., London, 1964), pp. 36–39, 43–55, 57. Reproduced by permission of the publishers.

gan which transformed beyond recognition the society de Tocqueville had known and described. When in 1869 the first railroad to span the American continent was completed at a remote spot in Utah, the United States "ceased to be an Atlantic country in order to become a continental nation" of a new, highly industrialized pattern.

What happened in the closing decades of the nineteenth century was not, however, simply an expansion of the process of industrialization which had begun in England a century earlier, until it became worldwide. I have already referred to the distinction between the first industrial revolution and the second, or (as it is sometimes called) between the "industrial" and the "scientific" revolutions. It is, of course, a clumsy distinction, which does less than justice to the intricacy of the historical facts; but it is a real one. The industrial revolution in the narrower sense—the revolution of coal and iron—implied the gradual extension of the use of machines, the employment of men, women and children in factories, a fairly steady change from a population mainly of agricultural workers to a population mainly engaged in making things in factories and distributing them when they were made. It was a change that "crept on," as it were, "unawares," and its immediate impact, as Sir John Clapham made clear, can easily be exaggerated. The second industrial revolution was different. For one thing, it was far more deeply scientific, far less dependent on the "inventions" of "practical" men with little if any basic scientific training. It was concerned not so much to improve and increase the existing as to introduce new commodities. It was also far quicker in its impact, far more prodigious in its results, far more revolutionary in its effects on people's lives and outlook. And finally, though coal and iron were still the foundation, it could no longer be called the revolution of coal and iron. The age of coal and iron was succeeded, after 1870, by the age of steel and electricity, of oil and chemicals.

I

The technical aspects of this revolution do not concern us here, except insofar as is necessary in order to understand its effects outside the spheres of industry, science and technology. It would nevertheless be difficult to deny that the primary differentiating factor, marking off the new age from the old, was the impact of scientific and technological advance on society, both national and international. Even on the lowest level of practical everyday living it is surely significant that so many of the commonplace objects which we regard as normal concomitants of civilized existence today—the internal combustion engine, the telephone, the microphone, the gramophone, wireless telegraphy, the electric lamp, mechanized public transport, pneumatic tires, the bicycle, the typewriter, cheap mass-circulation newsprint, the first of the synthetic fibers, artificial silk, and the first of the synthetic plastics, Bakelite—all made their appearance in this period, and many of them in the fifteen years between 1867 and 1881; and although it was only after 1914, in response to military requirements, that intensive aircraft development began, the possibility of adapting the petrol-driven internal combustion engine to the airplane was successfully demonstrated by the brothers Wright in 1903. Here, as elsewhere, there was necessarily a time-lag before the problems of large-scale production were solved, and some of the things we have come to regard as normal —radio and television among them—obviously belong to a later phase. Nevertheless, it can fairly be said that, on the purely practical level of daily life, a person living today who was suddenly put back into the world of 1900 would find himself on familiar ground, whereas if he returned to 1870, even in industrialized Britain, the differences would probably be more striking than the similarities. In short, it was around 1900 that industrialization began to exert its influence on the living conditions of the masses in the West to such an extent that it is hardly possible today to realize the degree to which even the well-to-do in the previous generation had been compelled to make shift.

The basic reason for this difference is that few of the practical inventions listed above were the consequence of a steady piecemeal development or improvement of existing processes, the overwhelming majority resulted from new materials, new sources of power, and above all else from the application of scientific knowledge to industry. . . .

II

The scientific, technological and industrial changes I have briefly recapitulated are the starting-point for the study of contemporary history. They acted both as a solvent of the old order and as a catalyst of the new. They created urban and industrial society as we know it today; they were also the instruments by which industrial society, which at the close of the nineteenth century was still for all practical purposes confined to Western Europe and the United States, subsequently expanded into the industrially undeveloped parts of the world. Technology, it has been observed, is the branch of human experience people can learn most easily and with predictable results.

The new industrial techniques, unlike the old, necessitated the creation of large-scale undertakings and the concentration of the population in vast urban agglomerations. In the steel industry, for example, the introduction of the blast furnace meant that the small individual enterprise employing ten or a dozen workmen quickly became an anachronism. Furthermore, the process of industrial consolidation was accentuated by the crisis of overproduction which was the sequel of the new techniques and the immediate cause of the "great depression" between 1873 and 1895. The small-scale family businesses, which were typical of the first phase of industrialism, were in many cases too narrowly based to withstand the depression; nor had they always the means to finance the installation of new, more complicated and more expensive machinery. Hence the crisis, by favoring rationalization and unified management, was a spur to the large-scale concern and to the formation of trusts and cartels; and the process of concentration, once begun, was irreversible.

It went ahead most rapidly in the new industries, such as chemicals, but soon spread in all directions. In England at this time Brunner and Mond were laying the foundations of the vast ICI combine. In Germany the great Krupps steel undertaking, which had employed only one hundred and twenty-two men in 1846, had sixteen thousand on its payroll in 1873 and by 1913 was employing a total of almost seventy thousand. Its counterpart in France was Schneider-Creusot, employing ten thousand in 1869; its counterpart in Great Britain was Vickers-Armstrong. In the United States Andrew Carnegie was producing more steel than the whole of England put together when he sold out in 1901 to J. P. Morgan's colossal organization, the United States Steel Corporation. But these were the giants, and in many respects the average performance, as illustrated by the

German statistics, is more informative. Here, in the period between 1880 and 1914, the number of small industrial plants, employing five workmen or less, declined by half, while the larger factories, employing fifty or more, doubled; in other words, the number of industrial units declined, but those that remained were substantially larger and employed no less than four times the total of industrial workers recorded for 1880. Furthermore, outworkers, domestic weavers and the like, who had still been a considerable element in the German textile industries in the early days of the Second Empire—in 1875 nearly two-thirds of the cotton weavers in Germany were domestic outworkers—were virtually eliminated by 1907, as industrial concentration gathered pace. In short, the workers were being gathered into factories and the factories concentrated in industrial towns and urban areas.

The process of herding mill-hands and factory workers into fewer but larger combines was common to all the industrialized countries. It completely changed their physiognomy. The towns devoured the villages and large cities grew faster than small ones. Areas like the Ruhr valley in Germany and the "Black Country" of the English midlands became sprawling belts of contiguous urban development, divided theoretically by artificial municipal boundaries but otherwise without visible break. A further factor hastening and accentuating the influx into the cities was the agricultural crisis caused by the large-scale import of cheap foodstuffs from overseas. The result was the proliferation of social conditions unknown at any time in the past, the rise of what has usually been called a "mass society." As a consequence of the progress of hygiene and medicine the death rate, which had been virtually static between 1840 and 1870, declined abruptly in the following thirty years in the more advanced countries of Western Europe—in England, for example, by almost one-third from twenty-two to a little over fifteen per thousand—and the population soared. Compared with an increase of thirty millions between 1850 and 1870, the population of Europe—taking no account of emigration, which drew off 40 percent of the natural increase—rose by no less than one hundred million between 1870 and 1900.

It is a striking confirmation of the shift that was taking place that the whole of this immense increase in population was absorbed by the towns. In Germany, where the census of 1871 recorded only eight cities of over one hundred thousand inhabitants, there were thirty-three by the end of the century and forty-eight by 1910. In European Russia the number of towns in this category had risen by 1900 from six to seventeen. By this time also one-tenth of the inhabitants of England and Wales had been drawn into the vortex of London, and in the United States—although three million square miles of land were available for settlement—nearly half the population was concentrated on 1 percent of the available territory and one-eighth lived in the ten largest cities. Whereas before the revolution of 1848 Paris and London were the only towns with a population exceeding one million, the great metropolis now became the hub of industrial society. Berlin, Vienna, St. Petersburg and Moscow in Europe, New York, Chicago and Philadelphia in the United States, Buenos Aires and Rio de Janeiro in South America, and Tokyo, Calcutta and Osaka in Asia, all topped the million mark, and it is significant that the emergence of great metropolitan centers was worldwide and that in this respect at least Europe no longer stood out as exceptional.

This, without doubt, was the second most conspicuous aspect of the revolution that was taking place. If to change for all time the social structure of industrial society was its first consequence, its second was to achieve with fantastic speed the integration of the world. This was noted, as early as 1903, by the German historian, Erich Marcks. "The world," wrote Marcks, "is harder, more warlike, more exclusive; it is also, more than ever before, one great unit in which everything interacts and affects everything else, but in which also everything collides and clashes."

This does not imply, of course, that Europe had lost, or was losing, its preeminence; on the contrary, the rapidity and extent of their industrialization increased the lead of the European powers and enhanced their strength and self-confidence, and with the sole, if weighty, exception of the United States, the gap between them and the rest of the world widened; even the so-called "white" dominions, Canada, Australia and New Zealand, lagged far behind in 1900, and the industrialization of Japan, however remarkable in its own context, remained small by European standards until after 1914. But it is also true that the voracious appetite of the new industrialism, unable of its very nature to draw sufficient sustenance from local resources, rapidly swallowed up the whole wide world. It was no longer a question of exchanging European manufactures—predominantly textiles—for traditional oriental and tropical products, or even of providing outlets for the expanding iron and steel industries by building railways, bridges, and the like. Industry now went out into the world in search of the basic materials without which, in its new forms, it could not exist.

It was a fundamental change, one with far-reaching consequences, and it affected every quarter of the globe. Thus, for example, 1883 saw the discovery and exploitation of the vast Canadian nickel deposits, necessary for the new steel-making processes. By 1900 Chile, which had produced no nitrates thirty years earlier, accounted for three-quarters of the total world production, or 1.4 million metric tons. In Australia the Mount Morgan copper and gold mine was opened in 1882 and Broken Hill, the largest lead-zinc deposit in the world, the following year. At the same time the demands of the plating and canning industries for tin, and the rapid growth in the use of rubber in the electrical industry and for road transport, increased the trade of Malaya by very nearly a hundredfold between 1874 and 1914 and made it the richest of all colonial territories. This catalogue could be extended considerably, and it would be necessary in addition to include the stimulus to development in overseas and tropical territories arising from the requirements, already referred to, of growing industrial populations for cheap and plentiful food supplies. The result, in any case, was a transformation of world conditions without parallel in the past. The outer zone of primary producers was expanded from North America, Rumania and Russia to tropical and subtropical lands and further afield to Australasia, Argentina and South Africa; "areas and lines of commerce that had previously been self-contained dissolved into a single economy on a world scale." Improvements in ship-building, the decline of shipping charges, and the possibility of moving commodities in bulk, brought into existence for the first time in history a world market governed by world prices. By the close of the nineteenth century more of the world was more closely interlocked, economically and financially, than at any time before. In terms of world history—in terms even of European expansion as manifested down to the middle years of the nineteenth century—it was a situation that was entirely new, the product not of slow and continuous development, but of forces released suddenly and with revolutionary effect within the life span of one short generation.

III

It would have been surprising if these new forces had not sought a political outlet. In fact, as is well known, they did. Until a short time ago few historians would have denied that the "new imperialism," which was so distinctive a feature of the closing decades of the nineteenth century, was a logical expression or consequence of the economic and social developments in the industrialized countries of Europe and in the United States which I have attempted to describe. Latterly, however, there has been a growing tendency to challenge the validity of this interpretation. "New, sustained or compelling influences," it has been argued, were lacking in the 1880s; in particular, the evidence does not indicate that the direction of imperial expansion was influenced to any marked extent by new economic pressures. Some recent writers, indeed, have gone so far as to urge, paradoxically, that the last two decades of the nineteenth century witnessed not a gathering but a slackening of imperial pressures, and that the "informal" imperialism of the free trade period, though less concerned with political control, had been no less thrusting and aggressive. About these arguments it is sufficient to say three things. The first is that they have done little more, in the last analysis, than replace old conceptual difficulties by new. Secondly, because of their preoccupation with refuting the economic arguments of Hobson and Lenin, they have approached the question from too narrow an angle. And thirdly, by dealing with the problems almost exclusively from a British point of view, they have avoided the main issues. The central fact about the "new imperialism" is that it was a worldwide movement, in which all the industrialized nations, including the United States and Japan, were involved. If it is approached from the angle of Great Britain, as historians have largely been inclined to do, it is easy to underestimate its force and novelty; for the reactions of Britain, as the greatest existing imperial power, were primarily defensive, its statesmen were reluctant to acquire new territories, and when they did so their purpose was usually either to safeguard existing possessions or to prevent the control of strategic routes passing into the hands of other powers. But this defensive, and in some ways negative, attitude is accounted for by the special circumstances of Great Britain, and was not typical. It was from other powers that the impetus behind the "new imperialism" came—from powers that calculated that Britain's far-flung empire was the source of its might and that their own new-found industrial strength both entitled them to and necessitated their acquiring a "place in the sun."

It is not difficult to demonstrate that the specific arguments of Hobson and Lenin, according to whom imperialism was a struggle for profitable markets of investment, are not borne out by what is known of the flow of capital. That, however, is no reason to suppose that economic motives did not play their part; for the new imperialism was not simply a product of rational calculation, and business interests could be carried away by an optimism which subsequent events disproved.[1] Nor is it difficult to show at any particular point —for example, Gladstone's occupation of Egypt in 1882, or Bismarck's intervention in Africa in 1884—that the immediate causes of action were strategic or political; but these strategical considerations are only half the story, and it would be hard in the case of Bismarck to deny that it would have been difficult for him to envisage intervention in Africa if it had not been for the new frame of mind in Germany resulting from the rapid industrial development of the Reich after 1871. When we are told that the new imperialism was "a specifically political phenomenon in origin," the short answer is that in such a context the distinction between politics and economics is unreal. What have to be explained are the factors which distinguished late-nineteenth-century imperialism from the imperialism of preceding ages, and this cannot be done without

---

[1] For this reason it is difficult to follow the argument of A. J. Hanna, *European Rule in Africa* (London, 1961), p. 4, who seems to imply that the fact that the chartered company which Rhodes founded in 1889 was "unable to pay any dividends whatever" until 1923 disproves the generally accepted belief that "desire for economic gain" was an operative factor in Rhodes's enterprises. In any case failure to pay dividends does not necessarily mean that an undertaking is unprofitable to its promoters. As H. Brunschwig has said, *Mythes et réalités de l'impérialisme colonial français, 1871–1914* (Paris, 1960), p. 106, "*il apparut que des particuliers pouvaient s'enrichir aux colonies, même si, du point de vue général ... elles n'étaient pas rentables pour l'état.*" ["it appears that individuals could enrich themselves in the colonies even if, in a broader perspective, colonies were not profitable for the state."—Ed.]

taking account of the basic social and economic changes of the period after 1870. "I do not exactly know the cause of this sudden revolution," Lord Salisbury said in 1891, "but there it is." His instinctive perception that an abrupt change of mood and temper had occurred, was sound enough. Ever since Disraeli's Crystal Palace speech of 1872, ever since his realization in 1871 that "a new world" had emerged with "new influences at work" and "new and unknown objects and dangers with which to cope," statesmen were conscious of new pressures; and it was these pressures, stemming from the heart of industrial society, that were the explanation of the changed reactions to a power relationship that was substantially older. As the German historian Oncken put it, it was "as though a completely different dynamic governed the relations of the powers."

It was only to be expected that the impact of scientific and technological change should take some time to build up. Historians have made much recently of the fact that the doctrine of imperialism was only clearly formulated at "the very end of the century whose last decades it purported to interpret," but it would be surprising if it had been otherwise. Theory followed the facts; it was a gloss on developments which men like Chamberlain believed to have been building up over the last twenty or thirty years. In the first place, the industrial revolution had created an enormous differential between the developed and the undeveloped (or, as we would now say, the underdeveloped) parts of the world, and improved communications, technical innovations and new forms of business organization had increased immeasurably the possibilities of exploiting underdeveloped territories. At the same time science and technology had disturbed the existing balance between the more developed states, and the shift which now occurred in their relative strengths—in particular the rising industrial power of imperial Germany and the United States and the gathering speed of industrialization in Russia—was an incitement to the powers to seek compensation and leverage in the wider world. The impact of the prolonged depression between 1873 and 1896 worked in the same direction. Industry was confronted with compelling reasons for seeking new markets, finance for securing safer and more profitable outlets for capital abroad, and the erection of new tariff barriers—in Germany, for example, in 1879, in France in 1892—increased the pressure for overseas expansion. Even if only a marginal proportion of overseas investment went into colonial territories, the sums involved were by no means negligible, and it is clear that in some at least of the newly acquired tropical dependencies British finance found scope for investment and profit. The position was even clearer elsewhere—for example, in the Belgian Congo.[2]

From another point of view, the growing dependence of industrialized European societies on overseas supplies for foodstuffs and raw materials was a powerful stimulus to imperialism. Its most conspicuous result was the popularization of "neo-mercantilist" doctrines. Neo-mercantilism took hold with remarkable speed, first in France and Germany, then in Russia and the United States, and finally in England in the days of Joseph Chamberlain. Since in the new industrial age no nation could hope in the long run to be self-sufficient, it was necessary—according to neo-mercantilist arguments—for each industrial country to develop a colonial empire dependent upon itself, forming a large self-sufficient trading unit, protected if necessary by tariff barriers from outside competition, in which the home country would supply manufactured goods in return for foodstuffs and raw materials. The fallacies inherent in this doctrine have frequently been pointed out, both at the time and subsequently. They did nothing to lessen its psychological impact. "The day of small nations," said Chamberlain, "has long passed away; the day of Empires has come." In many ways the "new imperialism" reflected an obsession with the magic of size which was the counterpart of the new world of sprawling cities and towering machines.

In the arguments of the neo-mercantilists questions of prestige, economic motivations and sheer political maneuvers were all combined and it would be a mistake to try to pick out the one factor or the other and accord it priority. In France, Jules Ferry's speeches reveal a curious mixture of politics, prestige and crude economic arguments, in which the restoration of France's international standing, depressed by the defeats of 1870 and 1871, loomed large. The same mixture of motives was characteristic of German "world policy" after 1897, the advocates of which regarded a "broadening" of Germany's "economic basis" as essential as a means of ensuring it a leading place in the global constellation which now appeared to

---

[2] Here an investment of fifty million gold francs over a period of thirty years, between 1878 and 1908, produced revenues totalling sixty-six million gold francs by the latter date (Brunschwig, op. cit., p. 71).

be taking the place of the old European balance of power. In the United States, it may be true that the administration was interested primarily in securing naval bases for strategic purposes; but the "expansionists of 1898" had few doubts or hesitations on the economic score, demanding the Spanish colonies in the interests of trade and surplus capital. As for Russia, economic motives certainly played little, if any, part in the great Russian advance across central Asia between 1858 and 1876—it would be surprising if at that stage they had done so—but after 1893 the position was different. Witte, the great Russian finance minister, was a convinced and thoroughgoing exponent of neo-mercantilist principles; his monument is the trans-Siberian railway. In the famous memorandum which he addressed to Czar Alexander III in 1892, he set out his ideas on a grand scale. The new railway, Witte said, would not only bring about the opening of Siberia, but would revolutionize world trade, supersede the Suez Canal as the leading route to China, enable Russia to flood the Chinese market with textiles and metal goods, and secure political control of northern China. Strategically, it would strengthen the Russian Pacific fleet and make Russia dominant in Far Eastern waters.

With ideas such as these in the ascendant, it is not surprising that the scramble for colonies gathered pace at an unprecedented rate. By 1900 European civilization overshadowed the earth. In less than one generation one-fifth of the land area of the globe and one-tenth of its inhabitants had been gathered into the imperial domains of the European powers. . . .

There was, without doubt, something febrile and inherently unstable about the "gaudy empires spatchcocked together" in this way at this time; except for the Russian gains in central Asia few of the territories concerned were destined to remain in undisturbed possession for as much as three-quarters of a century. It was nevertheless a stupendous movement, without parallel in history, which completely changed the shape of things to come, and to argue, as historians have recently done, that there was "no break in continuity after 1870" or, still more, that it was an age not of expansion but of "contraction and decline," does less than justice to its importance. . . .

D. C. M. Platt

THE "IMPERIALISM OF FREE TRADE": SOME RESERVATIONS

D. C. M. Platt (b. 1934), professor of Latin American history at Oxford and director of the Centre of Latin American Studies, has specialized in the study of British–Latin American relations in the nineteenth century. His major works include Finance, Trade, and Politics in British Foreign Policy, 1815–1914 *(1968) and* Latin American and British Trade, 1806–1914 *(1972). He has also written several articles on the interpretation of nineteenth-century expansion, using his detailed knowledge of British finance and trade in that period to criticize some of the generalizations of Robinson and Gallagher, Fieldhouse, and others.*

Fifteen years ago the *Economic History Review* published an article by J. Gallagher and R. Robinson on "The Imperialism of Free Trade." It was an article attractive both for the novelty of its interpretation of mid-Victorian imperialism and for the skill with which this interpretation was presented—so attractive, indeed, that its main theme, controversial as it is, has remained unchallenged.

Gallagher and Robinson turned their attention to the "myth" of mid-Victorian anti-imperialism, to the traditional belief that statesmen and officials distrusted expansionism and were indifferent even to the maintenance of the existing empire. Drawing examples from both the "formal" and the "informal" empires, they argued that the mid-Victorian decades were in fact the "decisive stage in the history of British expansion overseas," and that British governments in this period—as in that of the "New Imperialism"—showed themselves willing at all times "to establish and maintain British paramountcy by whatever means best suited the circumstances of their diverse regions of interest." The object of paramountcy was the security of British trade and investment, on behalf of which the British government was prepared, if it were expedient to do so, even to undertake annexation and formal control overseas: "The usual summing up of the policy of the free trade empire as 'trade not rule'

From D. C. M. Platt, "The Imperialism of Free Trade: Some Reservations," *The Economic History Review*, 2nd ser., XXI, no. 2 (August 1968), 296–306 (with omissions). By permission of the author and the Economic History Society.

should read 'trade with informal control if possible; trade with rule when necessary.' "

Prof. MacDonagh[1] has since questioned the link which Gallagher and Robinson established between imperialism and free trade. Basing his argument primarily on the opinions of Richard Cobden, the most influential free trader of the day, he showed that the natural attitude of doctrinaire free traders was anti-imperialist: the phrase "the imperialism of free trade" is therefore a misnomer and, in fact, "suggests the opposite of the truth." But he left it at that, merely sketching in, in his concluding paragraphs, a few reservations about the core of the Gallagher and Robinson thesis—the continuity which they claim to have found in British imperial policy for mid- and late-Victorians alike.

The article which follows will concern itself with this "continuity," and with the portrait Gallagher and Robinson have drawn of British official policy in relation to overseas trade and investment.

I

Gallagher and Robinson describe the great efforts made by mid-Victorian governments, both in the formal and informal dependencies, "to open the continental interiors and to extend British influence inland from the ports and to develop the hinterlands." The object was to create "complementary satellite economies" supplying raw materials and food, and opening markets in return for manufactured goods. Traditionally, historians have interpreted the mid-Victorian period as one in which "the political arm of expansion was dormant or even withered." In fact, Gallagher and Robinson argue,

> *that alleged inactivity is seen to be a delusion if we take into account the development in the informal aspect. Once entry had been forced into Latin America, China and the Balkans, the task was to encourage stable governments as good investment risks, just as in weaker or unsatisfactory states it was considered necessary to coerce them into more cooperative attitudes.*

But is this really acceptable as a description of official policy to-

---

[1] Oliver MacDonagh, "The Anti-Imperialism of Free Trade," *Economic History Review* 2nd ser., 14 (1962), 489–501.

wards overseas trade and investment during the high summer of laissez-faire and free trade? It is true that the British government, in the century before 1914, regarded itself as bound, so far as possible, to open the world to trade. "It is the business of Government," Palmerston told Auckland in 1841, "to open and to secure the roads for the merchant," and no Victorian, however much he may have differed about the means by which this might be achieved, had any argument with the ends. In Latin America, in the Levant, and in the Far East, British governments took what action they could to open markets and to keep those markets open. But what they were prepared to do fell far short of the energetic promotion and intervention described by Gallagher and Robinson, and it fell short in the following respects: the range of government action on behalf of overseas trade permitted by the laissez-faire tradition of the time was extraordinarily narrow; official demands on behalf of British interests overseas never went beyond equal favor and open competition; nonintervention in the internal affairs of foreign states was one of the most respected principles of British diplomacy; and force, while often called for in the protection of British subjects injured by government action abroad, was rarely and only exceptionally employed for the promotion of British trade and investments.

No historian of the mid-Victorian period can ignore what was one of the most characteristic attitudes of Victorian government; its reluctance to extend its responsibilities beyond the minimum required to guarantee the free play of the market, the normal interaction of supply and demand. The attitude of those officials whose concern was primarily with trade and finance was overwhelmingly laissez-faire. E. A. Bowring (of the Board of Trade) claimed that the difficulty in 1860 was to make any selection from the mass of evidence which could be used to demonstrate the benefits brought, in a mere fifteen or sixteen years, by the adoption of the principles of free trade, "or, to speak more accurately, from the reversion to the simple precepts of Nature, which have been so well epitomized by a great Frenchman in five short words: *Laissez-faire et laissez aller.*" Lord Farrer, while still Permanent Secretary to the Board of Trade, concluded his work on *The State in its Relation to Trade* (1883) with the observation that the state's "chief praise in relation to trade has been that it has left as much scope as possible to the free energy and self-interest of its people." Even after the experience of a couple of decades of foreign competition—increasingly threatening in neutral and home markets—Sir Courtenay Boyle (Permanent Secretary to the Board of Trade, 1893–1901) maintained that the state could give only limited assistance in developing and increasing our competitive power; Britain's commercial position had been attained, and must be preserved, by individual effort, and what the state could properly do was limited to the supply of accurate commercial information.

Whatever may have happened later under pressure of commercial depression and international competition, there can be no doubt that, back in the mid-Victorian period, laissez-faire and its economic expression, free trade, were unchallenged dogma at the Board of Trade; and at this period it was the Board's Commercial Department, under Louis Mallet, unreservedly Cobdenite, which supervised the conduct of the government's commercial policy overseas. What is more, in determining British policy even in what were known as the "semi-civilized" sectors of the world, the tradition of laissez-faire in relation to overseas trade and investment was paralleled by an equally strong tradition in British political diplomacy: nonintervention in the internal affairs of foreign states.

II

Gallagher and Robinson chose Britain's "informal empire" in Latin America as the main prop of their argument for the mid-Victorian period, and in terms simply of volume of trade there was good reason for doing so. At the time, Latin America seemed by far the most promising of the new markets opening to Britain's expanding exports. Brazil in 1828 was the third largest foreign market for British produce and manufactures (after the United States and Germany) and sixth in the list of our suppliers. If the "imperialism of free trade" were to operate anywhere, Latin America was its most obvious target. But was this in fact the case?

In the first years of the nineteenth century, the disastrous episode of the British expeditions to Buenos Aires had taught British statesmen resolutely to refuse further intervention or entanglement in the internal political affairs of Latin America. In a cabinet memorandum of 1807 Castlereagh rejected altogether any prospect of territorial acquisition, any dream of exclusive British political influence, or any intention to intervene further in the political condition of the Spanish colonies; Britain's sole interest was in cutting off one of Napoleon's chief resources and in opening up the markets to British manufactures. And those markets were to be opened on equal terms to world trade. Late in 1815 Castlereagh refused outright Spain's offer of special trading privileges in return for British mediation and active assistance with the rebellious colonies. He advised the Spanish government that "the Prince Regent has never sought for any exclusive advantages. He has always recommended the commerce of South America to be opened to all nations upon moderate duties, with a reasonable preference to Spain herself."

Canning's policy for Latin America, and that of his successors down to Sir Edward Grey, followed precisely these lines: nonintervention in the internal affairs of the new republics, and a commercial objective restricted to maintaining fair and equal treatment for British trade in relation to the trade of other nations. "The situation of affairs changes so frequently and so rapidly in these South American states," Palmerston minuted in 1835, "that . . . the safest course for English authorities to pursue seems to be to abstain rigidly from all interference in the internal dissensions of these republics." And when Grey summarized British policy to the Dominion delegates at the Imperial Conference of 1911, he explained that it was a standing instruction to all British diplomatists in South America that they were not to take any hand in politics or attempt to acquire political influence; their work was limited to upholding British commercial interests, and British governments had kept, and would continue to keep, carefully clear of all entanglements in the complex interrelationships of the Central and South American republics.

It is not easy to reconcile this, the traditional British policy in Latin America, with the policy described by Gallagher and Robinson. For them, no more spectacular example existed of "a policy of commercial hegemony in the interests of high politics, or of the use of informal political supremacy in the interests of commercial enterprise" than Canning's recognition of the republics in and after 1824. Britain, it appears, aimed in South America at "indirect political hegemony . . . for the purposes of trade"; she had some success in establishing informal control over Argentina and Brazil by the last decades of the century, and her attempts to turn Texas, Mexico, and Central America into informal dependencies were thwarted only by

American political strength; her method was "to encourage stable governments as good investment risks," and to coerce "weaker or unsatisfactory states into more cooperative attitudes."

No doubt British trade and finance might have avoided some disasters, and encountered others, if the government had been prepared to act as Gallagher and Robinson suggest. But of course it was not. Canning, Temperley explains, was well aware that attempts to stabilize conditions in Latin America would only have resulted in that perpetual interference in their politics which he so detested. He hoped to promote political tranquillity by developing trade, "but he always refused to sanction their loans or to give direct financial aid, for he knew that such financial methods would bring political complications in their train." Repeatedly thereafter the British government refused to become engaged in any respect in the internal politics of the republics, even at the sacrifice of British trading and financial interests....

III

As a further illustration, Gallagher and Robinson use mid-Victorian policy in the Far East. They refer to the "spectacular exertions of British policy in China," where, apparently, Britain enjoyed a "political hold" over the Chinese government which she employed, unsuccessfully, to break down Chinese self-sufficiency.

It was certainly the case that Britain took the leading part, by the Treaties of Nanking and Tientsin, in opening China to trade. But Lord Elgin was instructed to bear in mind throughout the Tientsin negotiations that, in opening this trade, "Her Majesty's Government have no desire to obtain any exclusive advantages for British trade in China, but are only desirous to share with all other nations any benefits which they may acquire in the first instance specifically for British commerce." This remained as British policy until after the troubles of 1898, and although Britain maintained its "paramountcy" in Chinese trade until the end of the century, the paramountcy was created by the existing network of British commercial and financial interests in China and Hong Kong, and owed nothing to any deliberate action by the government against its trading rivals....

The violence which accompanied the opening of the Chinese ports to world trade, and the strong position traditionally enjoyed by British trade and finance on the China coast, have tended to distort the final picture both of what actually happened in China in the middle decades of the last century and of the extent to which it affected the imperial government at Peking. Events of importance to Europeans were mere pinpricks on the maritime fringes of a great empire. European trade never made any real impact on the interior of China, and the efforts of mid-Victorian officials were restricted almost exclusively to the regulation of trade at the treaty ports. To write, as Gallagher and Robinson have done, of "Britain's political hold upon China" is to exaggerate beyond recognition, to confuse the troubles of a provincial governor with the responsibilities of an emperor. British officials at the time were more realistic. "The magnitude of our commercial interest," Sir Thomas Wade[2] told Salisbury early in 1880, "is constantly mistaken for an equal measure of political influence, which we no more possess than any other barbarian state."

IV

... The quarrel with the "imperialism of free trade" is one of degree. Mid-Victorian governments were prepared to promote and protect British trade, but to what extent? Can their action, such as it was, be described as "imperialism," formal or informal? Was the government ready to seek out "paramountcy" in the interests of British trade, by informal control if possible, formal control if necessary? Or was this "paramountcy" automatic, created by Britain's industrial and financial lead, through the agency of British traders and investors and without government intervention?

Gallagher and Robinson seem to have assumed that the limits of action open to mid-Victorian governments were very generous indeed, and that apart from a preference for informal over formal control, the government was prepared to go to extreme lengths in support of British trade and investment overseas:

> It is absurd to deduce from the harmony between London and the colonies of white settlement in the mid-Victorian age any British reluctance to intervene in the fields of British interests. The warships at Canton are as much a part of the period as responsible government for Canada; the battlefields of the Punjab are as real as the abolition of suttee.

[2] Sir Thomas Wade was British ambassador in Peking in 1871–83.—Ed.

But Whitehall's preference for laissez-faire and the restrictions on official policy in Latin America and China suggest that there was indeed a reluctance to intervene. The government was always prepared to negotiate "open-door" commercial treaties, even, on occasions, in face of strong opposition from local interests. It was always ready to use its diplomatic and consular stations abroad for the defense of British subjects against outrage and injury, and for the compilation and transmission of commercial intelligence. But there its functions ended. The promotion of individual interests was no part of official responsibilities; the government's duty, Layard told the Commons in 1864, was not to watch over one interest to the exclusion of all others but to promote the general welfare of the community. "No rule," wrote Sir Robert Morier[3] twenty years later, "has been more absolutely insisted upon in the dealings of Her Majesty's Missions abroad than this one, that, unless there is denial of justice, or treatment of British subjects engaged in mercantile transactions contrary to Treaties or to the spirit of Treaties, no assistance shall be rendered to further private interests." The government took no responsibility for the issue or expenditure of foreign government loans; nor was it prepared to back commercial or financial enterprises outside the empire. Earl Percy[4] warned Mr. Joseph Walton, M.P., as late as 1904, that the British government had hitherto kept to its old system of drawing a clear line of demarcation between the province of the state and the province of the individual trader; it had "deliberately adopted an attitude of laissez-faire," and it altogether declined to use state credit for the purpose of financing and assisting industrial or commercial undertakings overseas. As for defaults and debt-collecting, British policy was modeled on Canning's outright refusal to intervene; Canning did not "consider it as any part of the duty of the Government to interfere in any way to procure the repayment of loans made by British subjects to Foreign Powers, States, or Individuals." . . .

What remains, then, to call by the name "imperialism"? Nonintervention and laissez-faire were the characteristic attitudes of mid-Victorian officialdom, and these attitudes were faithfully reflected overseas. It is *not* true, for example, that British government policy

---

[3] Sir Robert Morier: British diplomat at Lisbon (1876–81), Madrid (1881–84), St. Petersburg (1884–93).—Ed.
[4] Earl Percy was British Undersecretary for Foreign Affairs, 1903–1905.—Ed.

in Latin America was to obtain "indirect political hegemony over the new regions for the purposes of trade," or to create "a new and informal empire" in the interests of future British commercial expansion. It is *not* the case that the mid-Victorian Foreign Office, in any positive or consistent sense, encouraged stable governments in Latin America, in China, and in the Balkans as good investment risks, and coerced weaker or unsatisfactory states into more cooperative attitudes. It can *not* be argued that Britain had a "political hold" on China, nor can it be denied that the government was reluctant to intervene over a wide field of British trade and financial interest and was particularly anxious to avoid the use of force to promote a trade. Above all, the policy of a laissez-faire, noninterventionist government can *not* realistically be described as "trade with informal control if possible; trade with rule when necessary."

So far as an "imperialism of free trade" can be said to have existed at all—and Prof. MacDonagh has already warned us how misleading that title can be[5]—it was limited to the opening of world markets on equal terms to international trade: an action which, though it may have ended occasionally in violence, at no stage made any claim to exclusive political influence or control, to new territory, or to preferential treatment. Actual imperial annexations in Africa and the East during the mid-Victorian period were seldom directly connected with the interests of British trade; they were designed primarily to safeguard existing frontiers and to establish government control and discipline over existing British communities. Elsewhere, the restriction of British government intervention to the creation of a "fair field and no favor" for British trade meant that spheres of interest or influence—though existent for political purposes in some parts of the Levant and Southeast Asia—had no relevance to the needs of British trade and finance.

Gallagher and Robinson carry conviction only in their emphasis on the continued importance in British government policy of the security of British trade. In this respect there was an indisputable continuity in official policy. But there was no continuity as between the mid- and late-Victorians in the steps that they were prepared to take

---

[5] The obvious exception is Hong Kong. But the acquisition of this barren island as an administrative center and *entrepôt* for British trade on the China coast was no more intended as a *point d'appui* for imperialistic designs on China than the Portuguese settlement at Macao.

in defense of British trade. It is here that the conventional interpretation of a break in the character of British imperialism after 1880—of the emergence of a "new imperialism"—begins to make sense. For, up to this point in time (*pace* Gallagher and Robinson), the dominant characteristics of British commercial and financial diplomacy were nonintervention and laissez-faire, and imperialism, informal or formal, was the last thing to be expected from laissez-faire. British "paramountcy" was the creation of our head-start in industrialization—it was the creation of the British traders and investors themselves, who neither sought nor expected government intervention.

The revolution in policy after 1880 was the recognition that a continued equality of opportunity for British trade and investment depended on an altogether new concept of the scope of government responsibility—a concept which included preemptive annexation and the outright delimitation of spheres of interest and influence *in the interests of commerce and finance.* The pressure of renewed protectionism, the partition of the world into colonial or semicolonial enclosures surrounded by high tariff barriers, and the development of a new form of interventionist financial diplomacy made any less active policy an abandonment of an obligation to which all British governments subscribed—the official duty to maintain a "fair field and no favor" for British interests at home and abroad.

The error in the "imperialism of free trade"—by which alone the phrase can have any meaning—is in the assumption that the mid-Victorians anticipated and shared this enlarged view of government responsibilities; that "throughout, British governments worked to establish and maintain British paramountcy by whatever means best suited the circumstances of their diverse regions of interest"; that mid-Victorian statesmen and officials were as ready as the late-Victorians (under very different circumstances) to undertake informal control if possible, rule if necessary, in the interests of British trade. The official attitude to trade promotion overseas is more accurately described by Walter Bagehot in his biographical sketch of Lord Clarendon (for eight years Foreign Secretary during the mid-Victorian period). Clarendon, Bagehot explained, was always ready to use the agency of the Foreign Office to forward commercial interests, but he employed only "legitimate functions" for trade promotion, interesting himself above all in the provision of improved commercial intelligence. He was too much a man of his times to adopt an aggressive foreign policy in the interests of trade, since "the old notion of fighting for foreign markets, or of intriguing for their exclusive use, had completely died out."

D. K. Fieldhouse
IMPERIALISM AND THE PERIPHERY

David Kenneth Fieldhouse (b. 1925), Beit Lecturer in Commonwealth History at Oxford, has published extensively in the field of colonial and imperial history. His article, " 'Imperialism': An Historiographical Revision," Economic History Review (1961), was a sharp and widely known attack on the theories of Hobson and Lenin. His later book, The Colonial Empires (1966), and his collection of readings, The Theory of Capitalist Imperialism (1967), continued in this vein. Economics and Empire, 1830–1914 (1973), his most recent work, the one from which the following selection is taken, is a full-length attempt to deal with the whole problem of the origins and nature of nineteenth-century European expansion, in particular to balance economic and non-economic, and metropolitan and peripheral, factors.

Peripheral Explanations of Imperialism

All explanations of European expansion so far considered[1] have three common features. All were "Eurocentric" in that they concentrated on problems and ideas within Europe and North America. All treated imperialism as a positive phenomenon: Europe deliberately acquired new colonies because she needed or wanted them. Finally, the problem was considered in the restricted context of the last quarter of the nineteenth century. Excluding Schumpeter's atavistic theory, all assumed that expansion occurred when it did because of the special character of this period, so that there was little or no

Reprinted from D. K. Fieldhouse, *Economics and Empire, 1830–1914* (1973), pp. 76–84, 467–77. Copyright © D. K. Fieldhouse 1973. Used by permission of Cornell University Press and George Weidenfeld and Nicolson Ltd., London.

[1] I.e., Fieldhouse's previous discussion of certain economic and political theories. —Ed.

continuity in the history of European imperialism before and after the 1870s.

Preliminary analysis has, however, suggested that these theories were in some degree defective precisely because of their preoccupation with Europe and the fact that they ignored longer-term historical trends. In terms of geography it was seen that in almost every case a theory based on European needs or attitudes was only viable if it took account of conditions on the periphery. As two historians [Robinson and Gallagher] have put the point in relation to Africa:

> *Scanning Europe for the causes, the theorists of imperialism have been looking for the answers in the wrong places. The crucial changes that set all working took place in Africa itself.*

But Eurocentric theories were almost equally weak in terms of chronology. Even the most superficial examination of the imperialist process indicates that it is unwise to look for the explanation of events during the so-called "age of imperialism" merely within the short period of time after about 1880, and this suggests that the apparent discontinuity of the historical process may be an illusion.

Dissatisfaction with these aspects of conventional explanations of late-nineteenth-century European expansion is a logical reason for attempting to construct alternative hypotheses which avoid their defects by concentrating on developments on the periphery and which take a longer-term view of trends. But such an approach is not a mere *pis aller.* Any historian who begins a study of colonial history by examining evidence in the one-time colonies rather than in the archives of Europe would find it natural to regard European expansion as the product of peripheral rather than metropolitan developments. How far this approach will serve varies from one region to another. In some cases what Cecil Rhodes called "the imperial factor" became significant only at the end of the story, when a European government had to give its formal sanction to acts initiated by men on the periphery. In others Europe became directly involved at an early stage. But always the impression is that formal colonization was a response to situations which evolved far from Europe and beyond effective metropolitan control. This is a far cry from theories of imperialism in which the future colonies are regarded as lay figures in a drama which centers on the banks, warehouses, chanceries or hustings of Europe.

There would seem, therefore, to be a strong case for approaching the problem of modern imperialism from the standpoint of problems developing outside Europe and on the assumption that colonization may have constituted a response by the metropolitan powers to external stimuli rather than the expression of economic or other problems within Europe. Since this approach is generally adopted in the rest of this book it will be convenient by way of introduction to indicate some of the characteristic trends and situations on the periphery which demanded some form of action by European states. But one reservation must be made. By definition peripheral explanations are a residual category. Because they deal in specific events they cannot form the basis for any general theory of imperialism. At most, observation of recurrent patterns may justify the conclusion that since many peripheral problems stemmed from the same broad expansion of European activities they had common features and required similar remedies.

In all regional studies of situations in Africa, Asia and the Pacific which ultimately led to formal European rule during or after the nineteenth century the underlying theme is that a fundamental change took place in the relations between Europeans and other peoples. Such changes took two forms. First, the partial or total insulation of other places from Europe was ended. Second, the power relationship between Europeans and other peoples changed dramatically. These processes occurred simultaneously and stemmed from the same roots. Together they generated the peripheral problems from which European empires eventually grew.

During the nineteenth century Europe at last breached the geographical limits of its influence during the previous three centuries. European exploration, trade and settlement had expanded spectacularly since the fifteenth and sixteenth centuries, yet huge areas of the world remained unaffected and largely unknown until the nineteenth century. To some extent this was the result of deliberate choice, but far more of technical factors—the relative inefficiency of sailing ships for long-distance bulk carriage, the small marginal advantage provided by European armaments, problems of health in tropical climates, and so on. During the early nineteenth century these obstacles to European expansion were removed by economic, technical and political developments within Europe. In nontechnical terms it can be said that in this period Europe underwent a "power revolution" which had no complement in other civilizations. This was most obvious in technology and industry. In about 1750 Europe possessed practically no industrial or technical advantages over producers in the more sophisticated Asian countries. A century later this was no longer true. Mechanization of production had given the European manufacturer an immense advantage in quality and price. The evolution of the heavy iron and steel industry had revolutionized machinery and armaments and was affecting ship construction. The steam engine both contributed to industrial efficiency and provided motive power for railways and ships, thus stimulating a revolution in the means of transport. At the same time population growth provided a labor force for expanding industry and a reservoir of potential emigrants. In some states there was a comparable improvement in the efficiency of government which was reflected in the armed forces and capacity to intervene in distant parts of the world.

This power revolution was bound to affect relations between the industrialized states of Western Europe and the rest of the world. Until other societies adopted the new technology Europe was in a uniquely dominant position. She could penetrate all markets, tap all sources of raw materials and impose her will on all indigenous governments. The vital question was what precise political form the new relationship would take. Would Europe and her existing communities of white colonists be content to exploit the new economic opportunities without also imposing formal political control as had once been done in America and India? Conversely, even if Europeans were content with that degree of "informal empire" which was inseparable from economic and military predominance, recognizing and cooperating with indigenous governments in Africa and the East, could these unreconstructed states and societies sustain the impact of accelerating European penetration?

In retrospect, of course, the general answers are clear. Though with considerable hesitation, European influence was eventually converted to empire in most, though not all, parts of Africa, Asia and the Pacific. But why did this occur and why in some places and not in others? There are two ways of approaching this question. One is to ask whether "informal empire" eventually proved unsatisfactory to those in Europe who were active on the periphery, so that these men demanded more complete political control to serve their own economic or other interests. The other is to see whether things broke down at the periphery, so that European governments were pulled in to deal with incipient or actual crises whatever their chosen policy. How can the historian best investigate the facts along these two lines?

To consider first the question of European attitudes to peripheral problems, it is possible that an approach along these lines may make some "Eurocentric" explanations of imperialism more credible than they would be in the form outlined above. It was seen that a major weakness of such theories was that they specified a positive demand for colonies which is difficult to substantiate. But if cause and effect are inverted and we consider whether imperialism might be a reaction to unsatisfactory conditions on the periphery, any of these hypotheses may make better sense. Thus merchants, who had not previously thought that tropical colonies were particularly valuable for trading purposes, might turn imperialist if and when existing or prospective markets in Africa or Asia were threatened by new obstacles created by indigenous governments or another European state. European capitalists, who took an entirely nonpolitical view of the world's investment potential, might nevertheless demand political action, even colonial rule, if an indigenous government reneged on loans made by European banks. Those engaged on capitalist enterprises overseas might equally welcome the imperial factor if they could not otherwise obtain satisfactory political conditions for plantations, mines and so on. This is very different from saying that merchants and finance capitalists wanted colonies because these were the *sine qua non* for their activities; but it does suggest that business interests might on occasion come to favor formal as opposed to informal empire. Similar considerations may have affected the views of European statesmen or nationalists. Though perhaps not initially enthusiastic about imperial expansion, they might be roused by evidence that changing conditions on the periphery were threatening real or imagined national interests. In short, and without at present evaluating the hypothesis, it may be possible to rehabilitate certain elements in most "Eurocentric" explanations of imperialism by inverting their assumptions. European imperialism may be explicable as a reaction of merchants, bankers, statesmen and jingoes to changes on the periphery which made it inconvenient or even impossible to preserve "informal empire" during the last decades of the nineteenth century. . . .

The obverse and complement to this modified exposition of European imperialism is to investigate why crises occurred on the periphery and why in some cases they led to alien rule. This, of course, requires detailed examination of each case. . . . It may, nevertheless, clarify the nature of the peripheral approach to imperialism to construct models of three of the more common situations which tended to destroy the existing balance between Europeans and other peoples and possibly lead to full annexation.

Colonial Sub-Imperialism. One of the more obvious factors in the extension of formal empire was the tendency of existing European possessions to expand into their environment. Two characteristic situations can be defined, one typical of colonies of European settlement, the other of colonies in which a small minority of Europeans ruled an indigenous society. Settler expansion was as old as European overseas colonization. Any group of emigrants who established an initial settlement on the tidewater of America, South Africa or Australia regarded the hinterland as a providential endowment for its future existence and growth. In the still colonial world the most probable regions for future settler expansion were Australia, Southern and Central Africa, the South Pacific, Southern Siberia and North Africa. During the period covered by this study these tendencies were at the root of many of the problems facing metropolitan governments on the periphery and, as will be seen, were primarily responsible for territorial expansion in these regions. In this respect imperialism may be seen as a classic case of the metropolitan dog being wagged by its colonial tail.

Settler sub-imperialism is an obvious phenomenon. Less obvious was the tendency of almost all European colonies or even small trading bases in Africa and Asia to expand into their environment, irrespective of the needs or wishes of the imperial power. The reasons were as various as the character of the territories: frontier insecurity, real or imagined; the need for more customs revenues from nearby ports; desire to control areas of production or trade routes on which the colonial economy depended; the ambitions or ideals of individual administrators, soldiers, missionaries and other Europeans temporarily employed there. Equally important, it was remarkable that many if not most colonial officials came to see local problems with local rather than metropolitan eyes, responding chameleon-like to the sub-imperialism of the frontier, whatever the established policy of the imperial government. In this way the official mind of the metropolis had its parallel in virtually every petty tropical or subtropical dependency, each generating its own form of autochthonous imperialism.

Important though it was as a force making for the extension of formal empire, sub-imperialism in existing European colonies does not exhaust the potential stock of peripheral explanations of imperial expansion. In many cases the key to events lies in analysis of the attitudes of non-Europeans or of the effects of informal European contacts on indigenous societies and governments.

Non-European Reactions. A basic weakness of many Eurocentric theories of imperialism is that they treat non-Europeans as lay figures, whereas modern research has emphasized the vast and decisive importance of the way in which indigenous peoples reacted to the intrusion of Europeans and its associated problems. Such reactions are intrinsic to a peripheral approach to European expansion, for in many places it is clear that the main if not the only stimulus to alien occupation and formal rule was the problem of deteriorating relations with non-Europeans. Obviously such problems varied immensely and cannot be reduced to a formula. But to clarify the concept it is proposed to indicate three characteristic situations which . . . might well eventually lead to the imposition of formal empire by one or other of the European powers.

The first was particularly characteristic of states and societies of considerable political or ideological strength and cohesiveness: for example, most of the Islamic states of the Mediterranean and Middle East, the civilized and sophisticated states of Southeast Asia and the stronger "pagan" states of sub-Saharan Africa. In these regions almost all indigenous states sooner or later reacted strongly against the presence of Europeans, either as intrusive neighbors or as infiltrators demanding political or religious rights. In the Islamic states of North Africa resistance came late, usually after an indigenous ruler had been forced by financial or some other weakness to transfer part of his sovereign power to alien "advisors," and it then took the form of a xenophobic popular movement or religious *jihad* to throw off foreign interference. In different circumstances comparable resistance occurred in Afghanistan, Turkestan, Burma and Indo-China; and in each case except that of Afghanistan indigenous resistance led ultimately to formal annexation. Conversely many other powerful states, including a number in sub-Saharan Africa, never willingly accepted informal European suzerainty or the need for peaceful coexistence; and in the course of time those which were thought to constitute a danger to the security of nearby European possessions or obstructed European commercial or other objectives were attacked and annexed. Thus, while by no means all indigenous states which resisted European penetration became formal dependencies, resistance was often the prelude to annexation when European interests were of sufficient importance to justify such action.

An alternative reaction to the European presence was to accept and make use of it. Indeed many non-European rulers obtained considerable short-term advantages from alliance with Europeans, acquiring money, guns or political support against indigenous rivals for power or territory in return for collaboration of many kinds. But in the end all such alliances became the kiss of death. Sooner or later the balance of local power turned against those who had treated Europeans as allies and equals. Some rulers found themselves ousted from effective power and used as puppet heads of state in a European protectorate; others were deposed when they tried to end an agreement or stand on their rights. In virtually every case indigenous collaboration ended in alien rule before 1914.

A third consequence of European informal penetration was to be found in weak indigenous states whose political and social systems could not withstand foreign pressure. In many parts of Africa and the Pacific, where political units were small and religions primitive, the presence of small numbers of European traders, planters, missionaries and beachcombers could erode indigenous institutions and social cohesion. Matters were made worse by rivalry between Europeans and by intermittent intervention by European military or naval forces. In the end such places, particularly in the Pacific, frequently reached a state of domestic disintegration which can be described as a "crack-up." At this point many rulers asked for formal European protection and in due course this was usually given, sometimes reluctantly, because European governments felt a responsibility both for the welfare of their nationals and for the preservation of the indigenous society. Empire was thus an unplanned product of the chronic disorder caused by informal European penetration.

Along these and similar lines it is possible to explain many aspects of European colonization without reference to Eurocentric theories of imperialism. Empire becomes a largely self-generating organism, growing fungus-like from a multiplicity of spawns scattered around the world by the dispersion of an expanding European civilization. This is an attractive line of argument and, as will be seen below, contains substantial elements of truth. Yet two reservations must be made. First, while peripheral factors may well have been the genesis of most problems from which formal annexation actually grew, the decision to resolve these problems by formal annexation had ultimately to be taken in the metropolitan capital. In the last resort, therefore, the historian must turn back to examine the working of the official mind in Europe as it reacted to problems flowing in from the frontiers. Second, the time factor must be considered. Many of the tendencies indicated above existed long before the 1880s. Why did the climax come during the following two decades rather than before or later and why did it simultaneously affect territories so widely different in place and circumstance? Clearly all these peripheral developments were in some sense pulled into a single historical pattern at some period in the later nineteenth century; otherwise one could not legitimately speak of imperialism as a collective phenomenon. The onus is therefore on the historian who starts his investigation at the periphery to demonstrate how and why this happened; and again he must turn to Europe to discover why the rulers of different states should have decided to solve so many disparate questions in much the same way at the same time. . . .

*   *   *

The Role of Economic Factors

. . . The men who made European policy in the later nineteenth century . . . inherited two alternative methods of dealing with those

economic issues on the periphery which generated some noneconomic difficulty and were not deemed to raise questions of major
national importance. The really important fact is that they continued
until 1914 and beyond to use both techniques. In the first instance
most powers still preferred to use diplomatic weapons or to rely
on informal influence; and in some places they never found it necessary to go further. In 1914 European and North American interests
in the Ottoman Empire, the Persian Gulf, Afghanistan, Siam, Japan,
China and Latin America were still for the most part based on a
complex of treaties and informal influence. In other places which
ultimately became colonies or protectorates the powers clung to
"spheres of influence" or relied on protectorate treaties not involving effective political control until well into the 1890s: for example in much of East and Central Africa, in Madagascar and the
Pacific. When it was eventually adopted formal rule was still commonly regarded as a crude and expensive way of dealing with
economic problems if they did not raise matters of strategic or
political importance to the metropolis.

There was, therefore, no point in time when the official mind of
European states entirely rejected the assumptions and techniques
which had served mid-century governments well enough. Yet it is
also undeniable that recourse to territorial control became far more
frequent in the 1880s and that in the 1890s this became the accepted
way of dealing with peripheral problems arising from European
economic and other activities. Why was this? The evidence suggests
two possible answers, complementary rather than contradictory.
First, that the acceleration of existing trends on the periphery,
coupled with growing international rivalries, meant that economic
enterprise generated political problems more frequently than they
had done previously. Second, that statesmen and permanent officials
became inured to using political means to solve these problems,
accepting the inevitable in a changing world—or that they gradually came to believe in the positive desirability of empire. The first
hypothesis can be tested by briefly recapitulating the evidence
region by region, the second by considering the changing attitudes
of officials in each major "imperialist" state.

There are, in fact, strong grounds for thinking that increasing
readiness to resort to formal rule was primarily a response to the

growing pressure of events after about 1880. It has been suggested above that one possible nondogmatic explanation for the timing of the "new imperialism" in the 1880s and 1890s is that this was a period of "general crisis," when outstanding problems in many places on the periphery were exacerbated by the intervention of an ever-increasing number of Europeans. It may, therefore, be desirable once again to survey the field to demonstrate when and why after 1880 statesmen seem increasingly to have felt that political problems associated with alien economic enterprise required formal political solutions.

In West Africa the long-standing French project for tapping the wealth of the Sudanese interior seemed from the start to require and justify military conquest and occupation because by about 1880 officials and soldiers were convinced that the Islamic states of the region constituted an otherwise insoluble problem. In this case, however, it must be recognized that the timing reflected impatience on the part of temporary holders of office in Paris rather than radically altered circumstances on the periphery. On the west coast political action became necessary for all interested powers because the long-term fiscal and juridical problems of small existing settlements were intensified after 1880 by growing international competition and because there was mutual fear that some other power would close existing markets by imposing protectorate treaties on African rulers in key areas. In the Congo region Leopold's plans for a highly informal commercial enterprise led to formal territorial division between the Congo Free State and other powers because in the first instance the French assumed that treaty-making on Leopold's account would give him exclusive political and economic control and therefore staked defensive counter-claims; and then because other powers were not prepared to accept a protectionist French regime throughout the Congo basin. In South-West Africa Bismarck decided to protect Lüderitz' concession in 1884 partly because he could not extract a clear British assurance of political security for this private economic venture. In East Africa Bismarck similarly supported Karl Peters' enterprise because it was reasonably feared that the British might otherwise try to block German acquisition of land in an area of traditional British primacy; while the British came to regard access to the Great Lakes as a major

British national interest. In Central Africa desire to satisfy Cape Colony imperialists, themselves primarily concerned with economic profit, constituted an essentially political motive for establishing a British sphere of interest and later protectorates.

In Southeast Asia and the Pacific the early and mid-1880s saw a similar shift from economic to political in the character of local problems. In Upper Burma the change came in 1885; in Indo-China between 1880–5, when the French had to recognize that an almost entirely commercial project to open a trading route through Tongking to China was blocked by political obstacles and, simultaneously, that informal control over Annam had become dangerously ineffective. In China the crisis came a decade later when the effects of the Sino-Japanese War seemed to threaten the established system of commercial rights based on informal political pressure. In this case, however, the powers were eventually able to avoid formal political solutions. In the Pacific Bismarck felt obliged to declare a protectorate over part of New Guinea because Queensland's attempt to annex the whole area, itself the product of concern for Australian political security as well as interest in the labor traffic, created a political threat to German economic activity. German claims in Samoa were equally the outcome of complex political factors, including an indigenous struggle for political power, the tactical political alignments of the foreign consuls and the symbolic importance attached to Samoa by metropolitan nationalists. Again the crisis was sparked off by a New Zealand attempt in 1883 to engineer a British takeover. The British had no desire at any stage to annex Pacific islands; but they found themselves under strong pressures from Australia and New Zealand to protect a number of islands which, in the eyes of the British colonists in the region, constituted a first-class national interest on grounds of security as well as a field for colonial trade, investment and missionary enterprise. The British eventually responded to these pressures for the political reason that they did not wish to alienate the self-governing colonies at a time when Britain was attempting to reintegrate her empire. The French took a similarly defensive and political view of Pacific islands close to Tahiti; and in the New Hebrides they were anxious to forestall expected British annexation which in turn was demanded by Australia as a defense against French occupation.

In general terms, then, the evidence seems very broadly to support the proposition that after about 1880 formal European rule was normally imposed by metropolitan governments in places where basic national interests were economic not because economic activity itself required formal empire but because in each case some noneconomic problem existed which could not be solved by informal means. It also strengthens the hypothesis that a new willingness to take such action developed in the 1880s, and not before, because outstanding problems happened to become more intense in the first half of that decade. So far as it goes this provides a conceptually satisfactory solution to the question why European statesmen used the political weapon of formal empire in situations which did not raise questions of major national importance. Unfortunately this conclusion leads back to the second problem: why were European statesmen more ready to act in this way than during the previous half-century? The answer suggested above is that officialdom was compelled to do so by the accumulation of otherwise insoluble problems. But there may be alternative or complementary explanations. Perhaps the statesmen were after all affected by new national economic problems or inspired by ideological enthusiasm for empire. To test these possibilities it is proposed briefly to review the chronology of change in the attitudes of officials in five leading imperialist states in the decades after 1880.

It is almost undeniable that the French were prepared to increase their use of annexation as a solution to political problems arising from economic problems on the periphery earlier than any other European state and that they eventually showed greatest positive enthusiasm for doing so. Despite official hesitation over Tunisia— essentially a political rather than an economic issue—France undoubtedly took the initiative in West Africa in 1879, responded quickly to the activities of Leopold in the Congo in 1882, accepted the need for military action in Tongking by 1883, risked major crises over Siam in 1893 and over the Nile in 1898, and was prepared to occupy Madagascar in 1898 when informal methods of control failed. Why was this? Four possible explanations have been suggested. First, that the propaganda of nonofficial imperialists during the 1870s had a measurable impact on some politicians and officials, conditioning them to regard solution of peripheral economic problems as a worthwhile object of national concern, provided these were not of interest only to a particular private concern. Second, mercantilist assumptions remained strong, despite the free-trading policy adopted in the 1860s; and the revival of tariff protection, coupled with concern for France's weak competitive position in commerce, encouraged a generalized belief that public support was necessary for economic interests. Third, republican political circles were extremely sensitive after the disaster of 1871 on questions affecting French power and prestige. Finally, the political and constitutional structure of the Third Republic enabled relatively small groups of politicians and officials, particularly those in the Colonial Department (later the Colonial Ministry) to obtain credits and undertake policies of which neither the Quai d'Orsay nor majority opinion in Parliament specifically approved. Whatever the reason, France was the first major state which was prepared to justify use of political means to deal with peripheral economic issues on the grounds that this served a general national interest, even where no major political or strategic objective was involved. Although challenged by many this doctrine was clearly enunciated by Ferry in 1885 and by the early 1890s seems to have become an accepted official principle.

It is impossible to talk of Russian imperialism in terms relevant to any of the constitutional states of Western Europe, for Russia did not possess a comparably informed or influential public opinion or Parliament, and the ministerial system was only partially developed. It is reasonably clear, moreover, that the distinction drawn in more sophisticated states between the national interest and that of private individuals had little meaning in St. Petersburg. Russian expansion in Central Asia and the Balkans resulted from historic modes of thought which approximate more closely to Schumpeter's model of atavistic behavior patterns than to the overseas policies of any advanced state in Western Europe. It is improbable, therefore, that nice distinctions were drawn in the 1880s and 1890s between specifically economic and political objectives in the Far East, for both were the concern of the government rather than of private interests and were seen as two elements in an agreed policy of preserving Russia's status as a major power in the Pacific leading to eventual predominance in China. The fact that Witte preferred to penetrate China by economic means rather than make territorial claims was due to the limited military and political resources available in the Far East until the trans-Siberian railway was completed rather than to distinctions drawn between economic and political objectives. It is therefore almost meaningless to attempt to date Russian willingness to use political means to save economic problems.

In Germany, however, this distinction was clear and important. Despite the adoption of domestic protection in 1879 and also the close personal links between many senior politicians, government officials and men of business, state power was not at the service of economic interests unless some important public interest would be served. Moreover, despite the volume of propaganda put out by imperialists, German ministers and senior officials do not, at least in the early 1880s, seem to have been convinced that colonies as such were necessary to the nation's economic interests. Hence the protectorates of 1884–5 were justified on highly conservative grounds: they provided specific solutions to otherwise insoluble problems facing German nationals on the periphery; they involved no diplomatic complications or large public expenditure; as protectorates, they could be renounced without difficulty. After about 1897, admittedly, increasing German aggressiveness in China, Morocco and the Pacific gave the impression that official attitudes had changed, that Bismarck's successors really believed in the economic importance of colonies to the metropolis and were ready to use state power to acquire territories in which no political obstacle to economic activity had arisen. But this is misleading. The evidence suggests that self-assertiveness on the periphery reflected a generally more chauvinistic foreign and naval policy, which were intended to assert the right of Germany to be consulted by other powers on all major international questions, rather than unqualified enthusiasm for colonization as an end in itself. Moreover it seems clear that the role of economic and political consideration was frequently reversed. The German state increasingly used economic weapons to further its political or military stratagems, forcing German commercial and investment interests to play a nationalistic role even against their inclinations. But the limits of political action in peripheral situations remained clear. Germany never seriously risked confrontation with any major power over a colonial issue because none was deemed to constitute a first-class national interest. The disgust of German imperialists at the Moroccan settlement of 1911 indicates that Bismarckian realism remained dominant in Berlin to the brink of the First World War.

American imperialism raises special problems of analysis and cannot be discussed at length. Fundamentally it is probable that, because of the character of the party system and the relative lack of continuity at the higher levels of the central administration, the official mind of Washington lacked those solidly established principles governing the foreign policies of all parties which could be seen in London, Berlin and to some extent at the Quai d'Orsay in Paris. Conversely, American policy was more susceptible to transient currents of public opinion. Until some point in the early 1890s it is clear that pressures from economic or other interests to acquire overseas territories for any purpose were slight, and conversely that no administration was prepared to use political methods to solve peripheral problems. Hence the refusal to partition Samoa or accept the invitation to incorporate Hawaii in 1893. Why, then, the dramatic change of policy in 1898–9 which produced formal empire in the Caribbean and Pacific? Was this due to a new consensus among politicians on the proper role of the state as protector and promoter of national economic enterprise after a period of economic hardship? It has been argued by some authors that this was so and that this change reflected both the growing political influence of the great financial corporations and pressing need during the slump of the later 1880s and early 1890s for new overseas markets. It is equally possible that concern for national security, and in particular for overseas possessions necessary for the effective exercise of naval power in an age of intensifying international naval rivalry, was partly responsible for this change of official attitude. The change must in any case not be exaggerated. The chosen limits of American imperialism after 1900 resembled those of Britain in the mid-nineteenth century rather than those of, say, France in the 1890s. The Americans showed almost no interest in possession of territory as a protected sphere of trade or investment. It was necessary only to secure commercial *entrepôts*, naval bases, the site for a strategic canal and to solve existing social and economic problems, in areas of established American influence, as in Samoa and Hawaii. The state should only use political or military methods when national security was at stake or to promote expanding trade when economic methods alone were inadequate.

There can be no doubt, finally, that in Britain the mid-nineteenth-century distinction between the proper role of state action and the sphere of private economic interests were never forgotten, even in the "age of imperialism." Despite "Manchester" influences earlier in the century British statesmen had never renounced the use of force or formal territorial control when dealing with political obstacles to economic enterprise. Thus the Chinese War of 1839–42 was based on the assumptions that would not have been out of period in the 1890s. Whitehall was extraordinarily unaffected by imperialist propaganda relating empire to economics until Chamberlain, in this as in many other respects a rebel against establishment assumptions, linked the two in the late 1890s. Officials and statesmen disliked the trend of events after about 1880 and were afraid that casual use of state power in connection with commercial difficulties would generate more expense and inconvenience than they warranted. Moreover, cabinet ministers and civil service mandarins distrusted the entrepreneurs of tropical empire as much as their predecessors had distrusted Wakefield fifty years earlier. Yet they could not be unaffected by the pace of events, and during the twenty years after about 1880 they gradually became inured to the fact that, when substantial British economic interests overseas were genuinely threatened by local political difficulties or by the political action of other powers, some form of political solution was inevitable. The stages of this reluctant descent from austere principles can be charted with some precision. It began in 1884–5 with the Niger Coast protectorate and the preliminary agreement with Germany over spheres of interest in East and Central Africa and the Pacific. It moved a stage further in 1886 when the Niger Company was given a charter to administer any territories it could effectively occupy. But until the early 1890s earlier principles remained almost unchanged. In each case state responsibility was kept to the minimum apparently required to secure the particular interest at stake —to preclude foreign political control of an area deemed important for British, Cape Colony or Australasian interests. The premiums Whitehall was ready to pay were, moreover, still small. A protectorate was expected to involve virtually no administration and a sphere of influence was merely a cartographical exercise. The real break came in 1897–8 when Chamberlain justified the cost of the West African Frontier Force in terms of the specific economic potential of the Middle Niger region, for this was to adopt the criteria of French and German unofficial imperialists, making imperial rule a gamble on the economic potential of semi-deserts. This was rare if not unique in the case history of British expansion after 1830; yet it is undeniable that by about 1900 British officialdom was reluctantly accepting the fact that empire had become a necessary solution to political and sometimes also economic problems on the periphery.

There were, therefore, significant differences in the time-scale of changing official attitudes to the proper role of the state when dealing with the consequences of European economic activity overseas. What determined the order of this procession? To answer the question fully, if indeed it can be answered, would require detailed analysis of many aspects of society and government in each main "imperialist" state and is beyond the scope of the present study. Yet, when all is said, such analysis would relate only to the chronology of reactions to external events. It could not rehabilitate the basic argument that the "new imperialism" was the product of influences operating merely within the metropolitan context. In the last resort the imperialism of the last two decades of the [nineteenth] century must be seen as a reaction to events outside Europe which swept all governments past the solid ground of mid-nineteenth-century assumptions into deep waters where they could survive only by striking out in new directions.

To summarize the argument without making vast generalizations or indulging in high-flown hyperbole the answer to the original question—the role of economic factors in European imperialism between 1830 and 1914—can be restated as a set of simple propositions.

Economic factors were present and in varying degrees influential in almost every situation outside Europe which led ultimately to formal empire; and the specific value of many of these territories to Europeans lay in trade, investment opportunities or other forms of economic activity.

But economic factors did not, on their own account, necessarily or even commonly generate need or desire for formal empire. The true "economic imperialism" of the European merchant and financier was frequently blind to politics. Formal ownership of territory was seldom essential or even relevant to economic activity and in some places might have positively inconvenient consequences for traders, planters, land speculators and others. Conversely the official mind of Europe for long assumed that economic interests could and should look after themselves without direct interference by the state.

The vital link between economics and formal empire was therefore neither the economic need of the metropolis for colonies nor the requirements of private economic interests, but the secondary consequence of problems created on the periphery by economic and other European enterprises for which there was no simple economic solution. At one extreme such problems directly affected what European officialdom regarded as "first-class" national interests. At the other they raised minor political difficulties such as the instability of an indigenous political regime or obstruction by other Europeans to satisfactory trade or investment. But in virtually every case the ultimate explanation of formal annexation was that the original economic issue had to some degree become "politicized" and therefore required a political solution.

In the crudest terms, therefore, it would seem that empire-building occurred on so large a scale in the last two decades of the nineteenth century, rather than at some previous time, and affected parts of Africa, Asia and the Pacific and not other regions, because it was in that period and in those places that relations between representatives of the advanced economies of Europe and other less-developed societies became fundamentally unstable. This fact can be explained according to initial assumptions. To the neo-Marxist it reflects the growing crisis of advanced capitalism which could only survive by absorbing and exploiting the less-developed regions of the world. To others it may suggest that, by coincidence, the activities of Europeans then became increasingly incompatible with preservation of indigenous economic, political and cultural systems in these areas. Probably, as the neo-Marxists held, though not for the economic reasons they gave, the whole process was historically inevitable. If so, it was inevitable only as a temporary expedient, to bridge the time-gap between a "modernized" Europe and a precapitalist periphery. And for the same reason empire eventually provided its own solvent. Half a century after 1914 Europe could withdraw the legions with reasonable confidence that the fundamental problems of international relations which had generated the imperialism of the late nineteenth century no longer existed. In the second half of the twentieth century European merchants and investors could operate satisfactorily within the political framework provided by most reconstructed indigenous states as their predecessors would have preferred to operate a century earlier but without facing those problems which had once made formal empire a necessary expedient.

Suggestions for Additional Reading

There are many thousands of books and articles on various aspects of the European expansion of the late nineteenth century. This brief list of suggested readings must concentrate on general matters. It will not be able to mention, therefore, a large number of useful sources, particularly those concerning the domestic histories and foreign policies of the different European countries, the nature of European activities in specific overseas areas, or the biographies of individuals.

While the bibliography of the various aspects of the subject is enormous, the number of works giving a broad, general coverage of the movement as a whole is itself quite small. Among the most useful are David K. Fieldhouse's concise *The Colonial Empires* (London, 1966), a comparative analysis of European expansion from the eighteenth century; Heinz Gollwitzer's *Europe in the Age of Imperialism, 1880–1914* (London, 1969), a brief survey with an emphasis on European attitudes and policies; and Volume 11 of the *New Cambridge Modern History,* entitled *Material Progress and World-Wide Problems, 1870–1898* (Cambridge, 1962), which has a great deal of factual detail. Taken together these books now supersede the old, once standard accounts of Mary E. Townsend and Cyrus H. Peake, *European Colonial Expansion Since 1871* (Philadelphia, 1941), and Parker T. Moon, *Imperialism and World Politics* (New York, 1926). None of them, unfortunately, has a really satisfactory bibliography. For general bibliographical purposes one should turn to John P. Halstead and Serafino Porcari's immense *Modern European Imperialism: A Bibliography of Books and Articles, 1815–1972* (2 vols.; Boston, 1974), which, although unannotated, is comprehensive and detailed. On more specific aspects of the subject, to be discussed below, there are also some excellent annotated bibliographies.

To begin with theory. The word "imperialism" itself presents a difficult but important problem. Its historiographical development may be found in Richard Koebner and Helmut Dan Schmidt, *Imperialism: The Story and Significance of a Political Word, 1840–1960* (Cambridge, 1964), which traces changing British attitudes toward empire. Recent attempts to define the word are Sidney Morgenbesser, "Imperialism: Some Preliminary Distinctions," *Philosophy and Public Affairs* 3 (Fall 1973): 3–44; Ronald J. Horvath, "A Definition of Colonialism," *Current Anthropology* 13 (Feb. 1972): 45–57; and Harrison M. Wright, " 'Imperialism': The Word and Its Meaning," *Social Research* 34 (Winter 1967): 660–74. Katherine West discusses the difficulty of the word in "Theorizing about 'Imperialism': A Methodological Note," *Journal of Imperial and Commonwealth History* 1 (Jan. 1973): 147–54.

The various theoretical interpretations represented in this volume (particularly those of Hobson, Lenin, and Schumpeter) are the subject of a growing body of literature. Also often discussed are such milestones of economic theory on the subject as Rudolph Hilferding's *Das Finanzkapital* . . . (Vienna, 1910), which connects expansion with capitalism's financial troubles; and Rosa Luxemburg's *The Accumulation of Capital* (London, 1951; published in German in 1913), which emphasizes the capitalists' need for markets. The economic theories are analyzed thoughtfully and in detail in Earle M. Winslow, *The Pattern of Imperialism* (New York, 1948), which is generally critical of them; and in Tom Kemp, *Theories of Imperialism* (London, 1967), which is generally sympathetic. (As might be expected, the two authors take the opposite positions on Schumpeter.)

Briefer discussions of theoretical interpretations may be found in a large number of periodical articles. A perceptive and largely sympathetic analysis of Hobson is Harvey Mitchell, "Hobson Revisited," *Journal of the History of Ideas* 26 (July 1965): 397–416. Useful recent articles basically critical of Hobson, Lenin, or other economic interpreters are, in chronological order: Raymond Aron, "The Leninist Myth of Imperialism," *Partisan Review* 18 (Nov.–Dec. 1951): 646–62; Daniel H. Kruger, "Hobson, Lenin, and Schumpeter on Imperialism," *Journal of the History of Ideas* 16 (April 1955): 252–59; David G. Smith, "Lenin's 'Imperialism': A Study in the Unity of Theory and Practice," *The Journal of Politics* 17 (Nov. 1955): 546–69; Hans Neisser, "Economic Imperialism Reconsidered," *Social Research* 27 (Spring 1960): 63–82; D. K. Fieldhouse, " 'Imperialism': An Historiographical Revision," *The Economic History Review,* 2nd ser., 14 (Dec. 1961): 187–209; David S. Landes, "Some Thoughts on the Nature of Economic Imperialism," *The Journal of Economic History* 21 (Dec. 1961): 496–512; G. Lee, "Rosa Luxemburg and the

Impact of Imperialism," *The Economic Journal* 81 (Dec. 1971): 847–62; and Trevor Lloyd, "Africa and Hobson's 'Imperialism,'" *Past & Present* 55 (May 1972): 130–53. Schumpeter was sympathetically reviewed by Eduard Heimann, in "Schumpeter and the Problems of Imperialism," *Social Research* 19 (June 1952): 177–97, an article which drew forth a sharp (and some think highly effective) attack by Murray Greene: "Schumpeter's Imperialism—A Critical Note," *ibid.* (Dec. 1952): 453–63. Horace B. Davis, "Conservative Writers on Imperialism," *Science and Society* 18 (Fall 1954): 310–25, excoriates all noneconomic interpretations. In a class by itself is the idiosyncratic essay by Arghiri Emmanuel, "White-Settler Colonialism and the Myth of Investment Imperialism," *New Left Review* 73 (May–June 1972): 35–57, which contains Marxist criticism of both Lenin and Hobson.

Recent books which discuss the theories of others in passing but which are largely concerned with propounding their own views support generally, as it happens, one or another form of economic interpretation. Such is *The End of Empire* (London, 1959), a general survey in a Hobsonian vein by the British socialist, John Strachey. Another work, *The Age of Imperialism* (New York, 1969), by the American Marxist, Harry Magdoff, is doctrinaire and somewhat narrowly tied to modern American examples. (It is criticized for theoretical failings by Alexander Erlich, "A Hamlet without the Prince of Denmark," *Politics and Society* 4 [Fall 1973]: 35–53.) A long, difficult, but powerful volume by the British Marxist, Michael Barratt Brown, *The Economics of Imperialism* (Harmondsworth, Eng., 1974) considers critically (and down to the present) the "classical," Keynesian, and Marxist interpretations; it largely supersedes his earlier *After Imperialism* (London, 1963; rev. ed., 1970). Another Marxist, George Lichtheim, discusses imperialism theoretically from Rome to the present in *Imperialism* (New York, 1971). In a somewhat different kind of volume, Roger Owen and Bob Sutcliffe have edited *Studies in the Theory of Imperialism* (London, 1972), which combines the Marxist assumptions of the editors with a heterogeneous and interesting collection of pieces by Marxist and non-Marxist authors alike. (The Marxist approach of the editors is criticized in Paul Wilkinson, "Neo-Marxist Theory of Imperialism," *Political Studies* 21 [Sept. 1973]: 388–93.) One noneconomic theorist is A. P. Thornton in *Doctrines of Imperialism* (New York, 1965), while Lewis H. Gann and

Peter Duignan, in *Burden of Empire* (New York, 1967), offer a rare apologia for expansion and colonialism, particularly in Africa.

Some of the older works of this type are still worth considering to obtain a deeper sense of the historiography of the controversy. On the Left there is Henry N. Brailsford, *The War of Steel and Gold* (London, 1914; 10th ed., 1918); Nikolai Bukharin, *Imperialism and World Economy* (New York, 1929; published in Russian in 1917); Leonard Woolf, *Economic Imperialism* (London, 1921); Maurice Dobb, *Political Economy and Capitalism* (London, 1937); and Paul M. Sweezy, *The Theory of Capitalist Development* (New York, 1942). Works with material critical of economic interpretations are Eugene Staley, *War and the Private Investor* (New York, 1935); Lionel Robbins, *The Economic Causes of War* (London, 1939); Hans J. Morgenthau, *Politics among Nations* (New York, 1948; 5th ed., 1974); and Schumpeter's own *Capitalism, Socialism and Democracy* (New York, 1942; 3rd ed., 1950).

The postwar interpretations of Robinson and Gallagher, their critics, and others have already generated a considerable body of literature. By and large this has revolved more around matters of fact and less around matters of general theory than did the works of their predecessors. Jane Pease, "The Imperialism of Status: A Synthetic Review," *The Review of Politics* 32 (1970): 461–75, does, however, make some reference to postwar theory as it relates to the British experience, while Eric Stokes, "Late Nineteenth-Century Colonial Expansion and the Attack on the Theory of Economic Imperialism: A Case of Mistaken Identity?" *The Historical Journal* 12 (1969): 285–301, is a highly theoretical (and critical) comparison of Robinson and Gallagher with Lenin.

Consideration of Robinson and Gallagher's "Imperialism of Free Trade" requires an investigation into mid-nineteenth-century imperial activity with an emphasis on Britain. The older works under attack, such as Robert Livingston Schuyler's *The Fall of the Old Colonial System* (New York, 1945), Klaus E. Knorr's *British Colonial Theories, 1570–1850* (Toronto, 1944), and Carl A. Bodelson, *Studies in Mid-Victorian Imperialism* (Copenhagen, 1924) are still provocative and worthwhile. While Robinson and Gallagher based their criticism of these works largely on trade and politics, others have reevaluated the economic theorists of the day. Such are Donald Winch, *Classical Political Economy and Colonies* (Cambridge, Mass., 1965), and, somewhat broader in scope, Bernard Semmel, *The Rise of Free Trade Imperialism . . . 1750–1850* (Cambridge, 1970). There is, of course, a substantial body of criticism of Robinson and Gallagher on the issue. In addition to the article reprinted in this volume, D. C. M. Platt has criticized them either explictly or implicitly in "Economic Factors in British Policy during the 'New Imperialism,'" *Past & Present* 39 (April 1968): 120–38; "Further Objections to an 'Imperialism of Free Trade,' 1830–60," *The Economic History Review,* 2nd ser., 26 (Feb. 1973): 77–91; and "The National Economy and British Imperial Expansion before 1914," *Journal of Imperial and Commonwealth History* 2 (Oct. 1973): 3–14. Other critical articles are Oliver MacDonagh, "The Anti-Imperialism of Free Trade," *The Economic History Review,* 2nd ser., 14 (April 1962): 489–501; B. A. Knox, "Reconsidering Mid-Victorian Imperialism," *Journal of Imperial and Commonwealth History* 1 (Jan. 1973): 155–72; and W. M. Mathew, "The Imperialism of Free Trade: Peru, 1820–70," *The Economic History Review,* 2nd ser., 21 (Dec. 1968): 562–79.

The partition of Africa, which is also central to any consideration of Robinson and Gallagher, has been the subject of many recent studies. The older works of Sir Charles P. Lucas, *The Partition and Colonisation of Africa* (Oxford, 1922), for long the standard general account, or Roland A. Oliver, *The Missionary Factor in East Africa* (London, 1952), Cornelius W. de Kiewiet, *The Imperial Factor in South Africa* (Cambridge, 1937), and Sybil E. Crowe, *The Berlin West African Conference, 1884–1885* (London, 1942), excellent studies of particular problems, must all now be reconsidered in the light of the new issues raised. A number of new introductory texts on modern Africa by Robert W. July, Robin Hallett, and others provide useful background. Several collections of readings, such as Robert O. Collins, ed., *The Partition of Africa: Illusion or Necessity* (New York, 1969), and Raymond F. Betts, ed., *The Scramble for Africa* (Boston, 1966; 2nd ed., 1972), point up the particular nature of the debate. For an introduction to more advanced study one should turn to Volume 5 of Peter Duignan and Lewis H. Gann's *Colonialism in Africa, 1870–1960,* entitled *A Bibliographical Guide to Colonialism in Sub-Saharan Africa* (Cambridge, 1973), which is a full, judiciously annotated bibliography of great value. More specifically, a long and critical review of *Africa and the Victorians,* summing up the case against the book, may be found in Ronald

Hyam, "The Partition of Africa," *The Historical Journal* 7 (1964): 154–69. Two other criticisms, more specifically focused, are in the *Journal of African History* 3 (1962): Colin W. Newbury, "Victorians, Republicans, and the Partition of West Africa" (pp. 493–501), and Jean Stengers, "L'impérialisme colonial de la fin du XIXe siècle: mythe ou réalité" (pp. 469–91). While it is impossible to discuss here the literature on Africa in detail, one should mention a few significant studies that emphasize economic motives for the partition. A. G. Hopkins, *An Economic History of West Africa* (New York, 1973); Michael Crowder, *West Africa Under Colonial Rule* (London, 1968); G. N. Uzoigwe, *Britain and the Conquest of Africa* (Ann Arbor, 1974); and Jean Suret-Canale, *French Colonialism in Tropical Africa, 1900–1945* (New York, 1971), all provide evidence and interpretation opposed in one way or another to that of Robinson and Gallagher.

Robinson and Gallagher were not unique in recognizing the possible importance of activities on the periphery as an inducement to European expansion. About the time they wrote, other significant and suggestive studies—primarily based on English or African examples, or both—discussed the same phenomenon. John S. Galbraith, "The 'Turbulent Frontier' as a Factor in British Expansion," *Comparative Studies in Society and History* 1 (Jan. 1960): 150–68, used India, Malaya, and South Africa in the early and mid-nineteenth century as examples. J. D. Hargreaves, "Towards a History of the Partition of Africa," *Journal of African History* 2 (1960): 97–109, discussed peripheral involvement in its West African context, a theme later considered in his *Prelude to the Partition of West Africa* (London, 1963) and his *West Africa Partitioned: The Loaded Pause, 1885–1889* (Madison, Wisc., 1975). In the mid-1960s W. David McIntyre wrote *The Imperial Frontier in the Tropics, 1865–75* (London, 1967), with West Africa, Malaya, and the South Pacific as special areas. (An attack on the "peripheral," noneconomic approach may be found in P. J. Cain, "European Expansion Overseas, 1830–1914," *History* 59 [Jan. 1974]: 243–49, a critical review of Fieldhouse's *Economics and Empire*.)

As one considers the problem of late-nineteenth-century expansion in less general and theoretical terms, the subject tends to break up into detailed studies of particular problems, individuals, countries or, as with Africa, overseas areas. Discussing the imperialism of the period from the point of view of the relations between European states, William L. Langer's *European Alliances and Alignments, 1871–1890* (New York, 1931; 2nd ed., 1950) and *The Diplomacy of Imperialism, 1890–1902* (2 vols.; New York, 1935; 2nd ed., 1950) are still unmatched both in detail and in scholarly approach. The two works are further enhanced, especially in the second editions, by excellent, annotated bibliographies. On economic matters Herbert Feis, *Europe: The World's Banker, 1870–1914* (New Haven, 1930), examines in detail the direction and nature of European foreign investment. Individuals concerned with the European expansion of the late nineteenth century—both those in Europe and those overseas—have been written about in countless biographies. Chamberlain, Ferry, Crispi, Bismarck, Rhodes, Kitchener, Lyautey and others have all been the subject of two or more biographies apiece. Reading biographies is crucial to an understanding of the problems of generalization. Two particularly good ones are Roland A. Oliver's *Sir Harry Johnston and the Scramble for Africa* (London, 1957), and John E. Flint, *Sir George Goldie and the Making of Nigeria* (London, 1960). Two convenient if occasionally superficial collections of biographies are in the French *Colonies et empires* series directed by C. A. Julien: No. 1, *Les Techniciens de la colonisation* . . . (Paris, 1947), and No. 5, *Les Politiques d'expansion imperialiste* (Paris, 1949), which emphasize the importance of individual initiative.

For German expansion one should turn first to the excellent bibliographical essay of Hartmut Pogge von Strandmann and Alison Smith, "The German Empire in Africa and British Perspectives: A Historiographical Essay," in Prosser Gifford and Wm. Roger Louis, eds., *Britian and Germany in Africa* (New Haven, 1967), pp. 709–95, which covers an unusually wide range of material. The motives of Bismarck are of course crucial to any understanding of German expansion. There is still considerable value in three early studies: Mary E. Townsend, *The Rise and Fall of Germany's Colonial Empire, 1884–1919* (New York, 1930); William O. Aydelotte, *Bismarck and British Colonial Policy: The Problem of South West Africa, 1883–1885* (Philadelphia, 1937); and A. J. P. Taylor, *Germany's First Bid for Colonies, 1884–1885* (London, 1938). The most important work on Bismarck and German expansion is, however, Hans-Ulrich Wehler, *Bismarck und der Imperialismus* (Cologne, 1969). In English one can get a sense of Wehler from his articles: "Bismarck's Imperialism, 1862–1890," *Past & Present* 48 (August 1970): 119–55 (which criticizes Robinson and Gallagher and Fieldhouse), and "Industrial Growth and Early German Imperialism," in pp. 71–90 of the Owen and Sutcliffe volume described above. Discussions of Wehler's views may be found in Hans Medick, "H. U. Wehler: *Bismarck und der Imperialismus,*" *History and Theory* 10 (1971): 228–40, and P. M. Kennedy, "German Colonial Expansion," *Past & Present* 54 (Feb. 1972): 134–41. In other brief assessments of Bismarck, P. M. Kennedy, "Bismarck's Imperialism: The Case of Samoa, 1880–1890," *The Historical Journal* 15 (1972): 261–83, finds a commercial motive; H. Pogge von Strandmann, "Domestic Origins of Germany's Colonial Expansion under Bismarck," *Past & Present* 42 (Feb. 1969): 140–59, finds a domestic one; and Henry A. Turner, "Bismarck's Imperialist Venture: Anti-British in Origin?" in pp. 47–82 of the Gifford and Louis volume, above, finds a need for power and prestige. General ideologies are discussed in Woodruff D. Smith, "The Ideology of German Colonialism, 1840–1906," *Journal of Modern History* 46 (Dec. 1974): 641–62.

For France, the bibliographical essay of David Gardinier, "French Colonial Rule in Africa: A Bibliographical Essay," in Prosser Gifford and Wm. Roger Louis, eds., *France and Britain in Africa* (New Haven, 1971), pp. 787–950, though it concentrates on the period 1914–1960, still has some useful material on the literature for 1870–1914. The most important recent volumes on French expansion in general are Henri Brunschwig, *French Colonialism, 1871–1914: Myths and Realities* (London, 1966; published in French in 1960), which sees the phenomenon as primarily nationalistic; and Jean Ganiage, *L'Expansion coloniale de la France sous la Troisième Republique, 1871–1914* (Paris, 1968). Older works are Thomas F. Power, Jr., *Jules Ferry and the Renaissance of French Imperialism* (New York, 1944), an attempt to disprove economic motivation for Ferry; Herbert I. Priestley's now very dated *France Overseas: A Study of Modern Imperialism* (New York, 1938); the still useful (and opinionated) Stephen H. Roberts, *History of French Colonial Policy, 1870–1925* (2 vols.; London, 1929), with its excellent bibliography of primary sources; and Agnes Murphy, *The Ideology of French Imperialism, 1871–1881* (Washington, 1948), an account of the shaping of French attitudes. Another useful study of French thinking is Martin D. Lewis, "One Hundred Million Frenchmen . . . ," *Comparative*

Studies in Society and History 4 (Jan. 1962): 129–53. Detailed analyses of French expansion into particular regions are A. S. Kanya-Forstner, *The Conquest of the Western Sudan* (London, 1969); James J. Cooke, *New French Imperialism, 1880–1910* (Hamden, Conn., 1973), despite its title primarily on French policy in North Africa; and John F. Cady's *The Roots of French Imperialism in Eastern Asia* (Ithaca, N.Y.), important although it concentrates on the first three-quarters of the century.

As might be expected there are innumerable works on the different aspects of British expansion. For introductory purposes one should turn to the good, shorter standard texts of the empire by James A. Williamson, Charles E. Carrington, Paul Knaplund, and others. At a more advanced level the most useful introduction is Robin Winks, ed., *The Historiography of the British Empire-Commonwealth: Trends, Interpretations and Resources* (Durham, 1966), a series of interpretive bibliographical essays by specialists in different areas. For details of the period as a whole one should turn to the appropriate volumes of the *Cambridge History of the British Empire* (Cambridge, 1929–), which, although some of them are by now badly dated, have a wealth of material on British expansion in all parts of the empire and very full (if unannotated) bibliographies. In this series the central volume for the period is vol. 3, *The British Empire-Commonwealth, 1870–1919* (Cambridge, 1959). Besides studies of expansionism during the "free-trade era," as discussed above, there have recently been a number of works concerned with British attitudes toward the empire during the late nineteenth century. A general study is A. P. Thornton, *The Imperial Idea and Its Enemies* (London, 1959). Bernard Porter, *Critics of Empire* (London, 1968) is on radical attitudes. C. J. Lowe, *The Reluctant Imperialists: British Foreign Policy, 1878–1902* (London, 1969) is oriented toward the diplomatic side. Works considering the views of labor toward the empire are Tingfu F. Tsiang, *Labor and Empire* (New York, 1923), which sees it as hostile, and Richard Price, *An Imperial War and the British Working Class* (London, 1972), which sees it as indifferent. Proponents of empire are discussed in Bernard Semmel, *Imperialism and Social Reform: English Social-Imperial Thought, 1895–1914* (Cambridge, Mass., 1960); William L. Strauss, *Joseph Chamberlain and the Theory of Imperialism* (Washington, 1942), which associates Chamberlain with social Darwinism; and Richard Faber, *The Vision and the*

Need: Late Victorian Imperialist Aims (London, 1966). On the controversial issues of economics one can find trade discussed in detail in D. C. M. Platt, *Finance, Trade, and Politics in British Foreign Policy, 1815–1914* (Oxford, 1968), and Samuel B. Saul, *Studies in British Overseas Trade, 1870–1914* (Liverpool, 1960). (Platt's book is critically reviewed in an article of the same title by Zara Steiner in *The Historical Journal,* 13, 3 [1970]: 545–52.) For investments and finance there are L. H. Jenks's pioneering *The Migration of British Capital to 1875* (New York, 1923), for the early period; and Alfred R. Hall, ed., *The Export of Capital from Britain, 1870–1914* (London, 1968) and A. K. Cairncross, *Home and Capital Investment, 1870–1913* (Cambridge, 1953), for the later. It is impossible here to list even the most important books on late-nineteenth-century British expansion into the various parts of the world. The reader is referred again to Winks's *Historiography,* where the literature on the subject is discussed in the many different chapters that take up each colony or colonial area in turn.

Outside of Britain, France, and Germany the late-nineteenth-century expansion of most European countries was regional, rather than worldwide, in extent. Jean L. Miège, *L'Impérialisme colonial italien de 1870 à nos jours* (Paris, 1968), with an ample bibliography, is a first-rate introduction to modern Italian activity, primarily in Africa. For Belgium one might begin with Ruth Slade, *King Leopold's Congo* (London, 1962). There are several good books on Portuguese activity, also in Africa, particularly Eric Axelson, *Portugal and the Scramble for Africa, 1875–1891* (Johannesburg, 1967), a detailed study, and Richard J. Hammond, *Portugal and Africa, 1815–1910* (Stanford, 1966), which emphasizes noneconomic factors. Dutch expansion in Indonesia is introduced briefly but effectively in John D. Legge's interpretive essay, *Indonesia* (Englewood Cliffs, N.J., 1964). Russian expansion, into Central and East Asia, is discussed in Benedict H. Sumner's succinct lecture, *Tsardom and Imperialism in the Far East and Middle East, 1880–1914* (London, 1942), in David J. Dallin's somewhat pugnacious *The Rise of Russia in Asia* (New Haven, 1949), and, in a far more detailed work on a smaller scale, Richard A. Pierce's *Russian Central Asia, 1867–1917* (Berkeley, 1960).

For comparative purposes it is useful to consider the late-nineteenth-century expansionist tendencies of non-European powers, particularly the United States and Japan. The United States, largely because of its recent foreign policies, has been the subject of a most active debate. Economic revisionists, such as Walter LaFeber in *The New Empire* (Ithaca, N.Y., 1963) and William A. Williams in *The Roots of the Modern American Empire* (New York, 1969), both of whom find American expansion resulting from growing industrial and commercial needs, should be compared, for example, to the more traditionalist work of Ernest R. May, *Imperial Democracy* (New York, 1961). An up-to-date introduction to the debate is Robert L. Beisner, *From the Old Diplomacy to the New, 1865–1900* (New York, 1975). For details on Japanese expansion one may turn to Hilary Conroy, *Japan's Seizure of Korea* (Philadelphia, 1960), for a sympathetic (and controversial) view; C. I. Eugene Kim and Hankyo Kim, *Korea and the Politics of Imperialism, 1876–1910* (Berkeley, 1967), for a Korean perspective; and Akira Iriye, *Pacific Estrangement: Japanese and American Expansion, 1879–1911* (Cambridge, Mass., 1972), for competing imperialisms.

Finally, but certainly not least in importance, those interested in the subject should read as many original sources as possible in order to obtain a first-hand idea of contemporary European attitudes. This involves the works of Kipling, Seeley, Leroy-Beaulieu, Harmond, and other publicists, the writings and speeches of the various statesmen and active overseas participants, and popular opinion as expressed in the books, journals, and newspapers of the time.

1 2 3 4 5 6 7 8 9

DATE DUE